Innovation, Economic Growth and the Firm

In memory of Ehud Zuscovitch

Innovation, Economic Growth and the Firm

Theory and Evidence of Industrial Dynamics

Edited by

Jean-Luc Gaffard

University of Nice Sophia Antipolis, Institut Universitaire de France, Observatoire Français des Conjonctures Economiques, and SKEMA Business School, France

Evens Salies

Observatoire Français des Conjonctures Economiques, France

Edward Elgar
Cheltenham, UK • Northampton, MA, USA

Published by
Edward Elgar Publishing Limited
The Lypiatts
15 Lansdown Road
Cheltenham
Glos GL50 2JA
UK

Edward Elgar Publishing, Inc.
William Pratt House
9 Dewey Court
Northampton
Massachusetts 01060
USA

A catalogue record for this book
is available from the British Library

Library of Congress Control Number: 2009940637

ISBN 978 1 84720 832 3

Printed and bound by MPG Books Group, UK

Contents

Figures

Tables

Contributors

Taylor Aldridge, Max Planck Institute of Economics, Jena (Germany)

Mario Amendola, University of Roma La Sapienza (Italy)

David Audretsch, Max Planck Institute of Economics, Jena (Germany)

William Baumol, University of New York (USA)

Flora Bellone, University of Nice Sophia Antipolis (France)

Sergio Bruno, University of Roma La Sapienza (Italy)

Patrick Cohendet, University Louis Pasteur, Strasbourg (France) and HEC, Montréal (Canada)

Rodolphe Dos Santos Ferreira, University Louis Pasteur, Strasbourg (France)

Jean-Luc Gaffard, University of Nice Sophia Antipolis (France) Observatoire Français des Conjonctures Economiques (OFCE), Valbonne (France) and SKEMA Business School, Valbonne (France)

Sarah Guillou, Observatoire Français des Conjonctures Economiques (OFCE), Valbonne (France)

Jean-Alain Héraud, University Louis Pasteur, Strasbourg (France)

Jozef Konings, Catholic University of Leuven (Belgium)

Adam Lederer, Max Planck Institute of Economics, Jena (Germany)

Patrick Llerena, University Louis Pasteur, Strasbourg (France)

Stanley J. Metcalfe, University of Manchester (England)

Patrick Musso, University of Annecy (France)

Lionel Nesta, Observatoire Français des Conjonctures Economiques (OFCE), Valbonne (France)

Michel Quéré, Centre d'Etudes et de Recherches sur les Qualifications, Marseille (France)

Evens Salies, Observatoire Français des Conjonctures Economiques (OFCE), Valbonne (France)

Stefano Schiavo, University of Trento (Italy)

Patrick Van Cayseele, Catholic University of Leuven (Belgium)

Frédéric Warzynski, University of Aarhus (Denmark)

Ehud Zuscovitch, University Louis Pasteur, Strasbourg (France)

Preface

When we are looking for the determinants of innovation and growth, it is not appropriate to focus on the firm in isolation. Economic growth is not only a matter of productivity gains and hence of institutions and rules that create incentives to R&D expenditures by firms. It is, also and mainly, a matter of co-ordination between supply and demand decisions both at each moment and over time, and hence of relations which prevail among firms that interact with each other during innovation processes. Thus, in an echo of Adam Smith, it is worth drawing attention to the articulation between the division of labour and the extent of market as the real source of wealth creation. As should be well known, without an expansion of market size, there is no possibility for firms to capture the productivity or the variety gains associated with a deeper division of labour. And hence, there is no real opportunity for firms to invest in specific physical assets and to boost the growth process.

In exploring the main implication of increasing returns, which are at the heart of industrial life, for economic growth, we can see that markets stand at the core of economic processes insofar as they are considered as 'instruments to transmitting impulses to economic change' (Kaldor 1972, p. 1240).[1] Every re-organization or restructuring of productive activities is the source of further changes which can be characterized by permanent differences between supply and demand. As a matter of fact, supply does not automatically generate a demand of an equal amount. Market disequilibria are unavoidable as a consequence of imperfect information. The market process is then a dynamic process of selection. But competition, provided it is well oriented, is presumed to be a process of co-ordination that prevents any disequilibrium to be cumulative. It is not only aimed at equalizing demand and supply in a given market and technological environment. It 'has also to adapt structure and technology to the fresh opportunities created by expanding markets' (Richardson 1975, p. 353).[2] This evokes the creative function of the market. Innovation is inseparable from the competitive process. The relation is two-way and mutually reinforcing between free competition and, notably business experimentation.

Dealing with a process of change, which implies learning, requires establishing market relationships over successive periods as well as a wide range of co-operative relationships over time (not only internally but also between different firms, between firms and banks, and so on). This different image of the firm implies a different relationship with its environment. As long as we keep looking at a firm, the boundaries of which are defined by a given technology and which must operate in a given market to carry out its allocation task, we stick to the idea of environment as an exogenous constraint. But the technology and the market are precisely specific expressions of this environment. On the other hand when we move the attention to a process of change that the firm itself must organize, a process that most often involves learning and structuring anew, then the environment necessarily becomes a strategic variable, to be moulded according to and as a functional part of the strategy pursued (Amendola and Bruno 1990).[3]

We thus come to an image of the firm that overcomes both the distinction between a micro and macro definition and that between the firm itself and its environment. Organizing and implementing the process by which new productive options (and technologies) are brought about also entails simultaneously redefining intra- and inter-relationships which make the firm change its configuration and articulation within a context that itself becomes modified and redefined together with the firm. Business experimentation and entrepreneurship both explain firm differentiation and firm dynamics and appear as an endogenous response to change in the environment. Therefore, markets and firms are not substitutes but complements. Entrepreneurial activity exists and is stimulated because the market creates opportunities, and promotes growth enhancing activities. On the other hand entrepreneurial activity serves an important source of economic growth by creating competition and conducting knowledge spillovers.

In this perspective, firm differentiation or heterogeneity, market selection and firm survival, networks of firms, relations between small and large firms, firm's specialization or diversity and flexibility are always phenomena that contribute decisively to growth and development.

This book addresses the foundations of economic growth at the firm level combining both theoretical and econometric contributions by established scholars. Challenging ideas revisit Marshall's view on the management of innovation, investigate the decision of firms to venture into entrepreneurship and clarify some misunderstanding about Schumpeter's views. The book goes on to shed light on the classical specialization–flexibility trade-off and provides a vision on the role of the knowledge-based economy and firm networks on technology development. Firm survival and performance, price–cost margins and the determinants of research intensity are also investigated econometrically. Our objective is notably to cover these topics through theoretical and state of the art econometric analyses by authors who participated to the 2006 Schumpeter conference. Besides, we offer a comprehensive view by assembling evolutionary with orthodox approaches to those issues. Leading specialists contribute to this book. Among them, some have already edited best sellers. Other contributors have good research tracks with publications in international academic journals. There are two major new features in this book. First, Stanley Metcalfe provides a key contribution to industrial dynamics through the lenses of evolutionary economics. Second, the book may reach a large audience as it combines papers on theories of entrepreneurship and firm behaviour with papers relying on econometric evidences on these issues dealing with firm-level data. The authors analyse firm performance, price–cost margins, investments and expenditures in research and development. Several sectors are covered in the domestic and foreign markets. The book should be of relevance to the academic profession involved in research projects that address issues on firm growth and performance from theoretical and econometric perspectives. It should also have an appeal to practitioners seeking tangible results on the relationship between key economic variables at the level of firms and to policy-makers who must be aware of the impact on firms' performance of changes in the organization of industries such as markets liberalization, exchange rate policies or laws promoting the entry of small and medium enterprises. We also think that doctorate and postgraduate students might use the book as a supplementary reading for the understanding of firms' behaviour.

Part I contains contributions to the history of economic thought. It starts with an ambitious methodological paper (Chapter 1 by Stanley J. Metcalfe) that offers a more general theory of evolutionary economics by bringing Alfred Marshall back to the centre. Metcalfe draws attention to Marshall's open systems approach to economic development and its intimate connection to his evolutionary perspective on the development of knowledge and organization. He also shows evidence that Marshall's writing is not out of place in regard to much of the modern literature on corporate strategy and innovation. In addressing issues such as Marshall and Schumpeter's reservations about the continuation of the innovation process and the implied limits to economic progress, Stan Metcalfe grasps the point that there are two evolutionary Marshalls, one devoted to the organic system development view of economic change, and the other, the adaptive, variation, selection view of industrial competition and development. Metcalfe's paper also clearly emphasizes the importance of historical research into firms and industries and the complementary importance of history friendly modelling.

In Chapter 2, Mario Amendola, Sergio Bruno and Jean-Luc Gaffard show the complementarity between Richardson's and Hicks' contributions as regards the sketching out of a proper analytical framework for dynamic analysis that depends on dealing with issues that are in the nature of dynamic problems. They call for co-ordination over time of economic activity, to render viable the process of change in the productive structure due to innovation. According to the authors, this can only come about through a process which is in the nature of an out-of-equilibrium process. The analytical framework sketched out by the authors helps to understand the methodological flaws of the traditional theories of economic policy, be then of the Paretian or of the Tinbergen type. Mario Amendola et al. argue that the out-of-equilibrium process admits instead a plurality of dynamic paths which regarding economic policy implication suggests that there is a wide room for policy action.

The two remaining parts of the book each contain two theoretical contributions followed by two empirical contributions. In Part II, David Audretsch, Taylor Aldridge and Adam Lederer (Chapter 3) question the link between small and medium enterprises (SMEs), industry dynamics and economic growth. In this chapter, the authors utilize the lens provided by the new knowledge spillover theory of entrepreneurship to understand how (SMEs) can influence industry dynamics and ultimately economic growth. The knowledge spillover theory of entrepreneurship inverts the traditional approach to SMEs. Rather than taking the context to be given and then asking how variations across individual attributes shape the cognitive process underlying the decision to become an entrepreneur, the authors instead assume the individual characteristics to be constant and then analyse how the cognitive process inducing the entrepreneurial decision is influenced by placing that same individual in different contexts. In particular, high knowledge contexts are compared with impoverished knowledge contexts. This leads to a very different view of entrepreneurship. Instead of being a phenomenon that is exogenously determined by pre-conditioned personal attributes and family history, entrepreneurship instead emerges as an endogenous response to opportunities generated by investments in new knowledge made by incumbent firms and organizations, combined with their inability to fully and completely exhaust the ensuing opportunities to commercialize that knowledge. Thus, the knowledge spillover theory of entrepreneurship shows how entrepreneurship can be an endogenous response to investments in new knowledge where commercialization of that knowledge is constrained by the existence of a formidable knowledge filter.

Chapter 4 by William Baumol brings us back to Schumpeter's 1911 model which, with good reason, most recent writings on the theory of innovative entrepreneurship start off from. William Baumol points out, however, that a careful rereading of his text indicates that Schumpeter's story entails a number of clear misunderstandings which call for some degree of rectification, none of them trivial and some affecting the logic of his argument and the conclusions to which it leads. Some of those misunderstandings lie close to the heart of the theory, while others are peripheral, but all of them raise significant issues. Baumol begins with one of the slips that is relatively ancillary because the issue it raises is so clear, namely, Schumpeter's analysis of the work of the entrepreneurs–inventor partnership and their vital role in the growth process. He then insists on some misunderstanding regarding the role of pricing in the Schumpeterian scenario where firms cannot survive if in addition to using innovation as a primary competitive weapon their pricing approach precludes recouping those investments in R&D. According to William Baumol, this is all lurking in the background in Schumpeter, but it never emerges fully and hence it invites the misunderstandings discussed here. Relaying on his own micro theory of the entrepreneur, Baumol offers two explanatory mechanisms behind the empirical evidence that the economic profits of innovation are, as a whole, negative, a phenomena overlooked by Schumpeter, thereby leading him to a conclusion about entrepreneurial profit that is supported neither by a fuller theoretical analysis nor by the empirical evidence.

A contribution to the literature on industrial dynamics which relates the firm's decision to exit to the heterogeneity of performance among competing firms is given in Chapter 5 written by Flora Bellone, Patrick Musso, Lionel Nesta, and Michel Quéré. Their article provides a better understanding of the duration of both young and old firms and of their determinants from using a large-scale micro-level dataset on French manufacturing firms over the period 1990 through to 2002. Unlike most of the existing literature, the surveyed unit is the legal (not the production) unit, which means that the authors are dealing with a firm-level (not plant-level) dataset. They document how the determinants of firm duration – in terms of firm performance and industry characteristics – act differently according to the age of the firm. The authors find that conditional on survival, firms experience continuous productivity gains throughout their life cycles. In the first few years of existence, the productivity growth of surviving firms is higher than that of the industry average but then decreases continuously to finally vanish completely. More generally, their findings for French manufacturing industries support the recent theoretical industrial dynamics literature in that, on the whole, exiting firms display below-average productivity levels and are smaller than their surviving counterparts. If age and market opportunities can be considered acceptable proxies for firm size and technological opportunity respectively, this result may be a replication of the Schumpeterian debate on the inverted U-shape relationship between firm size and innovation. In this case, young firms are more flexible and reactive, allowing them to occupy strategic niches, whereas large firms may enjoy some size advantage in terms of higher internal economies of scope.

Evens Salies investigates the Schumpeterian hypothesis in a single industry often discarded in firm-level studies, namely, the electric utilities industry (Chapter 6). This industry drew the attention of energy economists, following the decline in R&D investment from the early 1980s in the U.S.A. and in the U.K. To understand the drivers of a similar decline for electric utilities in Europe since 2000, Evens Salies considers size as primary variable of interest, but also the effect of deregulation-induced factors likely to be responsible for the decrease in aggregated R&D efforts. Overall, model estimation leads to the result that R&D varies proportionally with size net of R&D. The financial variables (debt and dividends) are negatively related to R&D, which supports the observation that electric utilities spend considerable funds to make domestic and cross-border M&A operations. The result for dividends is more politically sensible as it would suggest that research is an alternative use of funds to paying dividends. Moreover, the non-significance of the cash variable in all our regressions would suggest that electric utilities are not financially constrained. Furthermore the author deduces a negative impact of electricity deregulation on R&D efforts.

Part III starts with a theoretical model by Rodolphe Dos Santos Ferreira and the late Ehud Zuscovitch (Chapter 7) that addresses the specialization–flexibility trade-off of economic agents, or how specialized should an economic agent become? As the price to pay for more and more specialization (with the resulting increase in efficiency) is less and less flexibility (with the consequent loss of adaptability), a basic trade-off shapes technological decisions. Besides, such decisions have often to be taken in a context of strategic interaction, where the choices of our potential rivals condition our own. The author accordingly addresses this trade-off within a symmetric spatial duopoly framework, such that firms sequentially choose technologies, locations and prices. The technological frontier expresses the trade-off, since the cost of producing one unit of output is a decreasing function of the transportation rate allowing moving one unit of output from a location to another. Locations have as usual an abstract interpretation, as points in some one-dimensional characteristics space. Firms compete in prices separately at each instant of time and at each location, so that the corresponding equilibrium prices are Bertrand prices (equal to the higher unit production plus transportation cost). Computation of sub-game perfect Nash equilibriums shows that the trade-off ends up in extreme (not necessarily symmetric) choices whenever there are increasing returns to specialization. By contrast, when returns are significantly decreasing, the trade-off leads to a symmetric compromise solution. In the intermediate case, multiplicity of equilibriums with different degrees of asymmetry may emerge, providing a clue to the diversity and fragility of observed market configurations. In any case, competition between firms enhances flexibility, and fails to provide the socially optimal level of specialization.

The next contribution (Chapter 8) by Patrick Cohendet, Patrick Llerena and Jean-Alain Héraud is an essay on Ehud Zuscovitch's modern theoretical perspectives on division of labour and division of knowledge in firms' innovative networks. According to Ehud Zuscovitch, the conditions of surplus creation associated with innovation have fundamentally changed with the emergence of what he called 'information intensive production systems' (IIPS) – a concept related to the present expression 'knowledge-based economy'. The challenge in the new (post-fordist) regime is to deal with increasing variety while maintaining economic efficiency, and this is the role of networks of firms. The view of the authors here is that, if networks envision firms as ultimate units of knowledge specialization, the system will face severe limitations. Patrick Cohendet et al. suggest that the necessary slack of innovative resources which constitutes the source of 'surplus' in the new regime comes from 'knowing communities'. The latter can exist within hierarchies but often extend across hierarchies, and become the indispensable complement for the survival of firms in a regime of permanent innovation. In IIPS, the firm must be viewed as a nexus of competencies that articulate hierarchical structures and knowing communities. As a consequence, networks should not be seen anymore as networks of firms simply understood as hierarchical structures. With such an extension, Ehud Zuscovitch's vision calls for an in-depth reconsideration of the evolutionary theory of the firm.

In Chapter 9, Jozef Konings, Patrick Van Cayseele and Frédéric Warzynski ask the question whether the European integration process is effective in fostering growth through the benefits of increased competition. The empirical literature has been surprisingly silent about it, while theoreticians and practitioners have been debating about the pro and contra of various aspects of antitrust policy enforcement. In this paper, the authors apply the so-called Roeger's methodology to analyse the dynamics of price–cost margins using a large microeconomic dataset of Belgian and Dutch firms and relate it to the introduction of a new competition law and to the importance of import competition. In addition to examining in details the importance of cyclicality and trade, one of the paper's contribution is to test whether the toughness of competition policy has an effect on the toughness of price competition, where the latter is approximated through a cross country comparison and through a within country dynamic comparison. The authors find that price–cost margins are still estimated higher in the Netherlands than in Belgium; second, however, they have declined in the Dutch manufacturing industry following the introduction of the new competition law and have converged to the level observed in Belgium; third, moreover, trade appears to discipline the industry as the margins are positively linked to import price index.

Finally, Sarah Guillou and Stefano Schiavo (Chapter 10) investigate the pricing behaviour of firms operating in foreign markets by comparing the export price strategies of France, Germany and Italy using a large and common pool of manufacturing products and destination markets. Their results suggest that pricing-to-market (PTM) is not widespread among French and German exporters, whereas Italian ones do adopt more often such a pricing strategy. The standard claim that product specific characteristics play a major role in determining PTM is only weakly supported by their results, which find very limited regularity across products. On the other hand, the hypothesis of an homogeneous behaviour across destination countries (even for the same products) is strongly rejected. This suggests that export price changes are mainly determined by source and destination market characteristics. A similar conclusion applies to profit margins as well: they move rather homogeneously across products but differently across destinations. Within this heterogeneity, Sarah Guillou and Stefano Schiavo find that on average profit margins have either remained stable or augmented in the last three decades, so that increased international integration seems not to have reduced firm market power.

NOTES

1. Kaldor, N. (1972), 'The irrelevance of equilibrium economics', *Economic Journal*, **82** (328), 1237–55.
2. Richardson, G.B. (1975), 'Adam Smith on competition and increasing returns', in Skinner A. and T. Wilson (eds), *Essays on Adam Smith*, Oxford: Oxford University Press.
3. Amendola, M. and S. Bruno (1990), 'The behaviour of the innovative firm: relations to the environment', *Research Policy*, **19** (5), 419–33

PART I

Evolutionary Theories of the Firm

1. The Open, Evolving Economy: Alfred Marshall on Knowledge, Management and Innovation

Stanley J. Metcalfe

INTRODUCTION[1]

Alfred Marshall's two great works, *Principles of Economics* and *Industry and Trade*, locate him as a major figure in a thread of evolutionary reasoning that explores the restless, dynamic nature of modern capitalism, a thread that begins with Adam Smith and leads on through Marx to Schumpeter and Hayek. Marshall's work, along with that of Schumpeter, provides a convincing structure in which to focus on the self-transforming as well as the self-organizing nature of capitalism. The central feature that I wish to draw attention to in this essay is Marshall's open systems approach to economic development and its intimate connection to his evolutionary perspective on the development of knowledge and organization. Marshall's knowledge creating capitalism denies the possibility of any economic equilibrium and has evolved an instituted structure that creates the incentives and opportunities to transform knowledge into economic wealth. This restless nature of capitalism does not of course mean that its operation is chaotic. Far from it, the system is highly ordered and the nature of its ordering strongly conditions the process of innovation and economic adaptation to innovation. What I am not seeking to do is privilege Marshall's thought relative to these other contributors to the evolutionary understanding of capitalism, rather my purpose is to point out the specific nature of his deep perspective on change, development and value. It is the generality of Marshall's approach to the problems of knowledge and organization that is particularly striking in his work. Moreover, he does so in an explicit evolutionary manner that I will explain below.

Apart from a concern with connecting principles, there are two other reasons for a renewed interest in Marshallian dynamics. The first is that advances in the modelling of evolving systems since Nelson and Winter (1982) provide tools to address the Mecca of evolutionary economics in a way which was denied to Marshall – among these the methods of replicator dynamics play a central role in our interpretation of Marshall's economics as variation selection theory. The second is that Marshall's writing would not be out of place in regard to much of the modern literature on corporate strategy and innovation and this raises the prospect of building on his thought, to better combine managerial and economic theory in a way which evolutionists and innovation scholars must surely find enticing. Thus the modern literatures on the resource based view of the firm, on capabilities and their accumulation, and on the evolutionary theory of the firm all have a natural affinity with a Marshallian perspective (Winter 1995).

Taken as a whole these claims provide a strong rationale to revisit Marshall and tease out his thinking on the relation between, innovation, or business experimentation as he termed it, and the problems of development, value and distribution. Indeed, the predominance in modern economies of innovation based competition does not render the theory of value and distribution irrelevant. Quite the contrary, it requires a different theory of competition for its elucidation which is what Marshall and Schumpeter, in their different ways, in the end provide.

PRELIMINARIES

To begin it is of central importance to any understanding of Marshall's economics to recognize the vital interplay between knowledge and organization in his thinking; they are the key concepts in his account of the growth and development of economies and the explanation of growth and development is his primary objective. Thus we are told on the opening page of book IV (*Principles of Economics*, IV, 1, p. 138) that knowledge and organization are the greater part of capital, that knowledge is the most powerful engine of production and that knowledge is aided by organization in its many different forms.

Not only is knowledge organized but the flows of information characteristic of any society, a reflection of the distributed nature of knowing and acting, are also organized in three different ways: as firms, Marshall's basic unit of productive activity; as markets, Marshall's unit of exchange activity; and, as a plethora of other instituted activities, of which those in relation to education and research are of primary importance for his economic dynamics. In all three forms of organization, information flow is the basis of action via its role in correlating understanding. In relation to markets, for example, the degree of access to information by different sellers and buyers is crucial to the way they operate, which is why Marshall devoted many asides to the importance of developments in transport and communication technology. However, he devotes most of his theoretical discussion to the firm but while any firm has to take appropriate care of its internal organization it must just as importantly engage with the organization of markets and the other non-market activities if it is to survive and prosper. Organization is external as well as internal, which is exactly why economies of expansion and development are internal and external and are only harvested to the extent that the firm has appropriate, integrated internal and external organizational forms.

The twin themes of knowledge and organization have one purpose to bring together the theory of value and the theory of economic development, they are inseparable in Marshall, and their subsequent separation is the elementary reason why his writing is now confined to the margins of economic thought.[2] My claim here is the evolutionary economics will be greatly strengthened by bringing Marshall back to the centre, in so doing we are offered the prospect of a General Theory of Economic Evolution (GEE not GE) and a research programme devoted to identifying the diversity of economic behaviour and within that the ubiquitous role of innovation. I cannot in any way do justice to this ambition in one paper so I will concentrate on three aspects of Marshall as evolutionist, namely the role of management in his theory of firm and industry, the role of innovation and novelty and, most challenging of all, the relation between the representative firm and the theory of value.[3] Management and innovation connect directly to the variation/selection side of Marshallian though but they also connect to his organic, systems perspective through the discussion of the firm and the penumbra of activities that constitute its external environment and organization.

MARSHALL AND SCHUMPETER: COMPLEMENTS NOT SUBSTITUTES

I do not think I am alone in making a sharp separation in my mind between the economics of Marshall and Schumpeter that may not be warranted. It is not that there are not important differences in style and substance between them, compare Marshall's gradualism with Schumpeter's rather more saltation based view of the effects of innovation; it is rather that the similarities have been overlooked. First and foremost they both offer accounts of the self-transformation of capitalism through innovation and each makes clear that transformation presupposes a substrate of order that is transient which shapes the rate and direction of transformation.[4] In short organization is necessary for the possibility of non-random change. This is perhaps why neither found much use for the stationary state other than as an imperfect starting point for analysis, for the idea of a stationary capitalism had become in relation to the rest of their thinking a contradiction in terms.[5] Any proper model of capitalism would place the process of self-transformation at its core and for essentially the same reason, the organization of knowledge leads to the development of knowledge and if knowledge cannot be stationary how can an economy be stationary? As Marshall puts it, 'problems are imperfectly represented when they are treated as problems of statical equilibrium and not of organic growth' (*Principles of Economics*, V, 12, p. 461) and again "nothing of this (the stationary state) is true in the world in which we live" for there the problem to be addressed is,

> How changes in the volume of production, in its methods, and in its cost are ever mutually modifying one another; they are always affecting and being affected by the character and extent of demand (*Principles of Economics*, V, 5, p. 368).

Rather as Knight put it in his assessment of the forces leading to economic growth, they were both coming to terms with the nature of a self exciting system, a system in which the organization of the flow of information is not only the clue to the nature of order but the clue to the nature of economic evolution, though we had to wait for Hayek to make this clear in its full implications.

Moreover, innovation is a central part of the economic problem for Marshall just as much as for Schumpeter. For both, it equates to business leadership which individuals are endowed with to different degrees, and for both, business differentiation is a source of transient profit advantage. Marshall is just as capable as Schumpeter in distinguishing invention from innovation and in identifying great innovators as outstanding individuals, although for Marshall, innovation is more a part of business routine and he is far less explicit than Schumpeter in conceiving of barriers to innovation and the resistance of established interests.

Finally both Marshall and Schumpeter expressed grave reservations about the continuation of the innovation process and the implied limits to economic progress. For Marshall this lay in greater monopoly power and the elimination of multiple sources of innovation. For Schumpeter it lay in the rational bureaucratization of the innovation process and the euthanasia of the entrepreneur, although the dangers of bureaucracy for economic change are not lost on Marshall either, as we shall see below.

Thus it seems that a more careful comparison of the innovative stance of these two great economists would be fruitful; not least because while Schumpeter provides the link to Hayek, Marshall provides the equally significant link to Adam Smith. Taken together their writings spin a continuous thread that links the process of economic development to the growth of knowledge and organization as interwoven evolutionary processes.[6]

MARSHALL'S EVOLUTIONARY THEORY: ORGANIC SYSTEM AND VARIATIONAL CHANGE[7]

The point to grasp is that there are two evolutionary Marshall's, one devoted to the organic, system development view of economic change, the substance of book IV, and the other, the adaptive, variation, selection view of industrial competition and development, the substance of books V and VI. Marshall's difficulties in reconciling the first ecological perspective with the second adaptive perspective follow not only from the very different scope of the two books but also from the impossibility of treating questions of changes arising from within the system with the static mechanical method. He understood the restless nature of capitalism but found no method to hold in shape its system dynamics. The twin views of evolution are of course related. The organic, developmental view provides the matrix within which sits the variation-selection view so that the notion of evolution as cumulative unfolding and evolution as innovation and competitive process are linked together and operate at multiple levels. Marshall's organic system view is focused on patterns of economic differentiation and integration of economic activities, and the way their structures co-evolve over time in terms of changes in institutions, activities and individuals taken in their social and economic context (Limoges and Menard 1994; Hodgson 1993). For Marshall, however, it is the system changes that dominate his discussion, new parts are always being developed, connections made and broken and boundaries redrawn and this is the theme of book IV, an explanation of the high theme of economic progress expressed in terms of a cumulative unfolding of the division of labour and markets and the concomitant development of specialized skill, knowledge and machinery, together with the deeper integration of the ensuing parts through such factors as institutional development (credit) and new communications technologies (*Principles of Economics*, IV, 8, p. 241). It is a systemic view in which the parts and their interconnections evolve over time. It is through this discussion of the evolving division of labour that we reach the distinction between internal and external economies and the advantages of production on a large scale and so begin to form the precarious bridge with the concerns of value and distribution in books V and VI and, indeed, Marshall's second kind of economic evolution.

The second strand in Marshall's evolutionary thought is his population based account of individual variation and its economic consequences, for Marshall is no essentialist. Here we find the incessant emphasis on the individual, the differentiated person or organization that is at the centre of the evolutionary viewpoint. It is individualism that underpins variation and there is no more powerful source of variation in Marshall than individual differences in knowledge and ability. However, individuals find their meaning in an instituted social context, individualism is not atomism and 'the life of a society is something more than the lives of its individual members' (*Principles of Economics*, I, 2, p. 25) just as the history of an industry is more than the history of its constituent firms. Moreover, economics is the study of men 'as they live and move and *think* in the ordinary business of life' (*Principles of Economics*, I, 2, p. 14). The cognitive thread underpinning Marshall's theory of individual action in a social context is crucial to understanding the evolutionary spirit of his work. It underpins the importance of individual differences in human nature and motivation, in the variations in business ability, and most crucially of all in relation to the growth of knowledge. In relation to the latter, Marshall's concept of competition is a vitally important strand in his thinking. It is not perfect competition at all but a matter of rivalry (racing is his alternative description), a contest between competitors of different and changing abilities, grounded in the fundamental characteristics of modern industrial life – self reliance, deliberation and an awareness of the future consequences of actions. Competition not a dull, equilibrium state but rather a creative force promoting spontaneity and energy and what matters is its open character, it is a matter as he put it of *Economic Freedom* (*Principles of Economics*, I, 1, p. 10) that is to say, the freedom to use knowledge for economic advantage.

Competition in Marshall is a dual process, the generation of variation in activity, and the process of selection in which firms that are better managed are able to attract capital and grow but if they become 'slack in enterprise or weak in purpose' (*Industry and Trade*, II, 8, p. 315), they fail and make way for more vigorous competitors. It is not perfect competition as subsequently understood but its strength does depend on the degree of informational perfection of the market. This view of competition as a dynamic process of variation and selection underpins the principle of substitution, which is not restricted to the mechanical choice of options from a given list, as generations of text books have it, rather the lists of possible choices are actively and idiosyncratically created by each business in the course of its activity. The outcomes are then tested in the market so that 'society substitutes one undertaker for another who is less efficient in proportion to his charges' (*Principles of Economics*, V, 3, p. 341). Indeed, in introducing a discussion of profit in relation to business ability he is quite explicit that this principle of substitution is a special and limited application of the law of 'the survival of the fittest' (*Principles of Economics*, VI, 7, p. 597) and that the struggle for survival selects those best fitted to the extant environment but not necessarily those best fitted to benefit their environment. Here Marshall is fully aware that competition selects directly for immediate properties not necessarily those which might otherwise do good work for society.

We can now explore the two evolutionary strands in terms of Marshall's theory of management and his treatment of invention and innovation.

MARSHALL AND BUSINESS MANAGEMENT

Marshall's extended treatment of management provides clear evidence of the intertwining between his developmental and population dynamic views of economic progress. Indeed the managerial topic brings together the two high themes of knowledge and organization that is central to his treatment of economic dynamics. It is also worth noting that the main features of his treatment change little between the First and the Eighth editions; apparently Marshall's views on management were settled early in the development of the *Principles of Economics* and are elaborated in essentially the same form in *Industry and Trade*. I can think of no other comparable economic theorist who devoted so much attention to this topic. The reason for this is clear, the managerial function is a major route to explaining firm differentiation and firm dynamics both of which are central to the long run theory of value and to differential profitability. Echoes of Marshall's treatment are not to be found in modern economic textbooks but in major developments in managerial thinking, e.g. the distinction between strategy and implementation, of innovation versus routine, the matter of capability formation and the theory of the growth of the firm, following Penrose (1959).

In book IV Marshall sets out the central evolutionary question thus, ' . . . what are the causes which make different forms of management the fittest to profit from their environment, and the most likely to prevail over others . . . ' (*Principles of Economics*, IV, 9, p. 265). The answer is in two parts. Consider first the organic, developmental side of the argument and the rise of specialist managerial functions in business. This growth of specialized functions is of course a consequence of the wider organizing principle of the division of labour, for it is the increasing complexity of large scale business affairs that makes 'handicraft' managerial methods quite inappropriate to the task of modern business management. This requires a new division of administrative labour, premised on organizational innovation, with specialized businessmen who collectively undertake risks, bring together capital and labour, engineer the general plan and superintend minor details of the business. The distinguishing feature of these tasks is the distinctive knowledge and mental effort that they entail. The small businessman in a traditional trade, the village artisan for example, may be taxed by continued physical effort but, in a telling phrase 'his brain was seldom weary' (*Principles of Economics*, IV, 12, p. 292) and for Marshall, management in its new forms was a matter for the intellect and involved much more than the superintendence of labour.

Managerial services fall within two broad categories of action: first, the ability to appoint and lead a team of subordinates and to make the most of their abilities while preserving order and unity in the plan of the business; and, secondly, to 'know the trade'. By this short phrase, Marshall means activities that are closely tied to enterprise and innovation, and included in this category are the ability to forecast demand (expectations, as always, play an important role in Marshall's assessment of how people act and different individuals hold substantively different expectations),[8] the facility to judge risks boldly but with care and, finally, the capacity to innovate through the perception of opportunities to supply new commodities or for improving processes of production. Thus Marshall's organic view of the managerial team, consisting of grades of different ability carrying out interlinked tasks, organized on different lines whether partnerships or private companies, for example, but always held together by business leadership. In *Industry and Trade*, the list of attributes of a business leader and his chief subordinates is spelt out even more clearly, as follows: the personal qualities of judgement and enterprise, prudence and fortitude in risk making; an alertness to adopting new techniques and initiating them; a high power of organization; the ability to read and handle character in subordinates; and, finally, the skill to allocate employees to tasks at which they are most suited. All these Marshall notes are needed even in a head of business of moderate size and *a fortiori* in the larger business they are required of the senior management team and its head in particular.[9] It cannot be said from this that Marshall did not have innovation and enterprise very firmly in his grasp when he wrote about the distinctive contribution of management to economic organization.

Turning now to the population dimension of Marshall's treatment we find the twin concerns that underpin his dynamic treatment of value, namely, the differentiation of managerial ability and the tendency for managerial ability to develop with experience and age. In broad terms business leaders are divided into those who open up new and improved business methods and, as in Schumpeter, those who follow beaten tracks (*Principles of Economics*, VI, 7, p. 597).[10] In relation to variety very few employers combine the multifarious managerial abilities to a high degree and scarcely any two owe their business success to the same combination of advantages. Consequently each business is an 'individual', differing in some degree from its rivals, and no two persons pursuing the same aims follow exactly the same route and, importantly, we are told, this tendency to variation is the chief source of progress (*Principles of Economics*, V, 4, p. 355). The immediate consequence of the differences in managerial ability is the variation in the profitability of their business organizations, and their prospects for survival such that average ability brings forth quite low returns but exceptional ability allows fortunes to be amassed (*Principles of Economics*, VI, 12, p. 685).

However, Marshall insists that managerial ability is not a given. There is first the simple consequence of natural life span and the need to hand the business on to successors who if they are family members are unlikely as a general rule to have the business ability of the founder, despite the advantages of training in business that they might have enjoyed. In Marshall, business dynasties are short lived, at least that is until the innovation of limited liability for joint stock companies which fundamentally changed the nature of the competitive process. There is secondly the process of accumulating experience, overcoming obstacles and establishing a sound footing in a trade, what modern scholars would call 'learning'.[11] In Marshall, age and experience are intertwined with energy and purpose in offsetting ways through time. This is the theme of the 'trees in the forest' and of the rise and fall of individual firms[12] in the population, and, of course, this organic view poses a central problem of managerial continuity. Marshall's answer lies in the innovation of new forms of business organization: cooperative arrangements, of which he is in favour but doubts their viability, business partnerships in which the partners may specialize in different business functions, private companies and, more troublesome, the joint stock company with its publicly traded capital and separation of ownership from control. The fact that the later form might give the business a life beyond several generations of management was a continued source of concern in relation to the theory of competition in book V. Each of these different forms of organization has the effect of distributing the managerial task over a group of individuals, but what is significant about the joint stock form is that it opens up the possibility of managerial employment to individuals independently of their access to capital or prior business connection.

It is clear that Marshall considers the rise of professional management to give further advantages to the large scale organization, where the head can devote himself to 'the broadest and most fundamental problems of his trade' neither troubled with details nor with routine work but keeping 'his mind fresh and clear *for thinking out* the most difficult and vital problems of his business' (*Principles of Economics*, IV, 11, p. 284). While the smaller business may have advantages of direction and close control of fine detail, its most fundamental disadvantage is in making experiments (innovating) so that the small business must generally follow rather than lead. Here we see the division between the control of an existing business and the ability to change the business in technique, organization or market as a central managerial dichotomy. Yet, as always there are qualifications, the small business, exceptionally, may become large by overcoming formidable barriers. To do so, the businessman must adapt to the larger sphere, must retain his originality and versatility, his perseverance his tact and his good luck for very many years together (*Principles of Economics*, IV, 9, p. 285) so that a larger market can be secured, credit established, and subordinates attracted of more than ordinary zeal and ability. Yet bad luck may thwart such efforts and the ultimate barrier to growth may be decay if not of faculties then the willingness to work hard. For Marshall, it seems, great stress is placed on the fact that time is the ultimate scarce resource at the disposal of the individual.

The difference in business abilities which is central to Marshall's treatment is further reinforced by the operation of the capital market and this is an argument that foreshadows the treatment of long run values in book V. Differential ability translates into differential profitability and by making good profits a firm blessed with exceptional managerial ability and energy (*Principles of Economics*, VI, 8, p. 614) not only adds to own capital but increases the willingness of others to lend on more advantageous terms to the business. So vicissitudes apart, capital grows in proportion to business ability. The converse happens for weaker businessmen so that selection via the product market directly and the capital market by remove results in an unexpected correlation between size and business ability (*Principles of Economics*, IV, 12, p. 312).

INNOVATION AND THE GROWTH OF KNOWLEDGE

It is with regard to the discussion of innovation that Marshall's evolutionary thought reaches its most fundamental significance in relation to the development of knowledge in general and modern science and engineering in particular. Unlike Schumpeter, the focus on innovations as step, transformative changes is smoothed away in line with the gradualism that marks his approach. This is not to say that major, radical inventions are not countenanced but rather the economic mode of their development and application is gradual.[13] Indeed it is perhaps surprising to note how much Marshall, like Schumpeter, was in touch with the major inventions and innovations of his time, something which is manifest in even a cursory reading of *Industry and Trade*.[14]

What distinguishes Marshall most sharply from Schumpeter is that innovation is part of the normal routine for the discovery of business advantage, it is an intrinsic attribute of economic leadership in the economic systems that he analyses and observes (Moss 1982). The idea of the entrepreneur, 'the new man' breaking in discrete, saltationist fashion with the status quo, fits too uneasily with Marshall's avowed gradualism. The radical nature of any innovation only emerges with the benefit of hindsight, it is a historical fact, and depends on market and non-market responses as well as, normally, a stream of incremental innovations in technique, organization and instituted frame that have been stimulated by the information flux that trial and adaptation generate. Thus Schumpeter emphasizes the discontinuity of the original innovation opportunity, and Marshall emphasizes the ensuing continuity of adaptations: surely they are complements not substitutes. This is also manifest in Marshall's attitude to inventions, they are usually the culmination of many contributors over extended time that bring to a head 'constructive movements that have long been in preparation' (*Principles of Economics*, Preface, p. xiii).

Scattered across *Principles of Economics* and *Industry and Trade* is an account of the invention and innovation process that is thoroughly modern in outlook. As with the treatment of management the organic perception of the division of labour holds sway but now in relation to the generation of new knowledge, and with regard to the internal and external organization of the firm. Given this outlook it is not surprising to find Marshall claiming that the advances in the sciences of chemical, electrical and biological sciences will open up the prospect of increasing returns to effort for many generations to come. Knowledge for Marshall develops cumulatively in paradigm fashion in chains of related sequences of discoveries, ' . . . each new knowledge being the offspring of others that went before, and the parent of many that follow' (*Industry and Trade,* II, 2, p. 206). Moreover, its production has to be organized in such a way that '*imagination* [my emphasis] creates movement; *caution* checks reason by working out parallel but independent chains of thought, and each general rule is *confirmed or discredited* by experiments or observations of specific facts' (*Industry and Trade*, II, 2, p. 203). This is not too far removed in broad outline from a variation-selection view of the growth of knowledge that an evolutionary epistemologist might hold.[15] Furthermore, innovation is inseparable from the competitive process. For the advantages of economic freedom 'are never more strikingly manifest than when a business man endowed with genius is trying experiments, at his own risk, to see whether some new method or combination of old methods, will be more efficient than the old.' (*Principles of Economics*, V, 8, p. 406). The relation is two-way and mutually reinforcing between free competition and business experimentation.

Consider next the question of innovation and the firm. Here it is worth drawing attention to how much innovation figures in Marshall's treatment of the managerial function in large and small firms. As always, the argument is carefully nuanced and surrounded by a penumbra of qualification, for Marshall's method is a population method; there is always a statistical distribution of the phenomena in hand. Just as firms differ in their efficiency they are presumed to differ in the ability to change the underpinning activities. The importance of the problem is first posed in terms of discharging a characteristic task of the modern manufacturer, to create new wants where none previously existed (*Principles of Economics*, IV, 11, p.280). Thus in regard to the matter of business experimentation, Marshall's term for innovation, the general rule is that there are economies of large scale, such that the advantages generally lie with large firms unless age and size have fostered (Schumpeter-like) bureaucratic methods that inhibit innovation in technique and organization. But there are countervailing arguments in favour of the alert small business. Here Marshall deploys one of his favourite examples of external economies, namely, the ready access to a supply of trade and scientific literature that makes new discoveries public information, so shifting advantages in favour of the small firm, though only if that firm is led by an exceptionally strong individual with the ability for 'availing himself of the modern facilities for obtaining knowledge', and if the risks of experimentation can be born with a small capital base.[16] As always with Marshall, essentialism doesn't work, different behaviours and possibilities co-exist and any point generalizations are almost certainly false. Economic life is a distribution and a changing distribution at that.

When we turn to the determinants of the innovation process it is no longer sufficient to focus on the firm in isolation, its external organization in relation to the growth of knowledge matters, and so it is not an overstatement to see Marshall as propounding an innovation systems perspective which, of course, is simply another angle on the division of labour and its co-ordination. But in order to benefit from external economies the firm needs an external organization, external economies do not come for free and access to them has to be organized and co-ordinated. For Marshall the firm's internal knowledge generating process are embedded in a broader matrix of national and sectoral arrangements of two broad kinds, the industrial district and the national system of research. The first is well known, the co-location of firms facilitates the communication of information, thus it correlates knowledge so that 'the mysteries of the trade become no mysteries' and ideas are readily interchanged and, crucially, become 'the source of further new ideas', a perfect Marshallian combination of restless knowledge and restless activity (*Principles of Economics*, V, 10, p.271). The second information generating and disseminating structure is not well known perhaps because it is only found in *Industry and Trade*. It is articulated in terms of a tripartite ecology of research laboratories, as follows: those of the first order, charged with extending knowledge in the large and normally the province of publicly funded universities, the originators of scientific advances that revolutionize the methods of industry; those of the second order, charged with generating knowledge directed at the requirements of a particular branch of industry and either organized by single giant businesses or in collaborative association between businesses;[17] and those of the third order, quality control laboratories for particular establishments that check that their output meets the standards required. As with any division of labour its functioning depends on how it is interconnected, not in this case by markets but by personal scientific contact and reference to the published literature. Thus, the technical research laboratory of an industry benefits from keeping in touch with the chief scientific laboratories, and the later may gain much and loose nothing by keeping in touch with the industries whose methods may be improved by the fruits of fundamental research. Thus Marshall's account of innovation processes is one in which advances in knowledge are made by different men, of different capabilities and specialisms, with different motives and different methods. Thus, the businessman as innovator is supported by the role of students, 'men who labour not with reference to the attainment of any particular practical end, but in search of knowledge for its own sake' (*Industry and Trade*, II, 2, p. 203) and this pursuit is generally richer in its outcomes than knowledge pursued for particular practical ends.

Deeper still, the division of labour applies not only to organizational form across universities, laboratories and firms it also applies within laboratories. In an echo of Adam Smith and his 'philosophers and men of speculation', Marshall draws attention to the increasing importance of team activity in knowledge production in which a problem is broken down into smaller tasks carried out by lesser researchers but coordinated by a 'chief who sets each man his task' (*Industry and Trade*, I, 7, p. 134). It is where fundamental principles are not understood that vast numbers of random experiments must be made and this requires teamwork as in chemistry where many materials may be tried before a discovery is made. Not surprisingly then the team principle applies in the engineering workshops as well as the scientific laboratories. The organization of knowledge production is further facilitated by the emergence of standards for the conduct of research and the classification of knowledge and both are important for the possibility of its cumulative growth and diffusion. There should be little doubt now that Marshall was an early advocate of the systemic growth of knowledge and the related nature of the innovation process.

INNOVATION AND THE THEORY OF VALUE: MARSHALL'S DILEMMA

While our discussion of management and innovation in Marshall is of interest in its own right it has a wider significance in connection to his theory of value. Marshall's value theory addresses a fundamental question one that reflects the classical heritage that runs through the *Principles of Economics*. We may express it thus 'Is there an attractor that constitutes a long period focal point to guide the evolution of market price?' Or put with different emphasis, 'What governs long run value when individual firm cost structures

are different and changing?' Or again, 'Which firm if any can be said to
provide the anchor of the price system?' It cannot be the particular
circumstances of the firm just on the brink of survival, for it is shortly to
become extinct, and it cannot depend on the particulars of a new entrant for
its costs are yet too fluid to provide a benchmark. Instead the suggested
answer is to be found in the representative firm and it is here that the
difficulties begin; difficulties that rather quickly led to the marginalization of
Marshall's long period theory of value.[18] Of course, this is intrinsically a
dynamic issue and we should take Marshall's dynamic aspirations seriously
and accept that the theory of value is an integral component of his dynamics
of growth and development (O'Brien 1990; Loasby 1989). Indeed, behind
this traditional question is a deeper matter of the role of market processes and
the price mechanism in generating economic adaptation to the new
opportunities made possible by business experimentation. Whatever it is that
connects innovation and the pattern of order, it is central to the question of
the differentiation and growth of the firm, which, as we have already
established, is central to Marshallian dynamics, and, indeed, the
interdependent working of markets and the other institutions that foster
interaction and the correlating of beliefs and behaviour. Thus his theory of
value is premised on a, however rudimentary, account of the growth and
development of the innovating firm. It is, of course, captured in the statement
that the short-run effect of an increase in demand is normally to increase the
price of a commodity but that the long-run effect is normally the converse.[19]
This is none other than Smith's theme that extending the market increases the
efficiency and effectiveness with which resources are utilised, indeed we can
treat much of the *Principles of Economics* as being devoted to elaborating
this point in fine detail.[20]

   Thus the two sided view of an evolving economy that Marshall develops
in book IV is turned in books V and VI into a population dynamic analysis of
a long standing question in economics, the relation to be expected between
long-run normal prices and normal costs. It caused him endless difficulty and
as is generally accepted he failed in his chosen task (Hodgson 1993; Loasby
1989, 1990). Yet I want to establish here that he had assembled all the ideas
he needed to solve the relation between value and cost in an evolving
economy, in particular the necessity of beginning any discussion of
endogenous change from an account of the prevailing order, all that is
missing is the evolutionary toolbox.

   First and foremost, an understanding of Marshall's dynamic intent does
not involve abandoning a theory of economic order, quite the contrary.
Evolution is not possible without a substrate of order to give guidance and
purpose to change. So Marshall's reliance on statical methods was not
misguided but it was only half the story and here a paradox must be faced: to

exist and guide, any order requires stability in the small but evolution implies instability in the large, that the prevailing order must be capable of invasion by novelty.[21] This tension is worked out in Marshall in terms of his scheme of dynamic forces working at different velocities, the periodization scheme, and his theory of investment. In the short-run investment is tamed but in the longer and secular periods it has full sway with multiple kinds of investment, tangible or intangible, in capital goods (perhaps the lesser part), organization and knowledge driving the internal dynamic of the system. Thus Marshall repeatedly tells us of the importance of businesses pushing investment to the margin of profitability while at the same time warning us that the margin is different for different firms. On these differences in the investment margin hinge the foundations of variation, selection and ultimately organic change and, of course, they imply the vital importance of short period market phenomena.

Secondly, to link together value and development in his evolutionary way posed a problem, Marshall's central problem, how to explain endogenous change in the presence of diversity and order. As pointed out above, he had questioned whether the analysis of a stationary state could throw light on the problem, and in this he had much in common with Schumpeter, and for the same reason, that change in economically relevant knowledge arises from within the system. Elements of the 'statical' theory are needed to account for and describe the prevailing order but it is equally the case, we are repeatedly warned, that the chosen method is barely an introduction to the study of progress and industries which show a tendency to increasing return (*Principles of Economics*, V, 12, p. 461).

Thirdly, the fundamental reasoning behind these difficulties has already been explained in book IV, namely in terms of the co-evolution of knowledge and organization as expressed through the generation of internal and internal economies. However, woven into this analysis is another crucial evolutionary feature, these processes work very unevenly so that there is considerable variation across and within industries of these mutually modifying elements. It is this which poses the problem in relation to the theory of value for if all firms are different in their access to internal and external economies, it is the uncompleted resolution of this problem that book V, and book VI too, the latter particularly in relation to the profits of business power and organization, are devoted too.

To explore this in more detail it will help to first consider the meaning of order in Marshall, then move on to the representative firm and finally draw the threads together in an evolutionary, dynamic, population based exposition of the cost – price relationship.

EQUILIBRIUM, ORDER AND EVOLUTION

We should note that Marshall got off to a bad start in his use of the word equilibrium. He really meant that, depending on the calendar time allowed, there are the different, interlinked solutions to a particular problem of matching supply and demand in a particular trade but in such a manner that any short-period solution can only be provisional (Currie and Steedman 1990; Chick and Caserta 1997). For each solution is conditioned by the fact that both sides of the market are made up by information processors, individual firms and consumers who are knowledgeable and sentient. The solution to any information specific problem of reconciling demand with supply contains within it the information generating process that will revise beliefs and so change its determining conditions, due allowance for time being given. The Hayekian notion of an order is perhaps more apposite, for this avoids the real difficulty with the notion of equilibrium that whatever changes occur necessarily come from without; the balls in the famous bowl, it will be remembered, only change their configuration when acted on by an external agency. It is merely a matter of definition that a system that is in equilibrium cannot self-transform. Not so for Marshall's economy which, like Schumpeter's, is transformed continually from within as order generates flux: and the self-transformation of Marshall's economy, like Schumpeter's is founded on the ongoing transformation of knowledge. Hence the importance of the organization of flows of information within the market process that serve to challenge or confirm existing knowledge and belief. Here we might state boldly that self-organization depends on correlation of beliefs and understanding, while self-transformation depends on their de-correlation through the emergence of novelty. This is the theme of business experimentation and entrepreneurial action that binds Marshall and Schumpeter together.

The out of equilibrium logic is closely bound up in Marshall with the importance of time and the famous periodization scheme in which, as Shackle (1965) so perceptively recognizes:

> Equilibrium is a state of adjustment to circumstances, but it is fiction, Marshall's own and declared fiction, for it is an adjustment that *would* be attained if the very endeavour to reach it did not reveal fresh possibilities, give fresh command of resources, and prepare the way for inevitable, natural, organic further change (Shackle 1965, p. 36).

Thus in Marshall all economic order is transient; as the market period gives way to the short period, the later to the long period and everything is subservient to the secular period where knowledge and the character of man are allowed to change. If order is the solution to a problem it is a solution which, in its very emergence, changes the nature of the problem. Thus the long period is not an equilibrium stationary state in which long run forces have worked themselves out but rather a particular short-period order that has felt the effect of long-period forces over a defined period of history; and, as such, it is merely a staging post to a future period of history in which as yet to be identified long-period forces will hold sway. This is the essence of Marshall's open system dynamics, long-period forces are continually at work generating prospects for further change, the nature of which cannot be specified in advance of its occurrence. How much better would have been Marshall's reception if his followers had understood this fundamental point, had taken seriously his insistence on the dynamic nature of the value problem and its dependence on endogenous changes in organization and knowledge (Loasby 1990, 1991).

Of course, all these forces appropriate to the different 'periods' operate continuously and contemporaneously, so the pound *ceteris paribus* is simply a device to untangle not differing equilibria but forces that operate with different velocities with respect to each other and with respect to their differential effect on firms and industries. It should not be lost on the reader that non-uniform velocities of change are characteristic of evolutionary theory, in general, and that differential growth rates imply structural change and the redrawing of the pattern of order, in particular. Quite crucially, the different periods are not different states of affairs but different processes, defining forces working with particular velocities.[22] Everything happens, indeed only can happen, in the present but the future consequences of present action mean that expectations, that is to say imagination, are important and this is one of the major dimensions in which Marshall's individuals are different. In this way the past leaves its legacy through the knowledge it has generated and the effect this has on the interpretation of the future.

To sum up, there cannot be any long-run equilibrium in Marshall's system, only sequences of transient short-period orders that evolve with investment and the growth of knowledge. The different periods overlap, and between the long and secular period no sharp division could be drawn for in both knowledge changes but it is in each case different classes of knowledge that are in view. Thus the secular period allows for inventions and changes in the character of man while the long period includes not only the expansion of plant and equipment but the acquisition of trade knowledge and specialized ability together with adaptations of existing ideas. The long period in relation to a new entrant, for example, is obviously not the same as the long period for an established firm.[23] But these overlapping categories simply reinforce the idea of different forces working with different velocities in different industries. In this way Marshall was able to combine the idea of the out of equilibrium firm with the industry that is ordered, and in this dichotomy the concept of the representative firm plays a key role.

VALUE, COST AND THE REPRESENTATIVE FIRM

Marshall's answer to the question of long-period value and cost is subtle, but not at all transparent once we move beyond the central claim relating long-period value to the costs of the representative firm. At its core is a redrawing of Ricardo's argument on the differential rent of land, made applicable to the differential profit of business firms. Necessarily, for the reasons sketched above, the answer begins with a characterization of short-period order and, in the summary to book V, the argument begins, with the a claim that in any short-period situation (order), the price in an openly competitive market must cover the expenses of production 'of those producers who have no special and exceptional facilities' while more favoured producers will earn a producer's rent (*Principle of Economics*, V, 15, p. 499).[24] Thus the least viable of the current producers defines the margin of production as Shove (1930), Robbins (1928) and others subsequently insisted.

However, this pattern of order, and its associated particular expenses curve and pattern of profitability, or rather quasi rents, also engages the long-period forces that result in changes in the productive capacities in the different firms and their access to internal and external economies. This is the dynamic problem the representative firm is meant to handle, but it is a concept that is easily misunderstood.

Three problems arise, one with respect to meaning, one with respect to purpose and the third in respect of logic. Let me take them *seriatim*. What Marshall meant by the representative firm is not altogether precise. At one level it is expressed in terms of certain characteristic features of the firm; it enjoys its fair share of internal and external economies appropriate to the present scale of the industry (*Principle of Economic*, V, 12, p. 460), which suggests it is of average size for the industry; it is managed with normal ability which suggests it is not a new firm struggling into existence nor is it one at the end of its viable existence or even a firm that through ability and good fortune is more efficient than virtually any of its rivals; it is one in which the forces of managerial and organizational growth and decay are balanced, so that its characteristics are stationary; it is a firm that is always doing the same class of business to the same extent. These are not obviously compatible definitions but at least they suggest that representativeness is a central tendency perhaps best expressed as some kind of average firm but precisely what kind of average is not clear (*Principle of Economic*, IV, 13, p.318). Marshall also provides us with a quite different definition; a representative firm will have a constant output when the output of the industry is constant. All other firms may be and generally will be rising and falling in terms of relative output but the representative firm is held fixed in its market share. Thus, by implication, if the industry is growing, the representative firm is growing at the same rate, and keeps its market share constant, while all others are changing in their relative importance. This is a definition that helps greatly in unravelling the dynamic argument.

It is, naturally, a statistical concept made necessary by the forces of variation linked to management and innovation that mean that the firms in the relevant population are different in innumerable different ways. It is a neat, summary device for making use of these variations but Marshall wanted it to do much more, in two respects, to be the fulcrum around which the forces of evolution are gathered, and, to be the vehicle for the average attainment of internal and external economies that come with the expansion of the industry as a whole. These are two quite separate demands on the representative firm.

That the representative firm is an analytical device should be clear, although Marshall's quest for realism and perhaps continuity meant that he erred in hinting that the representative firm was a real firm; a point soon criticized by Sraffa (1930) and Robertson (1956) who rightly pointed out that there is 'no address in the Business Directory' for the representative firm. Marshall's quest for realism at this point was counterproductive, for it clouded the necessary insight that the characteristics defining the representative firm cannot be determined *a priori* but are a product of the evolution of the industry.[25] That it is a dynamic concept, that it is a concept that is defined by the process of establishing market order and changes with that order made it quite unsuitable for the demands of the static theory in which it was soon compressed.

Finally there is the matter of logic. The notion that the long-period costs of a representative firm define the long-period supply price faces an immediate objection. If price is equal to the average cost of the firms in the population (it makes no difference if we defined them in terms of the median) then at least one firm in this long run situation cannot be covering its full costs, prime and supplementary. It cannot therefore be presumed to be operating once long run forces have done their work on this particular firm. Either all the firms in the long run have identical costs, *contra* Marshall's reasoning about management and innovation, or the meaning of the relationship between supply price and costs in the representative firm cannot be as Marshall believed. Subsidiary to this is a further difficulty, how the notion of representativeness is to be interpreted when we accept that the competitive performance of the firm will depend on additional considerations that cannot be subsumed under the label 'costs'. Then if the firm is average in one dimension it may not be average in respect of the others and it is certainly very demanding to define representativeness in all relevant dimensions.

As is well recognized, the concept foundered quickly on the misinterpretation of its purpose by Marshall's followers. Marshall had meant it to be an open recognition of the fact that it is a summary of a distribution and would have no purpose if all firms are identical. Thus Pigou (1928) was soon emboldened to replace it by the equilibrium firm, or rather the uniform firm, and Viner (1931) to draw his cost curves the same for all firms, so that Marshall's evolutionary population methodology is unwittingly replaced by essentialist methodology (Hodgson 1993; Limoges and Menard 1994). Shortly afterwards, Robbins (1928) and Shove (1930) delivered the *coup de grace*, and within the own terms they were right so to do; unfortunately, they had lost sight of the fact that their terms were not Marshall's terms.

Shove and Robbins are simply dealing with a different, static problem, how to allocate heterogeneous resources in such a way as to best meet economic needs; a problem of 'sorting and fitting' as Shove put it, invoking in the reader's mind the image of the economic problem as a gigantic jigsaw puzzle with a given numbers of unchanging pieces. Their answer, the arbitrage principle of 'returns no worse than the next best use', had no more need for the concept of an average firm than it did for an average parcel of land or degree of human skill. It is the margin that matters in their characterization of any co-ordinated position and all talk of averages is redundant. The relevant supply curve is built from knowledge of the capacities of all the firms in a trade, and in the established order one firm, depending on circumstances forms the margin of viability. Thus a coherent account of price formation emerged that is not an account of any process but a characterization of a state of affairs. *Pace* Marshall, equilibrium of this kind is the equilibrium of every productive agent in the industry, though it is perfectly consistent with differential returns to entrepreneurs of differing ability including those at the margin who can at best expect normal returns to their vision and organizing ability.[26] Thus while Robbins and Shove kept population thinking but stripped it of any causal evolutionary force, Pigou and Viner went further and eliminated the population approach altogether. No bridge with Marshall remained (Raffaelli 2003, Ch. 6).

On both counts his critics got it wrong because they failed to treat seriously Marshall's insistence that his was a dynamic problem to be solved by evolutionary reasoning.[27] Thus his argument that the opportunities for exploiting increasing returns could be constrained by demand, that the investment required for their realization takes time and effort and, crucially, that other time dependent changes may take place in the interval to nullify their effects, fell on deaf ears – and why shouldn't they if the problem was no longer Marshall's problem.[28] Similarly, more recent attempts to resurrect the representative firm, several of which build on Viner's (1931, Appendix) insight that its place is in a stochastic theory of the industry, failed to catch on largely because the approach remained static in its fundamentals (Jenner 1964; Maxwell 1929, 1958; Newman 1960; Wolfe 1954; Newman and Wolfe 1961). It turns out that the developing theory of industrial dynamics associated with evolutionary economics may provide the necessary change of focus to complete Marshall's picture.

POPULATION THINKING AND MARSHALLIAN VALUES: A SUGGESTED RESOLUTION

How then to deal with these difficulties and reinvigorate the Marshallian case for an evolutionary approach? Here I suggest a particular resolution that draws on the modern theory of economic evolution as expressed in the concept of replicator dynamics. The starting point is the population perspective and the recognition that at every point in time firms differ in numerous dimensions relevant to their performance. In this context we can define a marginal firm, a best practice firm, real firms as it where, and an analytical firm we call the representative firm. Its purpose is dynamic and it acts as the fulcrum around which the industry evolves. Its origins and definition lie in the replicator dynamics of competition very much along the lines sketched by Nelson and Winter (1982) and much earlier by Downie (1955). As in Marshall, the prevailing short-period price defines a distribution of profitability in relation to business capability and thus a distributed system of incentives for long-period forces to operate. For the marginal producer the long period forces in terms of investment have ceased to operate and the managerial problem there is to deal with decline and extinction. For the other firms, some are expanding relatively some are declining relatively, while others are declining absolutely but the representative firm is defined, as in Marshall, as the one that keeps its market share constant, expanding at the general rate of the industry. It is a fulcrum around which three dynamic processes are played out, some firms are being driven to extinction, others are growing at different rates and yet others are entering the industry.[29] All, in general, are uniquely different in multiple dimensions and their uniqueness is continually changing under the forces of experimentation, the identity and experience of the specific managerial team and the normal forces of increasing returns, internal and external. In particular, the pattern of evolution of the relative outputs of the firms depends on their distance from the representative firm, this is the significance of the concept.

How the representative firm is identified depends on the nature of competition and the characteristics of the market environment, factor markets as well as product markets. When there are multiple dimensions to representativeness, it is defined in terms of a trade-off or surface, so that a firm need not be a strict average across all dimensions to be representative. Rather, it must simply have characteristics such that above average performance in one dimension is balanced by below average performance in some others; the balancing differences being such as to enable that representative firm to grow at the market average rate. Notice, again, that representativeness is an analytic concept, a pattern of characteristics that equates to growth at the market rate. Several firms or no firm in the population may qualify for the adjective representative at any point in the market section process.

The ensuing Marshallian dynamics are surprisingly clear, firms normally expand at a rate according to their profitability as dictated by the difference between the prevailing normal market price and their specific costs of production and this pattern of expansion of decline depends on the position of each firm relative to the representative firm – the distance from mean dynamic. Thus the long-period dynamic forces are distributed across the population of firms in accordance with their relative positions in terms of product and process characteristics. Apart from the representative firm, all the firms are growing at rates different from the market rate and so their relative market shares are changing over time, the firms with above average growth increasing market share, and conversely. The marginal firms are those that just break even by covering their long-run costs, they have ceased to invest in capacity and are gradually on their way to extinction unless they manage to lower their costs or the normal market price increase.

This dynamics of market selection has an obvious consequence, namely, the measure of the representative firm is changing endogenously and for two reasons. The selection process, augmented as necessary by entry and exit, is systematically changing the structure of the industry and redefining the relevant averages, and, the differential growth of the firms in relation to the growth of the industry distributes internal and external economies in an uneven fashion across the firms so that their individual characters change. This flux has an immediate consequence; the representative firm is a moving fulcrum for the evolution of the industry, hardly surprising that it is a fifth wheel in terms of statics.[30]

In sum, Marshallian competition is not working on given firms but on firms that evolve too in an industry that evolves, through innovations in organization, technique or product, in a population that is shaped by entry and exit and the differential growth of the firms. This is why the underlying discussion of management and innovation is an integral part of Marshall's approach. It is from this viewpoint an open system in which life cycle forces may not be entirely absent and in which luck and judgement cannot be ignored. Thus a firm at the forefront, an obvious candidate to monopolize the industry may fall back and find its promise negated by rivals with different business plans. All this is the familiar stuff of empirical industrial dynamics it fits well with Marshall and it requires a historical perspective to treat it properly – hence the importance of historical research into firms and industries and the complementary importance of history friendly modelling (Malerba et al. 2001; Malerba and Orsenigo 2002).

Thus the representative firm does have a clear role in the economic dynamics of long-period adjustment; it is not a ghostly spectre from the past as Robbins (1928) would have us believe. It is the fulcrum around which the industry evolves but this conclusion can never be uncovered by static methods. If we take Marshall seriously we take his evolutionary dynamics seriously too. Properly specified the representative firm is the moving attractor for long-run values but it in turn is attracted to the best practice firm the identity of which may also be changing for familiar Marshallian organic developmental reasons. If this comes at a price, the competitive process leads to concentration, so be it, it may be just how the world works.

SUMMING UP

Does this matter? Well it does, if we want to understand the way wealth is created from knowledge. To understand the open system dynamics of capitalism we cannot separate our account of innovation from our account of value formation and order in markets and other forms of organization, they stand in reciprocal relation to each other. The incentives to enterprise, the rewards to innovation, and the resources available to innovate are all dependent on the evolving structure of prices. It is a process in which variation and the differential dynamics of growth and decline are inseparable and which gives rise to many of the phenomena identified in the modern industrial dynamics literature (Metcalfe 2005). More fundamentally, they are the basis for any explanation of economic development and the consequential rates of economic growth: just as Marshall insisted development and value are one problem unified by increasing returns, as he appropriately summed up his position,

> Every increase in wealth tends in many ways to make a greater increase in wealth more easy than before (*Principle of Economics*, IV, 13, p. 314).

NOTES

1. Comments from Ammon Salter, David Gann, Annabelle Gawer, Mark Dodgson, Harry Bloch and colleagues in Manchester have helped in rethinking the structure of the argument. My indebtedness to the writings on Marshallian economics by Tiziano Raffaelli and Brian Loasby will I hope also be clear to the reader. This is an extended and amended version of Metcalfe (2007a).
2. Foster (1993) makes the important point that Marshall's treatment of organization and information is fundamental to his handling of time irreversibility. This theme clearly needs more exploration than I can provide here.
3. I draw primarily on the *Principles of Economics* 8th edition (1920) and *Industry and Trade*, 1st edition (1919).
4. Within modern evolutionary theory and the debates between 'developmentalists' and 'selectionists' the same point holds, change is premised on order, '...it is possible for natural selection to be effective in causing evolutionary change precisely because it works in and on a field of self organized entities subject to non-linear changes...' (Depew and Weber 1996, p. 399).
5. It is indeed a puzzle as to why economists have found a world without change to be of fundamental interest. It is for example a world in which one would not need markets, because the problem of co-ordination has necessarily been solved for all time.
6. See Raffaelli (2003, Ch. 6) for a good starting point.
7. This section draws heavily on my 'Alfred Marshall and Economic Evolution' to appear in Metcalfe (2006).
8. See Loasby (1990) for further elaboration. We note in passing that a business does not make profits or losses by having the same expectations as rivals.
9. *Industry and Trade*, II, 10, p. 355.
10. Not that leadership in innovation necessarily brings a full reward to the innovator, those that pioneer new paths may confer on society benefits that are disproportionate to their personal gains even if they 'have died millionaires' (*Principles of Economics*, VI, 7, p. 598).
11. Marshall was already distinguishing between general managerial knowledge applicable to many trades and the knowledge required for specific trades, and the concomitant roles of formal education and experience in the learning of capability.
12. There is some ambiguity here. On the one hand, rising and falling refers to the changing relative positions of firms in a market, on the other hand it refers to the different states of ability and leadership in the life of the firm and the implications for its cost structure.
13. Discontinuities are backward looking artifices as when Marshall explains the step change in economic society from that of traditional, custom bound agriculture and empirical knowledge to a world in which progress of technique depends on men trained in industry, in commerce or in scientific schools rather than the fields. In such a radically different modern society invention and innovation are endemic (*Industry and Trade*, II).
14. See for example the treatment of invention and innovation in relation to machines for making more exact machines (*Industry and Trade*, II, 2, pp. 210–11).
15. Vincenti (1990) for example.
16. *Principles of Economics*, IV, 11, pp. 284–5 and *Industry and Trade*, II,10, p. 360.
17. Marshall, who was generally enthusiastic about co-operative arrangements, notes that it may be advisable for such a co operative research venture to be partly funded by the public in order to exercise a degree of control (*Industry and Trade*, I, 5, p. 101).
18. Marshall's view was that the costs of the representative firm govern long run values. Thus, in the long run the value of a thing tends to correspond to its cost of production and this is of increasing importance as we depart from the short run (*Principles of Economics*, V, 3. p.348), while, in a stationary state cost of production governs value (ibid., p. 367).
19. One of the curiosities of Marshall's thought is that the distinction between long- and short-run supply response is not extended to the treatment of consumer demand. On this see Loasby (1990). Of course the distinction has to apply to the matter of the demand for factors of production.

20. In speaking of the example of watches, the long-run factors include, an enhanced supply of the appropriate skills, specialized machinery and resort to interchangeable parts and to this add the possibilities of invention (*Principles of Economics*, V, 12, p. 455).
21. See note 4 above.
22. Currie and Steedman (1990, Ch. 2), convincingly point out that the periods in Marshall are not analytic devices premised on specific decision processes but actual periods of calendar time. Thus the longer the period allowed the more the slower velocity forces impose their signature on events.
23. What a given stock of capital facilities means is not straightforward, since some existing capital goods can be diverted from other industries or brought out of retirement as they are in Marshall's discussion of the fishing industry. See Currie and Steedman (1990, Ch. 2) for further elaboration.
24. Here Marshall is inviting us to think of the population of firms defining a particular expenses curve that links capacity and different cost conditions, the curve being cut at a price which at least covers the expenses of the marginal producer.
25. However, the kind of average cannot be specified before the nature of the competitive process is agreed upon. It turns out that the representative firm is defined in terms of a weighted average of the firms operating in the population, with the weights contingent on the forces of competition. Since the weights are continually changing so must be the characterization of the representative firm. Since the concept does not refer to any real firm the objections raised by Shove (1930) in relation to Young's (1928) treatment of external economies does not arise.
26. Thus Shove says 'in equilibrium every unit of resources must be so placed that its owner does not consider that he would gain by moving it to another point in the industrial field' (Shove 1930, p. 99, footnote 1). But if so every firm must also be in equilibrium otherwise it would offer inducements to resource owners to come or go.
27. Marshall's position was further compromised in the eyes of his followers by the fact that his discussion of the representative firm was intertwined with a discussion of the forces of increasing returns, the internal and external economies of expansion whether of firm or industry. Marshall knew it, and strenuously tried to put barriers in the way but the inevitable conclusion that any 'equilibrium state' under increasing internal returns would be a monopoly (without explaining the process leading to that outcome) simply opened the door for Sraffa (1926) to state the obvious and tee up the theory of imperfect competition for Robinson and Chamberlin.
28. Thus when Sraffa (1928) called for the abandonment of the theory of perfect competition he did so by calling instead for the abandoning of Marshall's theory, wrongly believing the two to be the same. On this see Loasby (1989).
29. For Marshall, the entry decision is closely tied to the perception of costs of the representative firm for it is to this level of performance any entrant must aspire if it is to survive.
30. It should be noted that none of the above hinges on perfect product or factor markets, nor does it in fact, depend on any form of increasing returns, constant returns to scale is all the Marshallian process needs. The effect of increasing returns is on the one hand simply to speed up the competitive selection process, and, on the other hand, to hasten concentration as Marshall feared. I have explored the replicator dynamics of increasing returns in Metcalfe (1993).

REFERENCES

Chick, V. and M. Caserta (1997), 'Provisional equilibrium and macroeconomic theory', in P. Arestis, G. Palma and M. Sawyer (eds), *Markets, Unemployment and Economic Policy: Essays in Honour of Geoff Harcourt*, vol. 1, London: Routledge.

Currie, M. and I. Steedman (1990), *Wrestling with Time*, Manchester: Manchester University Press.

Depew, D.J. and B.H. Weber (1996), *Darwinism Evolving*, Boston: Bradford Books, MIT Press.

Downie, J. (1955), *The Competitive Process*, London: Duckworth.

Foster, J. (1993), 'Economics and the self organization approach: Alfred Marshall revisited', *Economic Journal*, **103** (419), 975–991.

Hart, N. (2003), 'Marshall's dilemma: equilibrium versus evolution', *Journal of Economic Issues*, **37** (4), 1139–1160.

Hodgson, G. (1993), 'The Mecca of Alfred Marshall', in *Economics and Evolution: Bringing Life Back into Economics*, Cambridge: Polity Press, pp. 99–108.

Jenner, R.A. (1964), 'The dynamic factor in Marshall's economic system', *Western Economic Journal*, **3** (1), 21–38.

Knight, F. (1935), 'Statics and dynamics', in *The Ethics of Competition*, London: George Allen and Unwin.

Limoges, C. and C. Menard (1994), 'Organization and division of labour: biological metaphors at work in Alfred Marshall's *Principles of Economics*', in P. Mirowski (ed.), *Natural Images in Economic Thought: Markets Read in Tooth and Claw*, Cambridge: Cambridge University Press.

Loasby, B.J. (1978), 'Whatever happened to Alfred Marshall's theory of value', *Scottish Journal of Political Economy*, **25** (1), 1–12.

Loasby, B.J. (1989), 'Knowledge and organization: Marshall's theory of economic progress and coordination', in B.J. Loasby (ed.), *The Mind and Method of the Economist*, Aldershot, UK: Edward Elgar.

Loasby, B.J. (1990), 'Firms, markets and the principle of continuity', in J. Whitaker (ed.), *Centenary Essays on Alfred Marshall*, Cambridge: Cambridge University Press.

Loasby, B.J. (1991), *Equilibrium and Evolution: An Exploration of Connecting Principles in Economics*, Manchester: Manchester University Press.

Malerba, F. and L. Orsenigo (2002), 'Innovation and market structure in the dynamics of the pharmaceutical industry and biotechnology: towards a history-friendly model', *Industrial and Corporate Change*, **11** (4), 667–703.

Malerba, F., R. Nelson, L. Orsenigo and S. Winter (2001), 'Competition and industrial policies in a "history friendly" model of the evolution of the computer industry', *International Journal of Industrial Organization*, **19** (5), 635–664.

Marshall, A. (1919), *Industry and Trade*, London: Macmillan.

Marshall, A. (1920), *Principles of Economics* (8th edition), London: Macmillan.

Maxwell, J.A. (1929), 'An examination of some Marshallian concepts', *American Economic Review*, **19** (4), 626–637.

Maxwell, J.A. (1958), 'Some Marshallian concepts, especially the representative firm', *Economic Journal*, **68** (272), 691–698.

Metcalfe, J.S. (1993), 'Competition, Fisher's principle and increasing returns in the selection process', *Journal of Evolutionary Economics*, **4** (4), 327–346.

Metcalfe, J.S. (2005), 'The evolution of industrial dynamics' mimeo, CRIC, University of Manchester.

Metcalfe, J.S. (2006), 'Evolutionary economics', in B. Loasby and T. Rafaelli (eds), *The Elgar Companion to Alfred Marshall*, Cheltenham, UK: Edward Elgar.

Metcalfe, J.S. (2007a), 'Alfred Marshall and the general theory of evolutionary economics', *History of Economic Ideas*, **15** (1), 81–110.

Metcalfe, J.S. (2007b), 'Alfred Marshall's Mecca: reconciling the theories of value and development', *Economic Record*, **83** (supplement), 1–22.

Moss, L. (1982), 'Biological theory and technological entrepreneurship in Marshall's writings', *Eastern Economic Journal*, **8** (1), 3–13.

Nelson, R.R. and S. Winter (1982), *An Evolutionary Theory of Economic Change*, Harvard: Belknap Press.

Newman, P. (1960), 'The erosion of Marshall's theory of value', *Quarterly Journal of Economics*, **74** (4), 587–599.

Newman, P., and J.N. Wolfe (1961), 'A model for the long-run theory of value', *Review of Economic Studies*, **29** (1), 51–61.

O'Brien, D.P. (1990), 'Marshall's industrial analysis', *Scottish Journal of Political Economy*, **37** (1), 61–84.

Penrose, E. (1959), *The Theory of the Growth of the Firm*, Oxford: Basil Blackwell.

Pigou, A.C. (1928), 'An analysis of supply', *Economic Journal*, **38** (150), 238–257.

Raffaelli, T. (2003), *Marshall's Evolutionary Economics*, London: Routledge.

Robbins, L. (1928), 'The representative firm', *Economic Journal*, **38** (151), 387–404.

Robertson, D.H. (1956), 'Some recent (1950–5) writings on the theory of pricing, in *Economic Commentaries*, London: Staples Press.

Shackle, G.L. (1965), *A Scheme of Economic Theory*, Cambridge: Cambridge University Press.

Shove, G.F. (1930), 'The representative firm and increasing returns', in 'Increasing returns and the representative firm: a symposium', *Economic Journal*, **40** (157), 94–116.

Sraffa, P. (1926), 'The laws of returns under competitive conditions', *Economic Journal*, **36** (144), 535–550.

Sraffa, P. (1930), 'Increasing returns and the representative firm: a symposium', *Economic Journal*, **40** (157), 79–116.

Vincenti, W. (1990), *What Engineers Know and How they Know It*, Baltimore: Johns Hopkins University Press.

Viner, J. (1931), 'Cost curves and supply curves', reprinted in G. Stigler and K.E. Bouldin (eds) (1953), *Readings in Price Theory*, selected by a committee of the American Economic Association, London: Allen and Unwin.

Winter, S.G. (1995), 'Four rs of profitability: rents, resources, routines and replication', in C. Montgomery (ed.), *Resource Based and Evolutionary Theories of the Firm*, Boston: Kluwer Academic Publishers.

Wolfe, J.N. (1954), 'The representative firm', *Economic Journal*, **64** (254), 337–349.

Young, A. (1928), 'Increasing returns and economic progress', *Economic Journal*, **38** (151), 527–542.

2. Hicks and Richardson on Industrial Change: Analysis and Policy

Mario Amendola, Sergio Bruno and Jean-Luc Gaffard

INTRODUCTION: CHANGE AS AN OUT OF EQUILIBRIUM PROCESS

Dynamic analysis depends on dealing with issues that are in the nature of dynamic problems rather than on referring to supposedly dynamic methods. Qualitative economic change – a change that implies a structural modification which can only be brought about through a process in real, irreversible time – is the crucial issue involved whenever a thorough dynamic problem is contemplated. Innovation, which implies creation of new resources and construction of different choice sets, is the foremost example of qualitative change; but also a speeding up of the growth rate or a simple change of the technique in use partake of the same nature. In all these cases, the previously existing productive structure is disturbed, its way of functioning is affected, its harmony over time, assured in the previous equilibrium state, is perturbed. As a result, problems of intertemporal complementarity arise which call for co-ordination over time of economic activity, to render the process of change undertaken viable. This process comes down to the construction (in the limit the creation anew) of a new productive structure which most of the times also implies the creation of new specific resources; in particular the appearance of new skills of the human resource, where the term 'skill' must be taken in a wider sense as referring not only to the intrinsic characteristics (qualifications, competences, etc.) of this resource, but also to its relations with the productive environment with which it interacts (organizational capabilities, institutional features, etc.).

New aggregates of elements that exhibit different complementarity relations among them have thus to be shaped up for a different productive structure with its distinctive way of functioning to emerge. This can only come about through a process which is in the nature of an out-of-equilibrium process; its viability is the crucial problem involved, and this depends mainly on being able to re-establish the harmony over time of productive activity broken up by the undertaken structural modification. In this perspective, complementarity and co-ordination over time appear as the relevant issues for viability.

This paper is aimed at showing the complementarity between Richardson's and Hicks' contributions as regards the sketching out of a proper analytical framework for dynamic analysis such as we just defined it.

INVESTMENT CO-ORDINATION AND THE DELAY OF TRANSMISSION OF INFORMATION

Standard equilibrium analyses, and models, are not suited to deal with the two essential aspects of the out-of-equilibrium analysis which qualitative change calls for: investment, in the sense of construction of productive capacity, and the relations which must be established for construction looked at as a process over time to be carried out.[1]

Both investment and relations between agents appear as strictly related problems in the analysis developed by Richardson (1960) in his book *Information and Investment*. This can be read in his very words: 'It is of the essence of the private enterprise that although its individual members are independent (in the sense that they are free from central direction) yet their activities are nevertheless interrelated' (ibid., p. 30). 'Any single investment will in general be profitable only provided, first, that the volume of competitive investment does not exceed a critical limit set by the demand available, and, secondly, that the volume of complementary investment reaches some minimum level' (ibid., p. 31).[2] On the other hand the decisions about the investment to be carried out are taken by entrepreneurs on the basis of expectations whose reliability depends on them being grounded on adequate information or evidence. According to Richardson 'the availability to entrepreneurs of this information . . . is a function of the nature of the particular form of organization or system within which they are presumed to operate' (ibid., pp. 29–30). The assumed market structure has therefore an important bearing on the way expectations are formed, and decisions taken as a consequence; and, as we shall see better in the last section of this paper 'some market imperfections may be essential to the process of successful economic adjustment' (ibid., p. 38).

If we put on the lenses represented by the above proposed interpretation of qualitative change we can see in which way Richardson's analysis helps to deepen our understanding of how, and due to which factors, a co-ordination problem arises and becomes the main issue to be dealt with in the out-of-equilibrium process on the viability of which the endeavoured change depends.

For a process of change to take place investments must be decided and actually undertaken which, after a phase of construction, will result in a new productive capacity to be matched by a corresponding demand for final output. As stressed by Richardson, the profitability of any investment project depends on the setting up of a satisfactory amount of both complementary and competitive investments along the way. If entrepreneurs had immediately complete information on all existing investment projects this profitability would be assured because the entrepreneurs themselves would behave in such a way that no imbalance between supply and demand would appear on the market for final output. However, this is not likely to happen in a '. . . private enterprise system; the larger the number of firms in each industry, and the less the co-operation between them, the more difficult it is to see how the required information could be obtained.' Thus

> it seems more reasonable to assume that entrepreneurs will generally learn of the investment commitments of others only after a certain period of time which, for convenience, will be called the 'transmission interval'. The duration of this interval, it seems safe to presume, would not be greater than the gestation period, after which the extra flow of goods would have themselves felt on the market, but could be shorter than this, where entrepreneurs were able to obtain evidence about the amount of construction under way (ibid., p. 51).

The very existence of this delay in the transmission of information implies that adequate market information is no longer obtainable and hence involves a co-ordination problem.

How – in particular, as the result of the establishing of which kinds and forms of relations – the required information can be made available is the specific object of the analysis developed by Richardson. However, he focuses on 'how entrepreneurs can be supplied with the information which will enable them to take the investment decisions required by a rational allocation of resources' (ibid., p. 45). What we are after, instead, is a theory able to explain change interpreted as the process by which new and different productive options are brought about: where the focus is on 'creation', not on 'allocation' of resources.

The problem of co-ordination, the existence of a delay of transmission of information and its relation with investment activity, the coherence of expectations formation – together with other interesting insights on the policy issues involved by the co-ordination problem, which, we shall see, Richardson's analysis also provides – are essential analytical ingredients of this theory. However, for the theory itself to be properly developed we still lack a crucial element: a representation of production as a time-structured process dealing explicitly with the intertemporal complementarity, which provides the adequate sequential framework for an out-of-equilibrium analysis.[3]

INTERTEMPORAL COMPLEMENTARITY OF PRODUCTION AND THE CONSTRUCTION LAG

Articulation over time of the production process is the distinctive feature of the Neo-Austrian model (Hicks 1970, 1973). In this model production appears as a scheme for transforming a sequence of primary labour inputs into a sequence of homogeneous final output. The production process is fully vertically integrated. This makes it possible both to exhibit explicitly the phase of construction of productive capacity by bringing it inside the production process and to stress that it must necessarily come before the phase of utilization of the same capacity.[4] Focus on the time structure of the production process, and on its intertemporal complementarity, allows to actually deal with the transitional dynamics of an economy, in the sense of bringing to light 'what happens on the way' (Hicks 1973, p. 10). In particular, the transition between two different techniques (a 'Traverse') is analysed by following the process through which this transition takes place in its sequential development (Hicks 1973). This allows important analytical insights: in particular it makes it possible a demonstration of Ricardo's 'machinery effect', according to which the introduction of machinery has an adverse effect on employment in the short run. The reason that the focus on the time structure of the production process renders evident is the temporal dissociation of inputs from output and of costs from proceeds during the Traverse (a consequence of the change in the age structure of productive capacity resulting from the modification of the balance between processes in the phase of construction and processes in the phase of utilization implied by a change in the technique in use) with the result of a temporary fall in final output, and hence in the resources available to sustain employment.

The message of the analysis of the Traverse is that any attempt to change a given productive structure implies bringing back into light the time articulation of the production process – its having to go first through a phase of construction of a different productive capacity in order to be able to use it later for current production – obscured by the synchronisation of production in a given equilibrium state. However it is a message the analytical potentiality of which cannot be fully exploited within the context sketched out by Hicks.[5] As a matter of fact no decision process is contemplated in this context. The barter economy dealt with in the analysis is made to move along the sequence of periods from the one technique to the other by means of the mechanism provided by the assumption of 'Full Performance'. This implies that all the output not absorbed by consumption out of wages paid to workers engaged on existing production processes or by consumption of other kinds, is in fact used to start new production processes. The rate of starts, thus made endogenous, sketches out the path followed by the economy, a fully predetermined path once the values of the technical parameters of the model are given. Full Performance, on the other hand, also implies flow equilibrium in each period, both in the sense that final output is totally absorbed by existing demand and in the sense that investment is equal to *ex ante* saving. Thus the existing productive structure is smoothly transmuted into the one adapted to the new technique as resources are gradually freed and invested into the building of the latter one. In this context no co-ordination problems can arise: Full Performance assures co-ordination.[6]

The importance of dealing with the decision moment of economic actions in a sequential context is recognized explicitly by Hicks himself in his attempt to define sequential causality as opposed to the contemporaneous causality concept prevailing in economic theory (Hicks 1979):

> Even the simplest case of sequential causation in economics has two steps in it: a prior step, from the objective cause to the decisions that are based on it, or influenced by it, and a posterior step, from the decisions to their (objective effects). With respect to the decision, the prior step is one of formation, the posterior of execution (ibid., p. 88).

We have thus a posterior lag (it could be Richardson's gestation lag, or the construction lag in the Neo-Austrian model) and a prior lag, the consideration of which might appear as the missing link for developing a thorough dynamic analysis along Neo-Austrian lines. But this is not so, at least in the way Hicks himself deals with the problem. Although stressing that the problem raised by the existence of a prior lag consists of two logical moments – the first one, which is a matter of information, concerning the decision in itself, and the second one, which is a matter of negotiation, concerning the arrangements for making the decision effective – he actually focuses only on the second moment. Thus the constraints, not the motivations of the decision process come into light.[7] This allows to put the accent on the existence and the role of reserves – and in particular on liquidity, which in this light appears as freedom from financial constraints as it gives ability to respond to oncoming opportunities – but not to grasp the implications of a decision process: in the first place, its interaction with the intertemporal complementarity of the production process interpreted as construction (or creation). It does not allow, in other words, passing from a sequence 'constraints–constraints' to a sequence 'constraints–decisions–constraints', which is the effective backbone of an out-of-equilibrium process of change.

THE CO-ORDINATION PROBLEM IN A DYNAMIC CONTEXT

This is where Richardson comes to the rescue. His analysis of the delay of transmission of information is the missing link that we need. It makes it possible to account for the specific co-ordination problem that characterizes a process of qualitative change; a problem that arises at the junction of two strictly related lags: the phase of construction of productive capacity – which entails sunk costs – and the delay of transmission of information – which implies uncertainty. Both lags must be taken into account in the analysis, because cancelling one of them also cancels the co-ordination problem.

This is why we stressed that it is indeed the absence of the latter lag in the Hicksian analysis of the Traverse that eliminates the problem of co-ordination by automatically assuring the equilibrium between supply and demand in each period of the sequence through which a superior technique is adopted by the economy. On the other hand overlooking of the lag represented by the construction phase, even in presence of incomplete information leading to mistakes in investment, allows not only a revision of plans, but this to be instantaneous, so as to cancel imbalances at the very moment of their appearance. In this case too, hence, no co-ordination problem arises.

When both lags are properly taken into account, and a co-ordination problem then arises, it can be shown that any kind of qualitative change that involves a modification of the productive structure of the economy may (and will actually do, failing very specific assumptions) bring about a distortion of productive capacity that implies that not only construction and utilization, but also investment and consumption, and supply and demand, are no longer harmonized over time. The initial distortion, through the interaction of the intertemporal complementarities of production and decisions, stirs an out-of-equilibrium process, which carries and possibly amplifies the existing imbalances over a sequence of periods. This process, via expectations, may become cumulative, so that its very viability may be hampered. The problem, then, is to bring to light the conditions for viability, that is, what is required to re-establish the consistency over time of the relevant interacting magnitudes of the economy (Amendola and Gaffard 1988, 1992, 1998; Amendola et al. 1993).

This means in the first place to re-establish the harmony between construction and utilization, so as not to have too strong imbalances between supply and demand of final output that might render the economy not viable. The required out-of-equilibrium strategy – which must be aimed in particular at dealing with the sunk costs due to the dissociation over time of inputs from output, and of costs from proceeds, as the result of the distortion of productive capacity – is more properly examined with reference to the most typical qualitative change, innovation interpreted as a process of creation of resources.

This strategy, as already mentioned above, needs market connections usually considered as market imperfections – that is, implicit or explicit agreements with other firms – but also to establish more complex relations than the market ones. Price relations, the only market relations usually considered, give information on what exists, allow learning in the sense of getting to know what is already there. A process of creation of resources, instead, needs creation of information, that is, creative learning that can only take place through an out-of-equilibrium process (Bruno 2004). Out-of-equilibrium contexts, on the other hand, need stressing non-price relations that allow focusing on quantity adjustments besides the price ones. Price rigidity – rendered by a fix-price hypothesis (Hicks 1965, 1989), which on one hand allows disequilibria to come to the surface through the appearance of stocks – is on the other hand the expression of a behaviour which, through the management of these stocks, tries to correct the sheer working of price adjustment mechanisms. In particular in the utilization phase, when the problem is harmonizing step by step final demand with the existing productive capacity, the role of sales intermediaries is paramount as regards avoiding strong fluctuations in prices which would be a threat to the required harmony over time between supply and demand.

In order to assure the viability of a process of change, co-ordination through co-operation or direct relations between firms may be more effective than co-ordination through anonymous market transactions, which may induce ever growing distortions in the structure of productive capacity. As a matter of fact, if demand and supply are continuously kept in equilibrium by flexible prices, strong (and may be erratic) variations of quantities exchanged may be recorded in a context of imperfect competition. Thus the practice not to allow prices to vary can be the correct method by which the relevant information is acquired (Richardson 1960, p. 66). However, while prices are kept fixed, the need for adaptability persists. This is assured by holding reserve assets – be they real or financial assets. As a matter of fact, the degree of synchronization between costs and proceeds 'will be either neither complete nor wholly predictable' (ibid., p. 154). Thus the possibility of making expenses in excess of income appears as a condition for adaptation and viability. Of course viability will be enhanced 'by the possession . . . of some source of readily-available purchasing power' (ibid.) whatever the way in which it is provided.

In order to better understand this point we can refer to an analysis of liquidity along Hicksian lines. Uncertainty calls for reserve assets (or borrowing power). Reserve assets reflect a precautionary motive: when information about the future is incomplete firms look for more liquid positions. Whatever the source of liquidity firms have access to (reserve assets, overdrafts, etc.) 'liquidity is not a property of a single choice, it is a matter of a sequence of choices, a related sequence' (Hicks 1974, p. 38). In this perspective, reserve assets belong to a bundle of complements. Firms need reserve assets to realize their choices and carry out production processes. Reserve assets and real (productive) assets appear as complements: they are complements over time (Amendola 1991). And this complementarity relation is essential for rendering viable a process of change out of equilibrium.

In *Information and Investment*, Richardson had already developed a similar argument. Indeed in discussing the way in which a firm selects a strategy under conditions of imperfect knowledge, he stresses 'it is necessary not only to construct the probability estimates, but also to judge how far the relevant information could be augmented by inquiry, by experiment or by the mere postponement of the decisions to be taken' (ibid., p. 147). Thus he recognizes that any choice, at any period of time, belongs to a related sequence of choices, and that this sequential character of the procedure of choice is the main reason for holding liquid assets or being able to rely on borrowing power. Summing up, Richardson's ideas and Hicks' insights evoke essential points for sketching out a proper out-of-equilibrium analysis and strategy; and their similarity – often a thorough complementarity – is striking. The focus on intertemporal complementarity and on co-ordination problems, the need for adjustment and the role of real and monetary reserves in this process, the role of fix prices in the acquisition of information, are but ones of these points.

CO-ORDINATION *EX ANTE* VERSUS CO-ORDINATION *EX POST*

The analytical considerations developed above are rich of normative suggestions. These concern both the firms and the governments wanting to foster development and change, though obviously in slightly different ways.

When we place ourselves in an *ex ante* perspective, only rather vague options for building up something new appear to the firms which are or might become involved in a process of innovation. Such options acquire increasingly definite features only as the process of exploration and experimentation takes place and sunk costs are met. In any case, in order to proceed in the construction of innovative options, the involved firms have to set up organizational strategies aimed at re-shaping through time the relationships of which the environment is made, because during the process of transformation the borders defining the environment itself cannot exist since the innovation consists exactly in the fact that some of the elements previously external to the activity performed by the firm are now made internal to its strategy, in accordance with the changes actually taking place in the process of production (Amendola and Bruno 1990, p. 420).

On the other hand the intertemporal co-ordination, required to carry out the above-mentioned strategy, involves several agents. However, the way the co-ordination of activities may be planned, at least in principle, and organized in the case of an outcome which is well specified *ex ante*, highly differs from the way the co-ordination of activities may be set up in the case of the creation of innovation. Consider the case of the inter-firm co-operative agreements, which are needed when the problem is that of 'the matching, both qualitative and quantitative, of individual enterprise plans' (Richardson 1972, p.98). The possibility of co-ordinating plans is actually open only at the condition that some fairly detailed knowledge about what should be planned does exist already within the cluster of companies that are deciding to co-operate. This might occur either in the case of the development or in that of the adoption of already existing innovations, but it cannot occur by definition in the case of firms that decide to co-operate in order to find out the way of setting up an innovation in the sense of creation of technology.

If firms decide to co-operate for the creation of innovation, therefore, the content of the agreement must be other than the planning of the activities regarded as actual pieces of production along an established time schedule. It cannot but be

1. The intention to establish a long-run co-operation in certain 'directions' for not precisely specified 'common aims';
2. The generic and specific resources they decide to put in common, at the purpose of engaging them in the innovative effort (and thus rendering them even more specific);
3. The rules and the procedures according to which to take future decisions 'on the way', and finally;
4. The rules and the procedures concerning the exploitation of the commonly produced outcome (Bruno and De Lellis 1992; Bruno 2004).[8]

On the other hand the more the setting up of an activity requires specific inputs, the more the involved agent is obliged to:

1. Take care and plan the time scheduling of his undertaking;
2. Establish reliable and specific relationships with the agents from whom he wants to obtain the desired inputs;
3. Meet the costs and face the risks which are connected to '1' and '2'.

And the more specific some, or many of the involved inputs are (up to the point of being new and unique, as in the case of absolute innovations), the more

4. The relationships with the other agents have to be personal, non-anonymous (as basically are, instead, the pure market transactions);[9]
5. The object of such relationships must be the establishment of co-operative 'activities' (as opposed to simple 'acts') the aim of which is the setting up of an environment for common learning (see in this direction Ciborra 1991).

The normative implications also concern the organizational patterns. A shift of the attention from how economic structures and systems 'are and function' to 'how do they change and why' also implies a shift of the focus from competitive relations[10] to co-operative ones, which are of interest from the viewpoint of the processes aimed at constructing them through time, efforts and investments.

Furthermore, the attention should be shifted from the 'organizational patterns' to the 'processes' of *'organizing'*, that is, to the activities that concern the organizational structuring of the relationships among the firms and within them. This implies that finding out what the optimal boundaries of the firm are – which is the crucial issue in modern industrial organization theory – is not what really matters. As also stressed by Richardson:

> . . . established positions are constantly under pressure not merely because of autonomous changes in taste and technique but also by virtue of the fact that at any point of time there will exist unexploited opportunities for the division of labour and the consequent regrouping of activities. For, according to Smith's theory of economic development, industrial structures will be in constant need of adaptation; the very process of adaptation, by increasing productivity and therefore market size, ensures that the adaptation is no longer appropriate to the opportunities it has itself created (1975, p. 358).

Thus what matters from an analytical as well as a business viewpoint, is not to know what the optimal organization of industry is but how this organization changes and why.

Of crucial importance, in this context, are the human resources: how are they formed before hiring and on the job, how are they cared and motivated within the companies industrial relations, which kind of hiring strategy is adopted by the firms. Once again the problem is far away from the standard optimality criteria: optimality requires that a firm has exactly the labour required for carrying on its present productive tasks with no excess both in its quantity and quality. But a firm that behaves optimally in this sense, which has no human resources whose skills and knowledge are above and beyond its present needs is blind: the firm cannot perceive the options for innovation, it cannot cultivate and develop them, it has difficulty to establish constructive relationships with other firms which could become the complementary partners of the development of the envisaged innovation. This observation has implications not only for the firms and their strategies, but also for governments, since high quality human resources are generated by a continuum of back-stages, which involve universities and the research network at large, and which require much in advance financial resources and care.

ECONOMIC POLICY IMPLICATIONS

The analytical framework sketched out also helps to understand the methodological flaws of the traditional theories of economic policy, be they of the Paretian or of the Tinbergen type.[11]

Again, Richardson gives the hint. As he puts it 'the Pareto optimum is conceived in terms of the categories of centrally planned allocation on the basis of full knowledge' (1960, p. 43). Now, in a context of incomplete information, efficiency cannot be considered by reference to a Paretian situation, that is, by reference to equilibrium with full co-ordination. It should be considered with reference to the process of adjustment. As a matter of fact those who consider perfect competition as a benchmark and those who advocate central planning have much in common. Both believe that it is always possible to obtain the right structure of information and ignore how the relevant information may be acquired, how the optimal state of affairs is to be brought about and what are the institutional and market arrangements required for the task. Thus while from a normative viewpoint the reference to Pareto optimum implies to look for the 'specific' incentives that are a good substitute for perfect information, the normative implication of Richardson (and ours) viewpoint is that what matters is to promote the 'general' rules that allow the firms to acquire the relevant information step by step.

But there is a deeper difference of perspective in the background. The traditional theory of economic policy has been established with reference to a world made of what we might call 'parametric optimizers'. By this we mean that the individual agents, as well as their aggregations, self-determine their behaviours through the solution of some problem of maximum (minimum), operated upon a set of functions whose general shape is uniform for the same kind of agents and whose parameters depend on the systemic forces and on the institutional set-up. In such a world, the policy instruments consist in a change of some of the parameters, which also implies a change – whose direction is known and whose intensity may usually be estimated – in the optimal solution adopted by each of the relevant agents. The so-called decision-makers are thus pure automata, which give basically mechanical responses to appropriate stimuli (Bruno 1993).

The out-of-equilibrium process outlined in this paper admits instead a plurality of dynamic paths. This implies that the system, though heavily bounded by its inner dynamic structure, is still open to a plurality of possible strategies on the side of the actors, who not only 'play within the system', but also contribute in 'shaping its patterns', while building up the productive capacity, while setting up cumulative systems of rules and relationships, while learning. This immediately suggests that there is a wide room for policy actions.

It is interesting to stress some of the most important consequences of the above outlined change of perspective:

1. No mechanical correspondence between policy actions and individuals' responses can be established, as it happens under traditional schemes based upon optimization hypotheses;
2. There are asymmetries of information not only among private actors, but also among institutions and between private actors and institutions (comprising governments, national and local, and government agencies);
3. Various forms of informational exchange may, and usually do take place, and have to be regarded as the key factor of the new economic policy.

The last point is paramount. As a matter of fact the common everyday perception is that the economic agents' interaction does not bring about chaotic results, so long as the decision-makers are characterized by roughly stable patterns of behaviour and/or as long as a fair amount of co-ordination takes place, through various forms of cognitive exchange. It is true, in fact, that if synchronous decisions undertaken by different subjects are shaped not only independently, but under conditions of reciprocal ignorance, this would hardly produce the regularities we observe in our societies; but the point is exactly this, that in our societies, under normal circumstances, 'some form of co-ordination among the subjects has been created in advance' through long lasting cumulative but someway differentiated processes.[12]

The adoption of routines, the compliance to rules and customs, communicative action, the sharing of expectations about the behaviour of the system, the use of signalling (encompassing the announcement of policies), explicit communication, the search for explicit agreements, are all mechanisms (or strategies) producing some degree of co-ordination, which confer order and stability to the environment and reduce the uncertainty or the risks and costs associated to it (North 2005).

It is finally worth spending a few words on the issue of monopolistic features. Richardson has been among the few to acknowledge that various forms of inter-firm agreements might play a crucial role in the fostering of development and innovation. According to him the entrepreneurs can obtain the required market information only if it exists a variety of restraints. These restraints, by definition, restrict freedom but provide secure expectations that allow the firms to commit themselves to irreversible investments. Thus 'they . . . constitute at worst a necessary evil' (1960, p. 69). Courage was needed to hold such a position in a world that is traditionally biased against oligopoly structures. As a matter of fact more attention should be paid to the fact that the attainment of extra profits constitutes the motivation (*ex ante*) and the reward (*ex post*) of previous efforts and costs for finding out new goods and/or new and less costly processes of production. The existence of such extra profits is thus the mechanism that induces the firms to continue to take risks and spend in research and development in order to introduce further innovation and to improve their competitive performance.

This should prescribe a selective attitude on the side of anti-trust authorities, which should be able to discriminate which are the actual features of oligopoly situations in single cases, abstaining from the application of exceedingly general rules, such as the traditional one, based on the actual existence of innumerable, powerless and fragmented firms. However, this calls for a change of analytical perspective along the lines pointed at in this paper. As a matter of fact:

> . . . in the great contemporary discussion of monopoly policy, the contribution of economic science has been, in the end, rather disappointing; an important reason for this . . . may be the inadequacy of the basic conceptual instruments with which we endeavour to analyze the process of economic adjustment in competitive conditions (Richardson 1960, p.71).

NOTES

1. Standard theory looks at production from the vantage point of trade and exchange, and production itself comes actually down to an analytically instantaneous assembling of given generic inputs. On the other hand co-ordination of economic activity – an activity interpreted as allocation, not as construction or creation of resources – is guaranteed by assumption by the price mechanism, and the theory is silent on how this actually takes place.
2. According to the author investment may be termed complementary (competitive) where the profitability of one is increased (reduced) by the carrying out of the other. Intermediate products or effective substitutes are examples of the one or the other, respectively.
3. The gestation period stressed by Richardson refers to the time lag required for obtaining the output from a given productive capacity; it has got nothing to do with the process through which this capacity is brought about, which represents the true time element of production.

4. The Neo-Austrian analysis of the production process is consistent with Richardson's vision of the nature of the firm. In his paper on Adam Smith, Richardson (1975) considers 'the implications of giving firms the freedom to practise a vertical division of labour', i.e. the implications of bringing back to the surface the temporal dimension of the production process. This leads him 'to regard firms as undertaking activities rather than making and selling products, these activities having to do with the discovery and estimation of future wants, with research development, and design, with the execution and co-ordination of processes of physical transformation, with the marketing of goods, and so on'. These activities look very much like vertically integrated (and separable) production processes as defined in the Neo-Austrian model.

5. This is the likely reason why there have been only scanty and unsuccessful attempts to pursue the line of research proposed by the Neo-Austrian model.

6. Which is rather odd, in a context where productive capacity is not adapted and that hence, in principle, should deny co-ordination.

7. Like in the analysis of the Traverse, where the assumption of Full Performance is made exactly in order to actually dispense with the problem of the constraints.

8. Both substantiate the hints by Hayek (1946, 1968).

9. This was well perceived by Richardson (1960). When the environment is large relatively to a single agent who decides to invest and the inputs are not specific, pure anonymous market transaction would be sufficient. If the magnitude of the devised investment is high relatively to the environment, as it happens in underdeveloped countries or areas and for investments presenting important indivisibilities, the relationships, which need to be established, tend to be unavoidably more personal. But even in a well developed environment, when the inputs must be specific and/or the magnitude of the orders is relatively large, explicit and direct co-ordination and co-operation will be likely to be needed or preferred.

10. Which are instead the focus of standard economic theory and that become interesting from a dynamic and transformation point of view only in so far as a change of the competitive rules is concerned.

11. In the Paretian tradition the public intervention is aimed at reaching a Pareto-efficient solution, given the distribution of individual endowments, or, for those who believe in the possibility of deriving or of having a 'social welfare function', 'the' Pareto-efficient and most equitable solution; such solutions amount to the maximum satisfaction of consumers' preferences. In the Tinbergen tradition, instead, the public action is aimed at optimizing an exogenously given set of objectives.

12. This explains also why sudden changes may impair or destroy regularity.

REFERENCES

Amendola, M. (1991), 'Liquidity, flexibility and processes of economic change', in L. McKenzie and S. Zamagni (eds), *Value and Capital Fifty Years Later*, London: Macmillan, pp. 333–351.

Amendola, M. and S. Bruno (1990), 'The behaviour of the innovative firm: relations to the environment', *Research Policy*, **19** (5), 419–433.

Amendola, M. and J.-L. Gaffard (1988), *The Innovative Choice*, Oxford: Basil Blackwell.

Amendola, M. and J.-L. Gaffard (1992), 'Intertemporal complementarity and money in an economy out of equilibrium', *Journal of Evolutionary Economics*, **2** (2), 131–145.

Amendola, M. and J.-L. Gaffard (1998), *Out of Equilibrium*, Oxford: Clarendon Press.

Amendola, M., C. Froeschle and J.-L. Gaffard (1993), 'Sustaining structural change; Malthus's heritage', *Structural Change and Economic Dynamics*, **4** (1), 65–79.

Bruno, S. (1993), 'The new theoretical limits of laissez faire', Working Paper Iside, University of Roma, La Sapienza.

Bruno, S. (2004), 'La concorrenza come 'viaggio esplorativo verso l'ignoto': dai giochi di prezzo alle azioni sperimentali', *Studi Economici*, 82.

Bruno, S. and A. De Lellis (1992), 'The economics of ex-ante co-ordination', Working Paper Iside, University of Roma, La Sapienza.

Ciborra, C. (1991), 'Innovation networks and organizational learning' in C. Antonelli (ed.), *The Economics of Information Networks*, Amsterdam: North Holland.

Hayek, von F. (1946), 'The meaning of competition', reprinted in F.A. Hayek (1949), *Individualism and Economic Order*, London and Henley: Routledge and Kegan Paul, pp. 92–106.

Hayek, von F. (1968), 'Competition as a discovery procedure', Lecture, reprinted in F.A. Hayek (1949), *New Studies in Philosophy, Politics, Economics and the History of Ideas*, London and Henley: Routledge and Kegan Paul, pp. 23–34.

Hicks, John R. (1965), *Capital and Growth*. Oxford: Clarendon Press.

Hicks, J. (1970), 'A neo-Austrian growth theory', *Economic Journal*, **80** (318), 257–79.

Hicks, John R. (1973), *Capital and Time*, Oxford: Clarendon Press.

Hicks, John R. (1974), *The Crisis in Keynesian Economics*, Oxford: Basil Blackwell.

Hicks, John R. (1979), *Causality in Economics*, Oxford: Basil Blackwell.

Hicks, John R. (1989), *A Market Theory of Money*, Oxford: Clarendon Press.

North, Douglass (2005), *Understanding the Process of Economic change*, Princeton: Princeton University Press.

Richardson, George B. (1960), *Information and Investment*, Oxford: Clarendon Press.

Richardson, G. (1972): 'The organization of industry', *Economic Journal*, **82** (327), 883–896.

Richardson, George B. (1975), 'Adam Smith on competition and increasing returns', in A. Skinner and T. Wilson (eds) *Essays on Adam Smith*, Oxford: Oxford University Press.

PART II

Firms' Formation and Growth

3. SMEs, Industry Dynamics and Economic Growth

David Audretsch, Taylor Aldridge and Adam Lederer

INTRODUCTION

What is the link between Small and Medium Enterprises (SMEs), industry dynamics and economic growth? This paper utilises the lens provided by the new knowledge spillover theory of entrepreneurship to understand how SMEs can influence industry dynamics and ultimately economic growth.

The knowledge spillover theory of entrepreneurship inverts the traditional approach to SMEs. Rather than taking the context to be given and then asking how variations across individual attributes shape the cognitive process underlying the decision to become an entrepreneur, we instead assume the individual characteristics to be constant and then analyse how the cognitive process inducing the entrepreneurial decision is influenced by placing that same individual in different contexts. In particular, high knowledge contexts are compared with impoverished knowledge contexts. This leads to a very different view of entrepreneurship. Instead of being a phenomenon that is exogenously determined by pre-conditioned personal attributes and family history, entrepreneurship instead emerges as an endogenous response to opportunities generated by investments in new knowledge made by incumbent firms and organizations, combined with their inability to fully and completely exhaust the ensuing opportunities to commercialize that knowledge. Thus, the knowledge spillover theory of entrepreneurship shows how entrepreneurship can be an endogenous response to investments in new knowledge where commercialization of that knowledge is constrained by the existence of a formidable knowledge filter.

Not only does holding the individual attributes constant but varying the knowledge context give rise to the knowledge theory of entrepreneurship, but the view of entrepreneurship as an endogenous response to the incomplete commercialization of new knowledge results in entrepreneurship as providing the missing link in economic growth models. By serving as a conduit of knowledge spillovers, entrepreneurship serves as an important source of economic growth that otherwise will remain missing. Thus, entrepreneurship is the mechanism by which society more fully appropriates its investments in creating new knowledge, such as research and education.

The next section explains how entrepreneurship combines the cognitive process of recognizing opportunities with pursuing those opportunities by starting a new firm. The third section introduces the knowledge spillover theory of entrepreneurship, which suggests that entrepreneurship is an endogenous response to investments in knowledge that are not fully appropriated by incumbent firms. The fourth section links endogenous entrepreneurship based on knowledge spillovers to economic growth. Finally, a summary and conclusions are provided in the last section. In particular, we suggest that entrepreneurship education and the transfer of technology from universities for commercialization make a key contribution to the societal values of economic growth, employment creation and competitiveness in globally linked markets by reducing the knowledge filter and facilitating the missing link to economic growth – entrepreneurship.

SMES AND ENTREPRENEURSHIP

Where do entrepreneurial opportunities come from? This question has been at the heart of considerable research, not just in economics, but throughout the social sciences. Herbert and Link (1989) have identified three distinct intellectual traditions in the development of the entrepreneurship literature. These three traditions can be characterized as the German Tradition, based on von Thuenen and Schumpeter, the Chicago Tradition, based on Knight and Schultz, and the Austrian Tradition, based on von Mises, Kirzner and Shackle.

Entrepreneurship has generally been viewed as involving the recognition of opportunities and the pursuit of those opportunities (Venkataraman 1997). The entrepreneurship literature has placed a particular focus on the cognitive process by which individuals reach the decision to start a new firm. As Sarasvathy, Dew, Velamuri and Venkataraman (2003, p. 142) explain, 'An entrepreurial opportunity consists of a set of ideas, beliefs and actions that enable the creation of future goods and services in the absence of current markets for them'.

The focus of the entrepreneurship literature on the cognitive process inherent in making the decision of starting a firm has generally involved a methodology of examining differences across individuals (Stevenson and Jarillo 1990). As Krueger (2003, p. 105) points out, 'The heart of entrepreneurship is an orientation toward seeing opportunities.' Thus, the central focus of research in entrepreneurship addresses the questions, 'What is the nature of entrepreneurial thinking and What cognitive phenomena are associated with seeing and acting on opportunities?' (Krueger 2003, p. 105).

Thus, the literature on entrepreneurship holds the context constant and then asks how the cognitive process inherent in the entrepreneurial decision varies across different individual characteristics and attributes (Shaver 2003; McClelland 1961). As Shane and Eckhardt (2003, p 187) summarize this literature in introducing the individual-opportunity nexus, 'We discussed the process of opportunity discovery and explained why some actors are more likely to discover a given opportunity than others.'

By contrast, a very different literature, associated with the model of the knowledge production function looked for opportunity exploitation for the unit of observation of the firm. This literature implicitly assumed that opportunity exploitation takes place within the same organizational unit creating those opportunities in the first place – the firm. By explicitly modelling and specifying the econometric estimation of the knowledge production function as linking firm innovative output to firm investments in new knowledge (Griliches 1984), such as R&D and human capital, this literature assumed that the creation and exploitation of new opportunities occurred within the same organizational unit. Just as the firm is viewed as providing the organizational unit for the creation of the opportunities, through purposeful investments in R&D, it is also viewed as appropriating the returns to those investments through innovative activity, such as patented inventions creating new intellectual property.

However, the empirical evidence from systematic empirical testing of the model of the knowledge production function contradicted the assumption of singularity between the organization creating the opportunities and the organization exploiting the opportunities. In particular, the empirical evidence pointed to a much more vigorous contribution to small- and new-firm innovative activity than would have been warranted from their rather limited investments in new knowledge, as measured by R&D and human capital (Audretsch 1995).

THE KNOWLEDGE SPILLOVER THEORY OF ENTREPRENEURSHIP

The discrepancy in organizational context between the organization creating opportunities and those exploiting the opportunities that seemingly contradicted Griliches' model of the firm knowledge production function was resolved by Audretsch (1995), who introduced *The Knowledge Spillover Theory of Entrepreneurship*,

> The findings challenge an assumption implicit to the knowledge production
> function – that firms exist exogenously and then endogenously seek out and apply
> knowledge inputs to generate innovative output. It is the knowledge in the
> possession of economic agents that is exogenous, and in an effort to appropriate
> the returns from that knowledge, the spillover of knowledge from its producing
> entity involves endogenously creating a new firm (Audretsch 1995, pp. 179–180).

What is the source of this entrepreneurial opportunity that endogenously
generated the startup of new firms? The answer seemed to be through the
spillover of knowledge that created the opportunities for the startup of a new
firm,

> How are these small and frequently new firms able to generate innovative output
> when undertaken a generally negligible amount of investment into knowledge-
> generating inputs, such as R&D? One answer is apparently through exploiting
> knowledge created by expenditures on research in universities and on R&D in
> large corporations (ibid., p. 179).

The empirical evidence supporting the knowledge spillover theory of
entrepreneurship was provided from analysing variations in startup rates
across different industries reflecting different underlying knowledge contexts.
In particular, those industries with a greater investment in new knowledge
also exhibited higher startup rates while those industries with less investment
in new knowledge exhibited lower startup rates, which was interpreted as a
conduit transmitting knowledge spillovers (Audretsch 1995; Caves 1998).

Thus, compelling evidence was provided suggesting that entrepreneurship
is an endogenous response to opportunities created but not exploited by the
incumbent firms. This involved an organizational dimension involving the
mechanism transmitting knowledge spillovers – the startup of new firms. In
addition, Jaffe (1989), Audretsch and Feldman (1996) and Audretsch and
Stephan (1996) provided evidence concerning the spatial dimension of
knowledge spillovers. In particular their findings suggested that knowledge
spillovers are geographically bounded and localized within spatial proximity
to the knowledge source. None of these studies, however, identified the
actual mechanisms which actually transmit the knowledge spillover; rather,
the spillovers were implicitly assumed to automatically exist (or fall like
Manna from heaven), but only within a geographically bounded spatial area.

As the previous section emphasized, while much has been made about the
key role played by the recognition of opportunities in the cognitive process
underlying the decision to become an entrepreneur, relatively little has been
written about the actual source of such entrepreneurial opportunities. The
knowledge spillover theory of entrepreneurship identifies one source of
entrepreneurial opportunities – new knowledge and ideas. In particular, the
knowledge spillover theory of entrepreneurship posits that it is new

knowledge and ideas created in one context but left uncommercialized or not vigorously pursued by the source actually creating those ideas, such as a research laboratory in a large corporation or research undertaken by a university, serve as the source of knowledge generating entrepreneurial opportunities. Thus, in this view, one mechanism for recognizing new opportunities and actually implementing them by starting a new firm involves the spillover of knowledge. The organization creating the opportunities is not the same organization that exploits the opportunities. If the exploitation of those opportunities by the entrepreneur does not involve full payment to the firm for producing those opportunities, such as a licence or royalty, then the entrepreneurial act of starting a new firm serves as a mechanism for knowledge spillovers.

Why should entrepreneurship play an important role in the spillover of new knowledge and ideas? And why should new knowledge play an important role in creating entrepreneurial opportunities? In the Romer (1986) model of endogenous growth new technological knowledge is assumed to automatically spillover. Investment in new technological knowledge is automatically accessed by third-party firms and economic agents, resulting in the automatic spill over of knowledge. The assumption that knowledge automatically spills over is, of course, consistent with the important insight by Arrow (1962) that knowledge differs from the traditional factors of production – physical capital and (unskilled) labour – in that it is non-excludable and non-exhaustive. When the firm or economic agent uses the knowledge, it is neither exhausted nor can it be, in the absence of legal protection, precluded from use by third-party firms or other economic agents. Thus, in the spirit of the Romer model, drawing on the earlier insights about knowledge from Arrow, a large and vigorous literature has emerged obsessed with the links between intellectual property protection and the incentives for firms to invest in the creation of new knowledge through R&D and investments in human capital.

However, the preoccupation with the non-excludability and non-exhaustibility of knowledge first identified by Arrow and later carried forward and assumed in the Romer model, neglects another key insight in the original Arrow (1962) article. Arrow also identified another dimension by which knowledge differs from the traditional factors of production. This other dimension involves the greater degree of uncertainty, higher extent of asymmetries, and greater cost of transacting new ideas. The expected value of any new idea is highly uncertain, and as Arrow pointed out, has a much greater variance than would be associated with the deployment of traditional factors of production.

As already discussed, a vigorous literature has identified that knowledge spillovers are greater in the presence of knowledge investments. Just as Jaffe, (1989) and Audretsch and Feldman (1996) show, those regions with high knowledge investments experience a high level of knowledge spillovers, and those regions with a low amount of knowledge investments experience a low level of knowledge spillovers, since there is less knowledge to be spilled over.

The knowledge spillover theory of entrepreneurship analogously suggests that, *ceteris paribus*, entrepreneurial activity will tend to be greater in contexts where investments in new knowledge are relatively high, since the new firm will be started from knowledge that has spilled over from the source actually producing that new knowledge. A paucity of new ideas in an impoverished knowledge context will generate only limited entrepreneurial opportunities. By contrast, in a high knowledge context, new ideas will generate entrepreneurial opportunities by exploiting (potential) spillovers of that knowledge. Thus, the knowledge spillover view of entrepreneurship provides a clear link, or prediction that entrepreneurial activity will result from investments in new knowledge and that entrepreneurial activity will be spatially localized within close geographic proximity to the knowledge source.

Thus, the first hypothesis to emerge from the knowledge spillover theory of entrepreneurship is what Audretsch, Keilbach and Lehmann (2005) term as the Endogenous Entrepreneurship Hypothesis, which suggests that Entrepreneurship will be greater in the presence of higher investments in new knowledge, *ceteris paribus*. Entrepreneurial activity is an endogenous response to higher investments in new knowledge, reflecting greater entrepreneurial opportunities generated by knowledge investments.

Systematic empirical evidence consistent with the knowledge spillover theory of entrepreneurship has been provided by Audretsch, Keilbach and Lehmann (2006) and Acs et al. (2004). Both studies find that entrepreneurship rates tend to be greater in the context of greater investments in new knowledge. In particular, Audretsch, Keilbach and Lehmann (2005) find that even after controlling for other sources of entrepreneurial opportunities access to entrepreneurial resources, those regions with a greater investment in new knowledge induces a greater degree of entrepreneurial startups, particularly in high-technology and other knowledge-based industries.

Additional support for the Endogenous Entrepreneurship Hypothesis is provided by Roberts and Malone (1996) who document the startup of new companies spawned by Stanford University. Similarly, Markman, Phan, Balkin and Giannodis (2005), O'Shea et al. (2005) and DiGregorio and Shane (2003) analyse the linkages between universities and the propensity of those universities to generate new-firm startups. Franklin, Wright and Lockett (2001), Ferguson and Olofsson (2004), and Lockett, Wright and Franklin (2003) all identify how universities spawn entrepreneurial activity.

The second hypothesis emerging from the knowledge spillover theory of entrepreneurship has to do with the location of the entrepreneurial activity. Access to knowledge spillovers requires spatial proximity. While Jaffe (1989) and Audretsch and Feldman (1996) made it clear that spatial proximity is a pre-requisite to accessing such knowledge spillovers, they provided no insight about the actual mechanism transmitting such knowledge spillovers. As for the Romer, Lucas and Jones models, investment in new knowledge automatically generates knowledge spillovers. The only additional insight involves the spatial dimension – knowledge spills over but the spillovers are spatially bounded. Since we have just identified one such mechanism by which knowledge spillovers are transmitted – the startup of a new firm – it follows that knowledge spillover entrepreneurship is also spatially bounded in that local access is required to access the knowledge facilitating the entrepreneurial startup: knowledge spillover entrepreneurship will tend to be spatially located within close geographic proximity to the source of knowledge actually producing that knowledge. Thus, in order to access spillovers, new-firm startups will tend to locate close to knowledge sources, such as universities.

While the knowledge spillover theory of entrepreneurship suggests that investment in the creation of new knowledge will generate opportunities for entrepreneurship as a mechanism for knowledge spillovers, the Locational Hypothesis places a spatial constraint on such spillovers, particularly from universities. Audretsch, Keilbach and Lehmann (2005) and Audretsch and Lehmann (2005) analyse a data base consisting of technology and knowledge-based startups making an initial public offering and find that, in general, those universities in regions with a higher knowledge capacity and greater knowledge output also generate a higher number of knowledge and technology startups, suggesting that university spillovers are geographically bounded. Geographic proximity is an asset, if not a pre-requisite, to entrepreneurial firms in accessing and absorbing spillovers from universities.

However, the findings of Audretsch, Keilbach and Lehmann (2005) and Audretsch and Lehmann (2005) also suggest that the role of geographic proximity in accessing university spillovers is considerably more nuanced than is suggested by the Locational Hypothesis. The importance of geographic proximity apparently depends on at least two factors – the particular type of university output and spillover mechanism. For those university outputs and spillover mechanisms which are more tacit in nature, geographic proximity plays a greater role in accessing and absorbing university spillovers. By contrast, for those university outputs and spillover mechanisms which are less tacit and more codified, geographic proximity is less important.

INDUSTRY DYNAMICS AND GROWTH

The knowledge spillover theory of entrepreneurship, which focuses on how new knowledge can influence the cognitive decision making process inherent in the entrepreneurial decision links entrepreneurship and economic growth, is consistent with theories of industry evolution (Jovanovic 1982; Ericson and Pakes 1995; Audretsch 1995; Hopenhayn 1992; Klepper 1996). While traditional theories suggest that small firms will retard economic growth, by imposing a drag on productive efficiency, these evolutionary theories suggest exactly the opposite – that entrepreneurship will stimulate and generate growth. The reason for these theoretical discrepancies lies in the context of the underlying theory. In the traditional theory, new knowledge plays no role; rather, static efficiency, determined largely by the ability to exhaust scale economies dictates growth. By contrast, the evolutionary models are dynamic in nature and emphasize the role that knowledge plays. Because knowledge is inherently uncertain, asymmetric and associated with high costs of transactions, divergences emerge concerning the expected value of new ideas. Economic agents therefore have an incentive to leave an incumbent firm and start a new firm in an attempt to commercialize the perceived value of their knowledge. Entrepreneurship is the vehicle by which (the most radical) ideas are sometimes implemented and commercialized.

A distinguishing feature of these evolutionary theories is the focus on change as a central phenomenon. Innovative activity, one of the central manifestations of change, is at the heart of much of this work. Entry, growth, survival, and the way firms and entire industries change over time are linked to innovation. The dynamic performance of regions and even entire economies, that is the 'Standort', or location, is linked to the efficacy of transforming investments in new knowledge into innovative activity.

Why are new firms started? The traditional, equilibrium-based view is that new firms in an industry, whether they be startups or firms diversifying from other industries, enter when incumbent firms in the industry earn supranormal profits. By expanding industry supply, entry depresses price and restores profits to their long-run equilibrium level. Thus, in equilibrium-based theories entry serves as a mechanism to discipline incumbent firms. By contrast, the new theories of industry evolution develop and evaluate alternative characterizations of entrepreneurship based on innovation and costs of firm growth. These new evolutionary theories correspond to the disequilibrating theory of entrepreneurship proposed by Shane and Eckhardt (2003).

For example, Audretsch (1995) analyses the factors that influence the rate of new firm startups. He finds that such startups are more likely in industries in which small firms account for a greater percentage of the industry's innovations. This suggests that firms are started to capitalize on distinctive knowledge about innovation that originates from sources outside of an industry's leaders. This initial condition of not just uncertainty, but greater degree of uncertainty vis-à-vis incumbent enterprises in the industry is captured in the theory of firm selection and industry evolution proposed by Jovanovic (1982). Jovanovic presents a model in which the new firms, which he terms entrepreneurs, face costs that are not only random but also differ across firms. A central feature of the model is that a new firm does not know what its cost function is, that is its relative efficiency, but rather discovers this through the process of learning from its actual post-entry performance. In particular, Jovanovic (1982) assumes that entrepreneurs are unsure about their ability to manage a new-firm startup and therefore their prospects for success. Although entrepreneurs may launch a new firm based on a vague sense of expected post-entry performance, they only discover their true ability – in terms of managerial competence and of having based the firm on an idea that is viable on the market – once their business is established. Those entrepreneurs who discover that their ability exceeds their expectations expand the scale of their business, whereas those discovering that their post-entry performance is less than commensurate with their expectations will contract the scale of output and possibly exit from the industry. Thus, Jovanovic's model is a theory of noisy selection, where efficient firms grow and survive and inefficient firms decline and fail. The links between entrepreneurship on the one hand and growth and survival on the other have been found across a number of social science disciplines, including economics, sociology and regional studies.

A series of survey articles by Sutton (1997), Caves (1998) and Geroski (1995) summarize the findings from a plethora of empirical studies examining the relationship between firm size and growth within the North American context. The early studies were undertaken using data from the U.S. These studies (Mansfield 1962; Hall 1987; Dunne, Roberts and Samuelson 1989; and Audretsch 1991) established not only that the likelihood of a new entrant surviving is quite low, but that the likelihood of survival is positively related to firm size and age. A stylized result (Geroski 1995) emerging from this literature is that, when a broad spectrum of firm sizes is included in samples of U.S. enterprises, smaller firms exhibit systematically higher growth rates than their larger counterparts. The growth advantage of small and new firms vis-à-vis large enterprises has been shown to be even greater in high technology industries (Audretsch 1995).

The performance of small and new firms is also conditional upon location. Fotopulos and Louri (2000) examine the impact that location within an agglomeration has on the likelihood of survival for Greek firms. They find that location in the Greater Athens area has a positive impact on the likelihood of survival, particularly for smaller enterprises.

Based on a panel data set consisting of firm-level observations, Scarpetta et al. (2002) provide evidence that there is a lower degree of firm turbulence, or what they call 'churning' in Europe than in the U.S. In particular, they identify that the distinguishing features of European SMEs from their American counterparts is that they start up at a larger size, have a higher level of labour productivity, and a lower level of employment growth subsequent to entry.

Thus, while there is somewhat more ambiguity in the studies linking growth and survival to firm size and growth, the results for Europe generally mirror the so-called 'Stylized Results' found within the North American context:

- Growth rates are higher for smaller enterprises;
- Growth rates are higher for younger enterprises;
- Growth rates are even higher for small and young enterprises in knowledge-intensive industries;
- The likelihood of survival is lower for smaller enterprises;
- The likelihood of survival is lower for younger enterprises;
- The likelihood of survival is even lower for small and young enterprises in knowledge-intensive industries.

What emerges from the new evolutionary theories and corroborative empirical evidence on the role of entrepreneurial small firms is that firms are in motion, with a lot of new firms entering the industry and a lot of firms exiting out of the industry. The evolutionary view of entrepreneurship is that new firms typically start at a very small scale of output. They are motivated by the desire to appropriate the expected value of new economic knowledge. But, depending upon the extent of scale economies in the industry, the firm may not be able to remain viable indefinitely at its startup size. Rather, if scale economies are anything other than negligible, the new firm is likely to have to grow to survival. The temporary survival of new firms is presumably supported through the deployment of a strategy of compensating factor differentials that enables the firm to discover whether or not it has a viable product (Audretsch et al. 2002).

The empirical evidence described above supports such an evolutionary view of the role of new firms in manufacturing, because the post-entry growth of firms that survive tends to be spurred by the extent to which there is a gap between the minimum efficient scale (MES) level of output and the size of the firm. However, the likelihood of any particular new firm surviving tends to decrease as this gap increases. Such new suboptimal scale firms are apparently engaged in the selection process. Only those firms offering a viable product that can be produced efficiently will grow and ultimately approach or attain the MES level of output. The remainder will stagnate, and depending upon the severity of the other selection mechanism – the extent of scale economies – may ultimately be forced to exit out of the industry. Rather, by serving as agents of change, entrepreneurial firms provide an essential source of new ideas and experimentation that otherwise would remain untapped in the economy. The impact of entrepreneurship is therefore manifested by growth – at the levels of the firm, the region and even at the national level.

But is this motion horizontal, in that the bulk of firms exiting are comprised of firms that had entered relatively recently, or vertical, in that a significant share of the exiting firms had been established incumbents that were displaced by younger firms? In trying to shed some light on this question, Audretsch (1995) proposes two different models of the evolutionary process. Some contexts can be best characterized by the model of the conical revolving door, where new businesses are started, but there is also a high propensity to subsequently exit from the market. Other contexts may be better characterized by the metaphor of the forest, where incumbent establishments are displaced by new entrants. Which view is more applicable apparently depends on three major factors – the underlying technological conditions, scale economies, and demand. Where scale economies play an important role, the model of the revolving door seems to be more applicable. While the rather startling result that the startup and entry of new businesses is apparently not deterred by the presence of high scale economies, a process of firm selection analogous to a revolving door ensures that only those establishments successful enough to grow will be able to survive beyond more than a few years. Thus the bulk of new startups that are not so successful ultimately exit within a few years subsequent to entry. By serving as agents of change, new firms provide an essential conduit of knowledge spillovers commercializing new ideas through experimentation that otherwise would remain untapped in the economy.

The SME life cycle is depicted in Figure 3.1. The production of new knowledge and ideas in the context of an incumbent organization, such as the research and development laboratory of a large corporation, or the research laboratory at a university, creates knowledge embodied in an individual knowledge worker, or team of knowledge workers. If divergences in the expected value or outcome from this new knowledge lead to the decision by the incumbent firms not to commercialize the new knowledge, the economic agent could remain employed by an incumbent firm and expect to earn incremental additions to her income over time, as depicted by the positive, linear incumbent earnings profile.

Alternatively, as a result of her endowment of ideas and knowledge that is not being appropriated or rewarded within the context of the incumbent organization, the knowledge agent could reach the decision to start a new firm, which is represented by point *A*. Why would a rational economic agent choose to settle for a lower return at point *A* than could be earned from a wage paid by an incumbent firm? Because of the expectation that there is some likelihood that the ideas upon which the firm is started will prove to be valuable, resulting in a growth of the firm and associated returns along the survival trajectory. As the evolutionary theories and systematic empirical evidence, shows, the likelihood of a new startup surviving is low. It is even lower for a knowledge-based startup. However, as discussed above, the same literature has provided theoretical insights and compelling empirical evidence showing that those knowledge-based startups that do survive will actually experience higher growth rates.

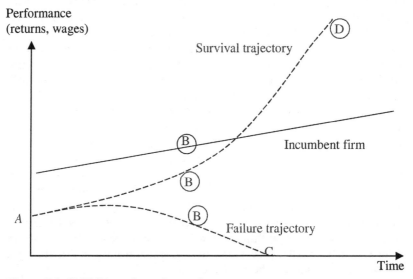

Figure 3.1 SME life cycle and growth

The likelihood that the new idea spawning the entrepreneurial startup is not compatible with market viability and sustainability is high. Thus, the evolutionary interpretation linking knowledge to entrepreneurship and ultimately economic growth suggests that the entrepreneurial act is to learn from the market about the viability and compatibility of a new idea that was rejected, or undervalued by incumbent organizations. The new startup serves as a conduit for knowledge spillovers from the source producing that knowledge to commercialization in a new firm.

One of the important findings of Glaeser et al. (1992) and Feldman and Audretsch (1999) is that economic performance is promoted by knowledge spillovers. However, their findings, as well as the corroborative results from a plethora of studies, focused on a spatial unit of observation, such as cities, regions and states. For example, Glaeser et al. (1992) found compelling empirical evidence suggesting that a greater degree of knowledge spillover leads to higher growth rates of cities. If the existence of higher knowledge spillovers bestow higher growth rates for cities, this relationship should also hold for the unit of observation of the (knowledge) firm. The performance of entrepreneurial firms accessing knowledge spillovers should exhibit a superior performance. Thus, the Entrepreneurial Performance Hypothesis states that 'The performance of knowledge-based startups should be superior when they are able to access knowledge spillovers through geographic proximity to knowledge sources, such as universities, when compared to their counterparts without a close geographic proximity to a knowledge source.'

The Competitive Advantage Hypothesis has been subjected to empirical scrutiny. Evidence supporting the Competitive Advantage Hypothesis at the firm level has been provided by Gilbert (2004), Audretsch, Keilbach and Lehmann (2006), Audretsch and Lehmann (2005) and Gilbert, Audretsch and McDougall (2004), all of whom find that the competitive advantage of new-firm startups within close geographic proximity to knowledge sources, such as universities. In particular, Audretsch, Keilbach and Lehmann (2006) and Audretsch and Lehmann (2005) show the exact relationship between location and the competitive advantage of entrepreneurial startups is complex. Whether or not geographic proximity to a knowledge source, such as a university, bestows competitive benefits to an entrepreneurial firm depends on a number of factors. In particular, the impact of geographic proximity on competitive advantage is shaped by the amount and type of knowledge produced at a particular university. If the research output of a university is meagre, close geographic proximity to a university will not bestow a superior competitive advantage. However, close geographic proximity to a university with a strong research output and spillover mechanisms enhances the competitive advantage of entrepreneurial startups. Similarly, Audretsch and Lehman (2005) and Audretsch, Keilbach and Lehmann (2005) show that the benefits of geographic proximity in enhancing competitive advantage are not homogeneous but apparently vary across academic fields and disciplines.

However, the Competitive Advantage Hypothesis and supporting empirical evidence not be interpreted as attributing the entire impact of entrepreneurship on growth to be restricted to the growth of entrepreneurial firms themselves. Such an extreme assumption of no external impacts is implicit in the analyses of new and small enterprises found in the pathbreaking Birch (1979) study, as well as the more recent Davis et al. (1996a and 1996b) update. While there is severe methodological disagreement between the Davis et al. and Birch approaches to measuring the impact of small firms on economic performance, both implicitly agree in an absence of external impact. Thus, in a type of statistical apartheid or segregation, in the Birch and Davis et al. studies, the impact of small and new firms is measured only within that set of firms.

By contrast, the impact of entrepreneurship on economic growth is not constrained to be limited to manifest itself solely in those entrepreneurial firms, but rather has an external impact of far greater significance. The link between entrepreneurship and economic growth should also exist at the more aggregated level of economic activity. A location, or Standort endowed with a higher degree of what Audretsch, Keilbach and Lehmann (2005) and Audretsch and Keilbach (2004) term as Entrepreneurship Capital, will facilitate knowledge spillovers and the commercialization of knowledge, thereby generating greater economic growth. The Growth Hypothesis states, 'Given a level of knowledge investment and severity of the knowledge filter, higher levels of economic growth should result from greater entrepreneurial activity, since entrepreneurship serves as a mechanism facilitating the spillover and commercialization of knowledge.'

In introducing the model of the production function, Robert Solow (1956) argued that economic growth is determined explicitly by the stocks of capital and labour. Technical change entered the production function exogenously as a shift factor. More recently Romer (1986), Lucas (1988) and others extended the neoclassical model of growth by suggesting that not only is knowledge an important factor generating growth, but because it spills over for use by third-party firms it is actually the most potent factor.

The knowledge spillover theory of entrepreneurship explained in the previous section suggests that this assessment of the role of knowledge overlooks some of the most fundamental mechanisms driving the process of economic growth. The spillover process that Romer and the endogenous growth theory assumes to be automatic is not at all automatic. Rather it is a process that is actively driven by economic agents. According to Audretsch et al. (2005), Entrepreneurship Capital serves as a mechanism facilitating the spillover of knowledge.

While Romer and Lucas added the factor of knowledge capital to the traditional factors of physical capital and labour, Audretsch et al. (2005) do not dispute the importance of the traditional factors, but suggest an additional factor as well – the degree of entrepreneurship capital specific to a Standort, or location. By entrepreneurship capital Audretsch et al. (2005) mean the capacity of the Standort, that is the geographically relevant spatial units of observation, to generate the startup of new enterprises.

While the neoclassical tradition identified investment in physical capital as the driving factor of economic performance (Solow 1956), the endogenous growth theory (Romer 1986, 1990; Lucas 1988) put the emphasis on the process of the accumulation of knowledge, and hence the creation of knowledge capital. The concept of social capital (Putnam 1993; Coleman 1988) could be considered as a further extension because it added a social component to those factors shaping economic growth and prosperity. According to Putnam (2000, p. 19),

> Whereas physical capital refers to physical objects and human capital refers to the properties of individuals, social capital refers to connections among individuals – social networks and the norms of reciprocity and trustworthiness that arise from them. In that sense social capital is closely related to what some have called 'civic virtue.' The difference is that 'social capital' calls attention to the fact that civic virtue is most powerful when embedded in a sense network of reciprocal social relations. A society of many virtues but isolated individuals is not necessarily rich in social capital.

Putnam also challenged the standard neoclassical growth model by arguing that social capital was also important in generating economic growth, 'By analogy with notions of physical capital and human capital – tools and training that enhance individual productivity – social capital refers to features of social organization, such as networks, norms, and trust, that facilitate coordination and cooperation for mutual benefits.'

A large and robust literature has emerged trying to link social capital to entrepreneurship (Aldrich and Martinez 2003; Thornton and Flynn 2003). However, while it was clear that Putnam was providing a link between social capital and economic welfare, this link did not directly involve entrepreneurship. The components of social capital Putnam emphasized the most included associational membership and public trust. While these may be essential for social and economic well being, it was not obvious that they involved entrepreneurship, per se.

Social capital and entrepreneurship capital are distinctive concepts that should not be confused. According to Putnam (2000, p. 19),

> Social capital refers to connections among individuals – social networks and the norms of reciprocity and trustworthiness that arise from them. In that sense social capital is closely related to what some have called 'civic virtue.' ... Social capital calls attention to the fact that civic virtue is most powerful when embedded in a sense network of reciprocal social relations ... Social capital refers to features of social organization, such as networks, norms, and trust, that facilitate coordination and cooperation for mutual benefits.

Audretsch et al. (2005) and Audretsch and Keilbach (2004) argue that what has been called social capital in the entrepreneurship literature may actually be a more specific sub-component, which we introduce as entrepreneurship capital. Entrepreneurship has typically been defined as an action, process, or activity. Entrepreneurship involves the startup and growth of new enterprises.

Entrepreneurship capital involves a milieu of agents and institutions that is conducive to the creation of new firms. This involves a number of aspects such as social acceptance of entrepreneurial behaviour but of course also individuals who are willing to deal with the risk of creating new firms[1] and the activity of bankers and venture capital agents that are willing to share risks and benefits involved. Hence entrepreneurship capital reflects a number of different legal, institutional and social factors and forces. Taken together, these factors and forces constitute the entrepreneurship capital of an economy, which creates a capacity for entrepreneurial activity (Hofstede et al. 2002).

It should be emphasized that entrepreneurship capital should not be confused with social capital. The major distinction is that, in our view, not all social capital may be conducive to economic performance, let alone entrepreneurial activity. Some types of social capital may be more focused on preserving the status quo and not necessarily directed at creating challenges to the status quo. By contrast, entrepreneurship capital could be considered to constitute one particular sub-set of social capital. While social capital may have various impacts on entrepreneurship, depending on the specific orientation, entrepreneurship capital, by its very definition, will have a positive impact on entrepreneurial activity.

Audretsch et al. (2005) and Audretsch and Keilbach (2004) include a measure of entrepreneurship capital, along with the traditional factors of production of labour, physical capital and knowledge capital, in a production function model to estimate economic growth. Their evidence suggests that entrepreneurship capital exerts indeed a positive impact on economic growth. This finding holds for different measures of entrepreneurship capital, ranging from the more general to the more risk oriented.

While the findings by Audretsch et al. (2005) and Audretsch and Keilbach (2004) certainly do not contradict the conclusions of earlier studies linking growth to factors such as labour, capital, and knowledge, their evidence points to an additional factor, entrepreneurship capital, that also plays an important role in generating economic growth.

The results from including measures of entrepreneurship capital in the context of estimating economic growth in a production function model are consistent with other studies also finding a positive relationship between various measures of entrepreneurship and economic growth. For example, Acs et al. (2004) find a positive relationship between entrepreneurship and growth at the country level. Thurik (1999) provided empirical evidence from a 1984–1994 cross-sectional study of the 23 countries that are part of the Organisation for Economic Co-operation and Development (OECD), that increased entrepreneurship, as measured by business ownership rates, was associated with higher rates of employment growth at the country level.

Similarly, Audretsch et al. (2002) and Carree and Thurik (1999) find that OECD countries exhibiting higher increases in entrepreneurship also have experienced greater rates of growth and lower levels of unemployment.

In a study for the OECD, Audretsch et al. (2002) undertook two separate empirical analyses to identify the impact of changes of entrepreneurship on growth. Each one uses a different measure of entrepreneurship, sample of countries and specification. This provides some sense of robustness across different measures of entrepreneurship, datasets, time periods and specifications. The first analysis uses a data base measuring entrepreneurship in terms of the relative share of economic activity accounted for by small firms. It links changes in entrepreneurship to growth rates for a panel of 18 OECD countries spanning five years to test the hypothesis that higher rates of entrepreneurship lead to greater subsequent growth rates. The second analysis uses a measure of self-employment as an index of entrepreneurship and links changes in entrepreneurship to unemployment at the country level between 1974 and 1998. The different samples including OECD countries over different time periods reach consistent results – increases in entrepreneurial activity tends to result in higher subsequent growth rates and a reduction of unemployment.

Holtz-Eakin and Kao (2003) examine the impact of entrepreneurship on growth. Their spatial unit of observation is for states. Their measure of growth is productivity change over time. A vector autoregression analysis shows that variations in the birth rate and the death rate for firms are related to positive changes in productivity. They conclude that entrepreneurship has a positive impact on productivity growth, at least for the case of the United States.

CONCLUSION

Why should SMEs affect economic growth? This paper has attempted to answer this question. When viewed through the lens provided by the knowledge spillover theory of entrepreneurship, SMEs have the potential to make a clear and compelling contribution to economic growth, innovation, and job creation.

The prevalent and traditional theories of entrepreneurship have typically held the context constant and then examined how characteristics specific to the individual impact the cognitive process inherent in the model of entrepreneurial choice. This often leads to the view that, given a distribution of personality characteristics, proclivities, preferences and tastes, entrepreneurship is exogenous. One of the great conventional wisdoms in entrepreneurship is 'Entrepreneurs are born not made'. Either you have it or you don't. This leaves virtually no room for policy or for altering what nature has created.

The knowledge spillover theory of entrepreneurship suggests an alternative view. In the knowledge spillover theory, the individual attributes constant and instead focus on variations in the context. In particular, we consider how the knowledge context will impact the cognitive process underlying the entrepreneurial choice model. The result is a theory of endogenous entrepreneurship, where (knowledge) workers respond to opportunities generated by new knowledge by starting a new firm. In this view entrepreneurship is a rational choice made by economic agents to appropriate the expected value of their endowment of knowledge. Thus, the creation of a new firm is the endogenous response to investments in knowledge that have not been entirely or exhaustively appropriated by the incumbent firm.

In the endogenous theory of entrepreneurship, the spillover of knowledge and the creation of a new, knowledge-based firm are virtually synonymous. Of course, there are many other important mechanisms facilitating the spillover of knowledge that have nothing to do with entrepreneurship, such as the mobility of scientists and workers, and informal networks, linkages and interactions. Similarly, there are certainly new firms started that have nothing to do with the spillover of knowledge. Still, the spillover theory of entrepreneurship suggests that there will be additional entrepreneurial activity as a rational and cognitive response to the creation of new knowledge. Those contexts with greater investment in knowledge should also experience a higher degree of entrepreneurship, *ceteris paribus*. Perhaps it is true that entrepreneurs are made. But more of them will discover what they are made of in a high-knowledge context than in an impoverished knowledge context. Thus, we are inclined to restate the conventional wisdom and instead propose that entrepreneurs are not necessarily made, but are rather a response – and in particular a response to high-knowledge contexts that are especially fertile in spawning entrepreneurial opportunities.

By endogenously facilitating the spillover of knowledge created in a different organization and perhaps for a different application, entrepreneurship may serve as the missing link to economic growth. Confronted with a formidable knowledge filter, public policy instruments emerging from the new growth theory, such as investments in human capital, R&D, and university research may not adequately result in satisfactory economic growth.

By serving as a conduit for knowledge spillovers, entrepreneurship is the missing link between investments in new knowledge and economic growth. Thus, the knowledge spillover theory of entrepreneurship provides not just an explanation of why entrepreneurship has become more prevalent as the factor of knowledge has emerged as a crucial source for comparative advantage, but also why entrepreneurship plays a vital role in generating economic growth. SMEs are an important mechanism permeating the knowledge filter to facilitate the spillover of knowledge and ultimately generate economic growth.

NOTE

1. As Gartner and Carter (2003) state, 'Entrepreneurial behavior involves the activities of individuals who are associated with creating new organizations rather than the activities of individuals who are involved with maintaining or changing the operations of on-going established organizations.'

REFERENCES

Acs, Z.J., D.B. Audretsch, P. Braunerhjelm and B. Carlsson (2004), 'The missing link: the knowledge filter and entrepreneurship in endogenous growth', *Centre for Economic Policy Research (CEPR) Discussion Paper*.

Aldrich, Howard E. and M. Martinez (2003), 'Entrepreneurship, networks and geographies', in Z.J. Acs and D.B. Audretsch (eds), *Handbook of Entrepreneurship Research*, New York: Springer Publishers, pp. 359–400.

Arrow, K.J. (1962), 'Economic welfare and the allocation of resources for invention', in R.R. Nelson (ed.), *The Rate and Direction of Inventive Activity*, Princeton, NJ: Princeton University Press, pp. 609-626.

Audretsch, D.B. (1995), *Innovation and Industry Evolution*, Cambridge: MIT Press.

Audretsch, D.B. (1991), 'New firm survival and the technological regime', *Review of Economics and Statistics*, **73** (3), 441–450.

Audretsch, D.B. (2005), *The Entrepreneurial Society*, New York: Oxford University Press.

Audretsch, D.B. and M.P. Feldman (1996), 'R&D spillovers and the geography of innovation and production', *American Economic Review*, **86** (3), 630–640.

Audretsch, D.B. and M. Keilbach (2004), 'Does entrepreneurship capital matter?', *Entrepreneurship Theory and Practice*, **28** (5), 419–430.

Audretsch, D.B. and E. Lehmann (2005), 'Does the knowledge spillover theory of entrepreneurship hold for regions?' *Research Policy*, **34** (8), 1191–1202.

Audretsch, D.B. and P.E. Stephan (1996), 'Company-scientist locational links: the case of biotechnology', *American Economic Review*, **86** (3), June, 641–652.

Audretsch, D.B, M. Come, A. von Stel, A. and R. Thurik (2002), 'Impeded industrial restructuring: the growth penalty', *Kyklos*, **55** (1), 81–98.

Audretsch, D.B., M., Keilbach and E. Lehmann (2005), 'The knowledge spillover theory of entrepreneurship and technological diffusion', in G.D. Libecap (ed.), *University Entrepreneurship and Technology Transfer: Process, Design, and Intellectual Property*, New York: Elsevier, pp. 69–92.

Audretsch, D.B., M. Keilbach and E. Lehmann (2006), *Entrepreneurship and Economic Growth*, New York: Oxford University Press.

Birch, D. (1979), *The Job Generation Process. MIUT Program on Neighbourhood and Regional Change*, Cambridge, MA: MIT Press.

Carree, M.A. and A.R. Thurik (1999), 'Carrying capacity and entry and exit flows in retailing', *International Journal of Industrial Organisation*, **17** (7), 985–1007.

Caves, R.E. (1998), 'Industrial organization and new findings on the turnover and mobility of firms', *Journal of Economic Literature*, **36** (4), 1947–1982.

Coleman, J. (1988), 'Social capital in the creation of human capital', *American Journal of Sociology*, **94**, 95–121.

Davis, S., J. Haltiwanger and S. Schuh (1996a), *Job Creation and Destruction*. Cambridge: MIT Press.

Davis, S., J. Haltiwanger and S. Schuh (1996b). 'Small business and job creation: dissecting the myth and reassessing the facts', *Small Business Economics*, **8** (4), 297–315.

Dunne, T., M.J. Roberts and L. Samuelson (1989), 'The growth and failure of US manufacturing plants', *Quarterly Journal of Economics*, **104** (4), 671–698.

DiGregorio, D. and S. Shane (2003), 'Why do some universities generate more start-ups than others?', *Research Policy*, **32** (2), 209–227.

Ericson, R. and A. Pakes (1995), 'Markov-perfect industry dynamics: a framework for empirical work', *Review of Economic Studies*, **62** (1), 53–82.

Feldman, M. and D. Audretsch (1999), 'Science-based diversity, specialization, localized competition and innovation', *European Economic Review*, 43 (2), 409–429.

Ferguson, R. and C. Olofsson (2004), 'Science parks and the development of NTBFs-location, survival and growth', *Journal of Technology Transfer*, **29** (1), 5–17.

Fotopulos, G. and H. Louri (2000), 'Location and survival of new entry', *Small Business Economics*, **14** (4), 311–321.

Franklin, S., Wright, M. and A. Lockett (2001), 'Academic and surrogate entrepreneurs in university spin-out companies', *Journal of Technology Transfer*, **26** (1-2), 127–141.

Gartner, W.B. and N.M. Carter (2003), 'Entrepreneurial behaviour and firm organizing processes', in Z.J. Acs and D.B. Audretsch (eds), *Handbook of Entrepreneurship Research*, New York: Springer Publishers, pp. 195–222.

Geroski, P.A. (1995), 'What do we know about entry', *International Journal of Industrial Organization*, **13** (4), 421–440.

Gilbert, B.A. (2004), 'The implications of geographic cluster locations for new venture performance, Strategic Management Society, 24th Annual International Conference, 31 October 31–3 November.

Gilbert, B.A., Audretsch, D.B. and P.P. McDougall (2004), 'The emergence of entrepreneurship policy', *Small Business Economics*, **22** (3-4), 313–323.

Glaeser, E., H. Kallal, J. Scheinkman and A. Shleifer (1992), 'Growth in cities', *Journal of Political Economy*, **100** (6), 1126–1152.

Granovetter, Mark S. 1983, 'The strength of weak ties: a network theory revisited', in Randall C. (ed.), *Sociological Theory*, San Francisco: Jossey-Bass, pp. 201–233.

Griliches, Z. (1984), 'Market value, R&D, and patents' NBER Chapters, in: R & D, Patents, and Productivity, NBER Conference Volume, Chicago: Chicago University Press, 249–252.

Hall, B.H. (1987), 'The relationship between firm size and firm growth in the US manufacturing sector', *Journal of Industrial Economics*, **35** (4), 583–606.

Herbert, R.F. and A.N. Link (1989), 'In search of the meaning of entrepreneurship', *Small Business Economics*, **1** (1), 39–49.

Hofstede, G., N.G. Noorderhaven, A.R. Thurik, A.R. Wennekers, L. Uhlaner and R.E. Wildeman (2002), 'Culture's role in entrepreneurship' , in J. Ulijn and T. Brown (eds), *Innovation, Entrepreneurship and Culture: The Interaction Between Technology, Progress and Economic Growth*, Chetenham, UK and Northampton, MA: Edward Elgar.

Holtz-Eakin, D. and C. Kao (2003), 'Entrepreneurship and economic growth: the proof is the productivity', *Center for Policy Research working Paper*, 50, Syracuse University, http://www-cpr.maxwell.syr.edu/cprwps/pdf/wp50.pdf.

Hopenhayn, H.A. (1992), 'Entry, exit and firm dynamics in long run equilibrium', *Econometrica*, **60** (5), 1127–1150.

Jaffe, A.B. (1989), 'Real effects of academic research', *American Economic Review*, **79** (5), 957–970.

Jones, C.I. (1995), 'R&D-based models of economic growth', *Journal of Political Economy* **103** (4), 759–784.

Jovanovic, B. (1982), 'Selection and evolution of industry', *Econometrica*, **50** (2), 649–670.

Klepper, S. (1996), 'entry, exit, growth, and innovation over the product life cycle', *American Economic Review*, **86** (3), 562–583.

Krueger, N.F Jr. (2003), 'The cognitive psychology of entrepreneurship', in Acs Z.J. and D.B. Audretsch (eds), *Handbook of Entrepreneurship Research*, New York: Springer Publishers, pp. 105–140.

Lockett, A., M. Wright and S. Franklin (2003), 'Technology transfer and universities' spin-out strategies', *Small Business Economics*, **20** (2), 185–201.

Lucas, R. (1988), 'On the mechanics of economic development', *Journal of Monetary Economics*, **22** (1), 3–42.

Mansfield, E. (1962), 'Entry, Gibrat's law, innovation, and the growth of firms', *American Economic Review*, **52** (5), 1023–1051.

Markman G., P. Phan, D. Balkin and P. Giannodis (2005), 'Entrepreneurship and university-based technology transfer', *Journal of Business Venturing*, **20** (2), 241–263.

McClelland, D. (1961), *The Achieving Society*, New York: Free Press.

O'Shea, R.P., T.J. Allen, A. Chevalier and F. Roch (2004), 'Entrepreneurial orientation, technology transfer and spinoff performance of US universities', *Research Policy*, **34** (7), 994–1009.

Putnam, R.D. (1993), *Making Democracy Work. Civic Traditions in Modern Italy*, Princeton: Princeton University Press.

Putnam, R.D. (2000), *Bowling Alone. The Collapse and Revival of American Community*. Clear water, FL: Touchstone Books.

Roberts, E.B. and D.E. Malone (1996), 'Policies and structures for spinning off new companies from research and development organizations', *R&D Management*, **26** (1), 17–48.

Romer, P.M. (1986), 'Increasing returns and long-run growth', *Journal of Political Economy*, **94** (5), 1002–37.

Romer, P.M. (1990), 'Endogenous technical change' *Journal of Political Economy*, **98** (5), 71–102.

Sarasvathy, S.D., N. Dew, S.R. Velamuri and S. Venkataraman (2003), 'Three views of entrepreneurial opportunity', in Z.J. Acs and D.B. Audretsch (eds), *Handbook of Entrepreneurship Research*, New York: Springer Publishers, pp. 141–160.

Scarpetta, S., P. Hemmings, T. Tressel and J. Woo (2002), 'The role of policy and instutions for productivity and firm dynamics: evidence from micro and industry data', *OECD Working Paper*, 329.

Shane, S. and J. Eckhardt (2003), 'The individual-opportunity nexus', in Z.J. Acs and
D.B. Audretsch (eds), *Handbook of Entrepreneurship Research*, New York:
Springer Publishers, pp. 161–194.
Shaver, K.G. (2003), 'The social psychology of entrepreneurial behaviour', in Z.J.
Acs and D.B. Audretsch (eds), *Handbook of Entrepreneurship Research*, New
York: Springer Publishers, pp. 331–358.
Solow, R. (1956), 'A contribution to the theory of economic growth', *Quarterly
Journal of Economics*, **70** (1), 65–94.
Stevenson, H.H. and J.C. Jarillo (1990), 'A paradigm of entrepreneurship:
entrepreneurial management', *Strategic Management Journal*, **11** (5), 17–27.
Sutton, J. (1997), 'Gibrat's legacy', *Journal of Economic Literature*, **35** (1), 40–59.
Thorton, P.H. and K.H. Flynn (2003), 'Entrepreneurship, networks and geographies',
in Z.J. Acs and D.B. Audretsch (eds), *Handbook of Entrepreneurship Research*,
Dordrecht: Kluwer Academic Publishers.
Thurik, A.R. (1999), 'Entrepreneurship, industrial transformation and growth', in
G.D. Libecap (ed.), *Advances in the Study of Entrepreneurship, Innovation, and
Economic Growth – The Sources of Entrepreneurial Activity*, vol. 11, Stamford,
CT: JAI Press, pp. 29–65.
Venkataraman, S. (1997), 'The distinctive domain of entrepreneurship research', in J.
Katz and R. Brockhaus (eds), *Advance in Entrepreneurship, Firm Emergence, and
Growth*, Greenwich, CT: JAI Press, vol. 3, pp. 119–138.

4. Some Significant Slips in Schumpeter's Scenario

William Baumol

INTRODUCTION

With good reason, most recent writings on the theory of innovative entrepreneurship start off from Schumpeter's 1911 model. Yet, a careful rereading of his text indicates that his story entails a number of clear misunderstandings, none of them trivial and some affecting the logic of his argument and the conclusions to which it leads. Several such items will be considered here. Some of them lie close to the heart of the theory, while others are peripheral, but all of them raise significant issues. I begin with one of the slips that is relatively ancillary because the issue it raises is so clear. Of course, none of the points raised here can be regarded as more than quibbles about the main argument, his original analysis that must surely be considered the first truly theoretical analysis of the work of the entrepreneurs and their vital role in the growth process. Still, even if no devil resides in the following details, they are matters that call for some degree of rectification.

ON RISK IN ENTREPRENEURIAL ACTIVITY

Both Cantillion and Knight place primary emphasis on the risk bearing entailed in entrepreneurial activity. But Schumpeter will have none of that. He tells us 'The entrepreneur is never the risk bearer . . . the one who gives the credit comes to grief if the undertaking fails.' (Schumpeter 1911; 1936, p. 187).

But this is surely wrong. Most important, it clearly ignores the role of opportunity cost. The inventor and his entrepreneur partner will normally have invested substantial quantities of time and effort in creating their invention, getting it ready for prospective users and actually bringing it to market. Nor are time and labour generally their only investments. They will often have used extensive amounts of materials and other inputs, though

Schumpeter is right that others may have provided the funds to cover the costs of those inputs. Even if others do not do so, he would undoubtedly have argued that this was a case in which the entrepreneur or the inventor had taken on the supplementary role of capitalist.

In any event, at least the opportunity cost of her effort is lost to the entrepreneur if the undertaking fails. And there are examples in abundance in which years of unstinting and substantial effort was entailed, as anyone has sampled some of the pertinent biographies must be aware. This surely makes the task an extremely risky one for the entrepreneur, who may well risk a very substantial share of her professional and even her private life in an undertaking such as is here in question.

ON THE ROLE OF SUNK COSTS

In Schumpeter's model, as is well known, two of the relevant features of the market are:

- Ease of entry by imitators of any profitable innovation, and;
- For the entrepreneur who wishes to continue to receive the earnings of his occupation, it is necessary to undertake one innovation after another.

Now, it is clear that in such a process the expected future sunk outlays (unlike those already incurred) cannot be ignored. The rational entrepreneur, or the investor in her enterprise must have the expectation of (at least) recovery of those not yet sunk investments, or else he would not lay out the requisite sums.

This means that what he calls 'the second act of the drama' must not just offer the prospect of repayment of the money laid out for input purchases at this later date. Its expected revenues must also promise, in addition, to provide some contribution toward recovery of the sunk investments, unless they can be recouped completely in the initial, pre-competitive entry period. Schumpeter himself, however, leaves out any such later contributions: 'But now comes the second act of the drama . . . the final result must be a new equilibrium position, in which, with new data, the law of cost again rules . . . in the sense of equality between value of product and value of means of production . . . ' (Schumpeter 1936, pp. 31, 39). From this, it seems fair to infer that, according to the author, returns in the second period will just equal the cost of the inputs used up in that period. But in this story, none of the R&D cost is incurred in this later period, so no contribution to this initial investment is allowed in the scenario we are offered. That, it must be conceded, is a possible variant of the state of affairs. The entrepreneur is alone in the market during the initial period of Schumpeter's drama. So he is able to recoup his R&D outlays in one blow, and he may be able to collect even more. But that is patently not the general case, particularly if the appearance of substitutes is very speedy, as it so often is in practice. If the entrepreneur takes this possibility or even likelihood into account, and if his goal is profit, as Schumpeter assumes (see below), then she will not embark on the project if she cannot expect to recoup the rest of her investment outlay in later periods.

Fortunately for her, in this scenario, if the imitators also have profit as their objective function, they too will enter only if there is reason for them to expect to be able to recoup their investments, and so the magnitude of entry should not normally proceed to the point where it can be anticipated that prices will be driven down to a level that precludes amortization. That is, in a market for the innovation with easy entry the expected trajectory of earnings should provide just enough of a stream of revenues sufficient for recoupment of the sunk outlays.

In this case it must be acknowledged that the author made no explicit mistake, but at the very least his account at this point overlooked an important element of the situation, and so his story is far less general than he implies. What he failed to recognise was not only the role of competition and easy entry on the prospect of total profit, but also a basic insight into the mechanism that determines the intertemporal pricing pattern. The story is an important example of what I call 'intertemporal price discrimination' that is subject to a profit constraint imposed by competition. The analysis is formally identical with that of the more widely discussed type of price discrimination, in which customers in several separated submarkets are charged different prices for the same products, even though there is no difference in the cost of supplying the different submarkets. In that case, in markets supplied by larger numbers of rival firms, any one of the firms, *ceteris paribus*, will face more elastic demand curves. And in those markets the profit maximizing prices will therefore be lower. The Schumpeterian scenario is guided in exactly the same way, only the different submarkets do not differ in, say, location, but in the time at which they are in existence. That is, there is the early submarket in operation soon after an innovation is introduced, in which the innovator faces few rivals, if any. And there is the later submarket in which the number of suppliers has expanded. Interpreted in these terms it is easier to analyse the determination of prices more concretely. This is all lurking in the background in Schumpeter, but it never emerges fully and hence it invites the misunderstandings discussed here.

THE PROSPECT OF ENTREPRENEURIAL PROFIT

To Schumpeter, it is a positive economic profit that is at the heart of the story: 'Without development there is no profit, and without profit there is no development.' (Schumpeter 1936, p. 184). That is, since his ultimate focus was economic growth, profit was important to him as a necessary requirement of his mechanism, and the relation is deemed reciprocal, with growth necessary (if not always sufficient) for profit, and profit necessary for growth.

But if entry into the innovation market is easy, zero profit is all the representative innovative entrepreneur can anticipate by way of earnings, because the availability of positive economic profits in the arena will attract more and faster entry. The imitators can be expected to speed their appearance and, as often happens, the appearance of several rival innovations may be virtually simultaneous. If so, as just asserted, the process can be expected to yield zero economic profits, but with a return sufficient to compensate for risk and recoupment of R&D outlays also to be expected, as we have just seen.

ENTREPRENEURIAL PROFITS IN REALITY

So much for what the theory, as formulated up to this point, should lead us to expect. But the empirical evidence paints a picture that is even more dramatic, and further from what was evidently believed at least by the earlier Schumpeter. There is systematic evidence (see, e.g., Freeman 1978; Benz and Frey 2004) that the average earnings of self-employed individuals are significantly lower than those of employees with similar qualifications, and the same is presumably true, in particular, of the self-employed innovative entrepreneurs. That is, the economic profits of the representative self-employed individual are clearly negative if the evidence is valid. There are at least two studies that do support this conclusion for innovative entrepreneurs and inventors in particular. Thomas Astebro (2003) reports on the basis of a sample of 1,091 inventions that,

> The average . . . internal rate of return on a portfolio investment in these inventions is 11.4 percent. This is higher than the risk-free rate but lower than the long-run return on high-risk securities and the long-run return on early-stage venture capital funds . . . the distribution of return is skew; only between 7–9 percent reach the market. Of the 75 inventions that did, six received returns above 1400 percent, 60 percent obtained negative returns and the median was negative (p. 226).

Perhaps even more striking is the recent work of Nordhaus (2004), whose calculations show how little of the efficiency rent goes to the innovator:

> Using data from the U.S. non-farm business section, I estimate that innovators are able to capture about 2.2 percent of the total surplus from innovation. This number results from a low rate of initial appropriability (estimated to be around 7 percent) along with a high rate of depreciation of Schumpeterian profits (judged to be around 20 percent per year) . . . the rate of profit on the replacement cost of capital over the 1948-2001 period is estimated to be 0.19 percent per year (p. 34).[1]

How does one explain this negative economic profit phenomenon, which may well be considered somewhat startling? This is not the place to go into detail, and I am preparing a fuller discussion for another paper. In short, there are at least two explanatory phenomena – first, the well documented over-optimism of entrepreneurs as a group (see, e.g., Astebro 2003). The other is the psychic benefits that innovative entrepreneurs appear to enjoy, first by avoiding subservience to the direction of higher management that is the fate of employees of a firm engaged in similar activities and, second, because of the pleasures of their creative activities themselves. The literature has recognised, at least as early as the *The Wealth of Nations*, that occupations that are less pleasant must offer higher wages in equilibrium. The role of excessive optimism should also be clear. And these are phenomena overlooked by Schumpeter, thereby leading him to a conclusion about entrepreneurial profit that is supported neither by a fuller theoretical analysis nor by the empirical evidence. In sum, he and I both appear to be in error, he when he concludes that the profits of the representative entrepreneur should be positive, and I, when my theoretical model requires them to be zero.

NOTE

1. See also the valuable study by Benz and Frey (2004), and these are by no means the only writings that reach the same result. There are also extensive and authoritative studies of the subject by David Audretsch and Zoltan Acs. See the recent volume of papers authored or coauthored and edited by Audretsch (2006).

REFERENCES

Astebro, T. (2003), 'The return to independent invention: evidence of unrealistic optimism, risk seeking or skewness loving', *Economic Journal*, **113** (484), 226–238.

Audretsch, D.B. (2006), *Entrepreneurship, Innovation and Economic Growth*, Cheltenham, UK and Northampton, MA: Edward Elgar.

Benz, M. and B.S. Frey (2004), 'Being independent raises happiness at work', *Swedish Economic Policy Review*, **11** (2), 95–138.

Freeman, R. (1978), 'Job satisfaction as an economic variable', *American Economic Review*, **68** (2), 135–141.

Nordhaus, W.D. (2004), 'Schumpeterian profits in the American economy: Theory and measurement', Cambridge, MA: National Bureau of Economic Research, Working Paper 10433.

Schumpeter, J.A., 1911, *The Theory of Economic Development*, Cambridge, MA: Harvard University Press. [English translation 1936.]

Schumpeter, J.A. (1936), *The Theory of Economic Development: An Inquiry into Profits, Capital, Credit, Interest, and the Business Cycle*, Cambridge, MA: Harvard University Press.

Smith, A. (1776), *The Wealth of Nations*, reprinted in E. Cannan (ed.) (1904), London: Methuen.

5. Market Selection Along the Firm Life Cycle

Flora Bellone, Patrick Musso, Lionel Nesta and Michel Quéré

INTRODUCTION[1]

One of the most salient findings in the recent empirical literature on industrial economics is that the competition and selection of heterogeneous firms contributes positively to aggregate economic growth. Basically, exiting firms are mostly concentrated in the lowest part of the productivity distribution, suggesting that markets contribute to aggregate productivity by rightly selecting against inefficient firms.[2] Moreover, conditional on survival, new entrants have been found to display higher productivity levels and size growth than incumbents. These robust stylized facts should not conceal the fact that market selection mechanisms may work more or less efficiently across countries, across industries and over time, depending on a potentially large host of factors.[3] Bartelsman et al. (2004, 2005) provide comparisons of the contribution of firm turnover to aggregate productivity growth for 10 Organisation for Economic Development (OECD) countries. They argue that the regulatory frameworks in Europe, and especially in France, have been less efficient than those in the U.S. at promoting the growth of new firms during the last decade. Their main conjecture is that higher entry and labour-adjustment costs in France encourage more pre-entry evaluation of business plans with consequently less market experimentation and ostensibly slower firm expansion. Then, start-ups in France tend to be larger and, on average, more productive than those in the US, but their survival probability is lower and their growth rates slower. This caveat is of particular importance as it suggests that market selection mechanisms to support young firms may be less efficient in some countries than in others.

Given that young firms play a crucial role in promoting growth by infusing markets with more modern technologies, a better understanding of the duration of both young and old firms and of their determinants is much needed. In this paper, we address this issue by examining firm survival and the determinants of market exit using a large scale micro-level dataset on French manufacturing firms over the period 1990 through to 2002. Based on this panel of data, we document how the determinants of firm duration – in terms of firm performance and industry characteristics – act differently according to the age of the firm.[4] We apply duration models to different sub-samples, of young and mature firms, to emphasize the role of market structures in shaping pre-exit selection processes. We use measures of firm performance – in terms of profitability and productivity – rather than size as proxies for efficiency, and measures of industry characteristics to proxy for market structure and turbulence. To our knowledge, although related to three different strands of the existing empirical and theoretical literature, this research is the first to consider explicitly that the determinants of firm duration differ with firm age.

First, our research follows the empirical literature by focusing on the determinants of firm exit hazard rates (Audretsch 1991; Mata and Portugal 1994). These are usually exemplified by firm performance, notably size and profitability, and a host of industry characteristics such as industry structures (i.e. concentration, minimum efficient scale, etc.) and industry turbulence (firm turnover, size of entrants and growth in overall sales, etc.). The observed vector of parameter estimates associated with these variables is then interpreted as the result of competition between firms in imperfect markets. The significance of some industry characteristics is generally interpreted as reflecting the fact that market selection mechanisms do not operate equally over uniform industries. However, none of these studies provides any evidence about whether these market selection mechanisms operate equally over the same set of firms within an industry.

Second, our research is linked to the theoretical literature on industrial dynamics, which relates the firm's decision to exit to its profitability. In the seminal papers by Jovanovic (1982), Hopenhayn (1992), and Ericson and Pakes (1995), firms are at birth endowed with different profitability parameters and/or learning abilities, which determine the distribution of their future profit streams. A central feature of these models is that a new firm does not know what its relative efficiency is (its cost function), but discovers it through a process of Bayesian learning. In these models, if successful the firm grows; if unsuccessful it shrinks or exits. At the industry level, these models predict that the rate of firm turnover is negatively related to entry costs and that, in turn, a low firm turnover rate is associated with large productivity gaps between exiting and surviving firms. Moreover, these models are based on the idea that aggregate economic growth is rooted in the heterogeneity of performance among competing firms.

Finally, our research relates to the work of Gort and Klepper (1982) which triggered a series of theoretical and empirical investigations concerning the so-called industry life cycle. The theoretical models of Klepper (1996; 2002a) and repeated empirical investigation by Klepper and Simmons (2005; Klepper 2002a) and Agarwal and Audretsch (1999) imply that the dynamics of product markets are likely to affect firm exit. The stylized facts predict that in the early stages of an industry, competition is mainly based on product innovation. Both firm entry and firm exit are frequent, although entry dominates over exit. At this stage, product competition is the rule, so that there is no decisive advantage in implementing large scale production. As the industry matures, process innovation dominates so that price competition plays a major role in dictating firm exit. At this stage, there is a natural advantage for large, generally older, firms in that they can spread unit cost reductions across larger scales of production. It follows that beyond and above the major role of firm profitability in accurately predicting firm exit, one should also consider market structures and industry turbulence as potential determinants of the fates of firms.

The paper is organized as followed. The next section describes the dataset and the methodology used to estimate productive efficiency. It also provides descriptive statistics on turnover by industry and captures post entry performance of young firms. Then we focus on the market selection process throughout the life cycle of the firm by means of duration models. The last section summarizes our main findings and provides some conclusions.

FIRM TURNOVER AND PRODUCTIVITY IN FRENCH MANUFACTURING INDUSTRIES

Data and Measurement

We use a unique micro dataset collected by the French Ministry of Industry (SESSI). The French Manufacturing Census (EAE) is a survey that gathers information from the financial statements and balance sheets of all individual manufacturing firms with at least 20 employees, from 1990 to 2002.[5] Unlike most of the existing literature, the surveyed unit is the legal (not the production) unit, which means that we are dealing with a firm-level (not plant-level) dataset. This has the advantage that it avoids potentially spurious effects when assessing the role of efficiency and market selection in determining firm survival. Indeed, a plant closure may not be the direct consequence of a market selection process, but rather the result of an internal decision process.[6] To assess the contribution of market selection to productivity growth, firm rather than plant-level datasets are at need.

In our sample, each unit is endowed at birth with an identifying number. This identifying number is what allows us to track the firm over time and to tabulate entry and exit flows. However, it does not allow us to discriminate between 'true' entries and exits on the one hand, and mergers and acquisitions on the other hand.[7] This limitation is common to most of the micro datasets used in the literature. Consequently, and in accordance with Bartelsman et al. (2005), we rely on the following standard definition of entrant, continuing, and exiting firms. An entrant is an identifying number that exists in the reference year t but not in $t - 1$; an exiting firm is an identifying number that exists in year t, but not in $t + 1$. A continuing firm is an identifying number that exists in years t, $t + 1$ and $t - 1$. When applied to our dataset, these definitions induce some re-entry phenomena, due essentially to the +20 employee threshold effect. In what follows, we correct for this bias by discarding re-entering firms from our sample.

Table 5.1   Entry and exit by year

Year	Entrants	Continuing	Exits	Turnover rate (%)
1990	1,887	19,351	1,738	18.7
1991	2,130	19,181	2,057	21.8
1992	1,683	18,896	2,415	21.7
1993	1,157	18,295	2,284	18.8
1994	1,961	17,785	1,667	20.4
1995	1,511	17,816	1,930	19.3
1996	1,644	17,679	1,648	18.6
1997	1,626	17,828	1,495	17.5
1998	1,374	18,007	1,447	15.7
1999	1,304	17,911	1,470	15.5
2000	1,345	17,758	1,457	15.8
2001	1,464	17,617	1,486	16.7

Note: Figures indicate firm counts, except the last column which reports yearly turnover rates, defined as the sum of entrants and exits relative to continuing firms.

Table 5.1 shows that firms' entry and exit rates average about 9% and 10% respectively. The turnover rate, defined as the sum of the entry and the exit rates, averages 18% per annum, displaying a slightly decreasing trend over the period. These numbers are slightly lower than those reported by Bartelsman et al. (2005) for France. Nonetheless, they show that France has a relatively high turnover rate compared to other OECD countries. Another feature of our dataset, which is in line with the literature, is that industries differ significantly in terms of their turnover rates. This is a potentially important phenomenon as it may have a strong influence on the fate of firms in terms of their hazard rate of exit.

Table 5.2 shows the average annual turnover rates for each of our 14 two-digit level industries. As expected, industries differ greatly in terms of turbulence, and firms' entry and exit rates are positively correlated across industries.

Table 5.2   Sectoral turnover rates, firm counts and employment weighted

Industry	Number of firms			Employment		
	Entry	Exit	Sum	Entry	Exit	Sum
Clothing and footwear	9.2	15.2	24.4	5.1	9.3	14.4
Printing and publishing	9.2	11.0	20.1	5.4	6.6	12.1
Pharmaceuticals	8.1	8.4	16.6	4.3	6.2	10.5
House equipment and furnishings	8.3	10.4	18.8	4.8	5.9	10.7
Automobile	7.3	7.1	14.4	7.2	6.6	13.8
Transportation machinery	8.9	9.4	18.2	5.5	3.5	9.1
Machinery and mechanical equipment	9.7	9.8	19.5	5.0	5.5	10.6
Electrical and electronic equipment	11.9	12.4	24.2	5.4	5.4	10.8
Mineral industries	7.6	8.6	16.2	3.9	4.7	8.6
Textile	7.6	10.0	17.6	4.7	6.5	11.3
Wood and paper	8.0	9.0	17.1	4.8	5.8	10.6
Chemicals	8.1	7.1	15.2	3.9	3.8	7.8
Metallurgy. Iron and Steel	8.0	7.9	15.9	6.1	5.2	11.3
Electric and Electronic components	9.5	8.9	18.4	5.2	5.7	10.9

Note: The turnover rate is defined as the sum of entrants and 'Exitors' relative to continuing firms.

As expected, industries differ greatly in terms of turbulence, and firms' entry and exit rates are positively correlated across industries. The highest turbulence is in 'clothing and footwear', 'printing and publishing', and 'electrical and electronic equipment', while the lowest is exhibited by the 'automobile', 'chemical', 'mineral' and 'metallurgical industries'. These cross-industry differences in terms of turnover rates may be a reflection of several phenomena. They may reveal differences in entry costs across industries (Hopenhayn 1992), differences in market sizes (Asplund and Nocke 2003) or difference in rates of technological progress (Jovanovic and Tse 2006). To fully understand these differences is beyond the scope of this paper. Rather, we are interested in the consequences of cross-industry variations in turnover rates. A major focus of this paper is to investigate how firm productive efficiency is related to hazard rates of exit. This involves measuring firm productive efficiency. We do this by applying two complementary indicators, namely Labour Productivity (hereafter, LP) and Total Factor Productivity (hereafter, TFP). 'Labour Productivity' is defined as the log-ratio of real value added on labour (hours worked):

$$\ln LP_{it} = \ln\left(\frac{V_{it}}{L_{it}}\right). \tag{5.1}$$

where V_{it} denotes the value added of the firm deflated by the sectoral price indexes published by INSEE (French System of National Accounts). We compute TFP by using the so-called 'Multilateral Productivity Index' first introduced by Caves et al. (1982) and extended by Good et al. (1997). This methodology consists of computing the TFP index for firm i at time t as follows:

$$\ln TFP_{it} \equiv \ln Y_{it} - \overline{\ln Y_t} + \sum_{\tau=2}^{t}\left(\overline{\ln Y_\tau} - \overline{\ln Y_{\tau-1}}\right) \tag{5.2}$$

$$-\sum_{n=1}^{N}\frac{1}{2}(S_{nit} + \overline{S_{nt}})\,(\ln X_{nit} - \overline{\ln X_{nt}})$$

$$-\sum_{\tau=2}^{t}\sum_{n=1}^{N}\frac{1}{2}(\overline{S_{n\tau}} + \overline{S_{n\tau-1}})\,(\overline{\ln X_{n\tau}} - \overline{\ln X_{n\tau-1}})$$

where Y_{it} denotes the real gross output of firm i at time t using the set of N inputs X_{nit}, where input X is alternatively capital stocks (K), labour in terms of hours worked (L) and intermediate inputs (M). S_{nit} is the cost share of input X_{nit} in the total cost (in Appendix we provide a full description of the variables). Subscripts τ and n are indices for time and inputs, respectively. Symbols with an upper bar correspond to measures for the reference point (the hypothetical firm), computed as the means of the corresponding firm level variables, for all firms, in year t. Note that Equation (5.2) implies that reference points $\overline{\ln Y}$ and $\overline{\ln X}$ are the geometric means of the firm's output and input quantities respectively, whereas the cost shares of inputs for the representative firms $\overline{S}$ are computed as the arithmetic means of the cost shares for all firms in the dataset.

This methodology is particularly well suited for comparisons of within firm-level panel datasets across industries and across years in that it guarantees the transitivity of any comparison between two firm observations by expressing each firm's input and output as deviations from a single reference point. Applying such a methodology to our dataset reveals strong variations in industry productivity growth over the period of investigation. Average TFP growth rates range from around 3% per annum in the fastest growing industries, to less than 0.3% per annum in the slowest growing industries. In the remainder of this work, we trimmed the dataset by screening out observations located in the top 1% and the bottom 1% of the TFP distributions, in order to control for the presence of outliers which could alter the results of the subsequent calculations.

CHARACTERISTICS OF ENTRANTS AND POST-ENTRY PERFORMANCE

Before investigating the determinants of firm exit, it is necessary to depict the post-entry performance of entrants. Examination of their survival rates shows that entrants in our dataset suffer from high rates of infant mortality (18% in the first year) but that the risk declines steeply with age to stabilize at 5% to 7% after the age of 10. Only half of a given cohort managed to survive beyond their sixth year. These preliminary statistics are consistent with most empirical analyses of firm demography (Caves 1998; Bartelsman et al. 2005). Because productive efficiency is traditionally considered to be a major determinant of firm survival, we estimate post – entry TFP performance by computing for a given year t the TFP of each firm i 'relative' to all firms with a different age in the industry:

$$\ln TFP_{it,a}^{ri} \equiv \ln TFP_{it,a}^{S} - \ln \overline{TFP_{t}^{S}} \qquad (5.3)$$

where $\ln \overline{TFP_{t}^{S}}$ is the arithmetic mean of the log of TFP of the firms in sector S at period t and is defined as:

$$\ln \overline{TFP_{t}^{S}} = \frac{1}{n} \sum_{i \in S}^{n} \ln TFP_{it,b \neq a}^{S}$$

and a and b stand for age.

The first two columns in Table 5.3 show these relative productivity distributions over the quintiles for two categories of entrants: those surviving at least one year ('Survivors'), and those exiting after only one year ('Exitors'). It is interesting that the two distributions are similar, suggesting that technical efficiency is not a crucial determinant of young firms' survival. For mature firms (13 years old), we can see from the last two columns of Table 5.3 that Exitors are clearly concentrated in the lowest part of the productivity distribution (Quintile 1), suggesting that for mature firms, productivity is closely associated with the hazard of exit. This is preliminary evidence to support the hypothesis that the determinants of survival change with firm age, allowing for a potentially inefficient market selection process affecting young firms. We return to this aspect in the next section. Another interesting result is that the relative productivity indexes of entrants are almost uniformly distributed across quintiles. This contradicts the basic vintage theory that entrants are more productive because they embody up-to-date technologies.

Table 5.3   Relative TFP distribution

	Age =1		Age = 13	
Quintile	Survivors	Exitors	Survivors	Exitors
1	22.02	23.36	20.02	35.03
2	18.32	19.42	21.48	21.66
3	18.48	18.15	20.71	15.29
4	19.52	18.19	20.34	15.92
5	21.67	20.87	17.45	12.10
	100	100	100	100

Note: See text for computational details.

To shed a more light on this, we follow the TFP dynamics of firms after entry. Figure 5.1 displays two sorts of TFP dynamics.

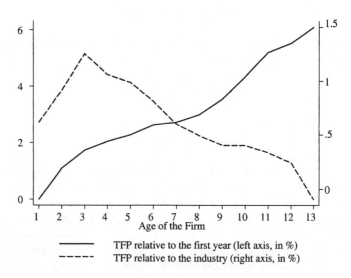

Figure 5.1 Post-entry TFP performance (in %)

The dotted line depicts the dynamics of firms' TFP relative to the sector average ($\ln TFP_{it,a}^{ri}$); the plain line represents the dynamics of firm TFP relative to the year of entry. Formally:

$$\ln TFP_{it}^{re} = \ln TFP_{it,a} - \ln TFP_{it,a=1} \qquad (5.4)$$

where $\ln TFP_{it,a=1}$ is the TFP of firm i in year t at time of entry.[8] Figure 5.1 shows that conditional on survival, the representative firm enjoys continuous productivity gains. Moreover, entrants have a significant productivity advantage over incumbents of around 0.6%. Conditional on survival, this relative advantage increases to 1.25% when firms have managed to exist for three years, then declines monotonically over the next ten years to the industry average. This initial rise is puzzling: it may result from a selection effect, i.e. only the most productive firms survive, or a learning effect, i.e. firms TFP increases over the course of their productive activities. In order to discriminate between these effects, we concentrate on successful entrants, defined as those firms that survive for a substantial period of time. Should the selection effect dominate over the learning effect, the peak at age 3 should simply vanish, implying that the observed increase in relative TFP is the result of an efficient market selection mechanism. Should the learning effect dominate, the general pattern would remain unchanged. Figure 5.2 displays measures of $\ln TFP_{it,a}^{ri}$ for four types of entrants: all entrants; entrants surviving at least 3 years; entrants surviving at least 5 years and entrants surviving at least 10 years.

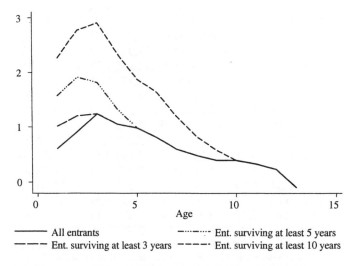

Figure 5.2 Post-entry TFP performance, by life duration (in %)

It shows that the general pattern is robust to entrant type. The initial increase persists until age 3 over all life durations, implying that the learning effect dominates over the vintage effect, at least for infant firms.[9] Moreover, the initial TFP advantage of entrants is positively associated with life duration, suggesting that successful entrants enjoy a greater productive advantage from birth onwards. This underlines the importance of initial conditions in shaping the fate of firms. Altogether, the data militate in favour of a model of industry dynamics in which a learning effect dominates when firms are young and a vintage effect when firms become mature. Importantly, both effects interact to drive aggregate productivity growth (Baldwin and Rafiquzzaman 1995).

To complete the picture, Table 5.4 provides additional information on the dynamics of firms after entry. Specifically, if we look at a series of variables x_{it}, where subscripts i and t stand for firm i at time t, x is alternately the log of TFP, the log of labour productivity (abbreviated as 'LP' in the table), the log of employment (L) and the log of capital intensity (K/L). We can examine their dynamics relative to either the rest of the industry or their own value at the time of entry. Again, values relative to the rest of the industry $x_{it,a}^{ri}$ are computed as the log difference between the observed value of firms of a given age, and the sectoral mean value of firms of a different age ($x_{it,a}^{ri} \equiv x_{it,a} - x_{it,b \neq a}$). Values relative to the year of entry $\ln x_{it}^{re}$ are computed as $\ln x_{it}^{re} \equiv \ln x_{it,a} - \ln x_{it,a=1}$.

Table 5.4   Post-entry performance of firms, by age (in %)

	Relative to industry average				Relative to firm year of entry				
Age	n	TFP	LP	L	K/L	n	TFP	LP	L	K/L
1	15,695	0.62	–6.02	–36.68	–50.83	15,695	*0.00*	*0.00*	*0.00*	*0.00*
2	13,630	0.91	–4.21	–30.43	–42.62	12,951	1.10	3.64	3.82	20.94
3	12,188	1.25	–2.30	–25.11	–33.97	10,158	1.73	6.09	8.38	36.92
4	11,359	1.06	–1.49	–21.99	–26.53	8,257	2.05	8.49	12.16	50.89
5	10,540	0.99	*–0.59*	–18.47	–20.16	6,797	2.28	10.69	16.29	64.28
6	9,742	0.81	*–0.21*	–15.86	–13.96	5,656	2.64	12.86	20.22	75.98
7	8,942	0.60	*0.54*	–12.41	–8.10	4,573	2.73	14.28	23.60	88.39
8	7,542	0.49	*0.34*	–10.03	–4.45	3,626	3.01	16.50	26.74	100.85
9	6,400	0.40	*0.91*	–7.70	*–0.94*	2,852	3.55	20.11	28.66	116.31
10	5,347	0.40	1.33	–4.41	2.83	2,077	4.34	23.12	29.95	132.81
11	4,653	0.33	*0.26*	–3.94	5.95	1,620	5.22	27.23	31.99	148.22
12	3,841	*0.24*	1.55	*–1.59*	9.20	1,032	5.54	30.05	33.07	174.41
13	3,085	*–0.10*	2.12	*0.92*	14.44	459	6.11	33.37	32.10	185.92

Note: Mean values $x_{it,a}^{ri}$ and $x_{it,a}^{re}$ reported. Significant differences are indicated in italics. See text for computational details of $x_{it,a}^{ri}$ and $x_{it,a}^{re}$. *n*: number of observations; TFP: Total Factor Productivity; LP: Labour Productivity; K/L: Capital Intensity.

We observe a well-documented result (Caves 1998): entrants are significantly smaller than incumbents (37%) and dramatically less capital intensive (50%). This lack of available productive capital translates into a significant disadvantage in labour productivity (–6.2%) despite the relative advantage in TFP previously mentioned. But, conditional on firm survival, firms grow quite quickly and, based on an impressively high investment rate, double their capital-labour ratio within eight years, caching-up with the average level of labour productivity.

MARKET SELECTION ALONG THE FIRM LIFE CYCLE

Econometric Models

In this section we develop an empirical model of the determinants of the hazard rate of exit. It is based on a discrete time duration model for grouped data following the approach introduced by Prentice and Gloeckler (1978). Suppose there are firms $i = 1,...,N$, that enter the industry at time $t = 0$. The hazard rate function is defined as the probability of failure in interval $[t, t + 1]$ divided by the probability of surviving at least until t. The hazard rate function for firm i at time $t > 0$ and $t = 1,...,T$ is assumed to take the proportional hazard form: $\theta_{it} = \theta(t) \cdot X_{it}' \beta$, where $\theta(t)$ is the baseline hazard function and X_{it} is a series of time-varying covariates summarising observed differences among firms. The discrete time formulation of the hazard of exit for firm i in time interval t is given by a complementary log-logistic function such as:

$$h_t(X_{it}) \equiv 1 - \exp\{-\exp(X_{it}'\beta + \theta(t))\} \tag{5.5}$$

where $\theta(t)$ is the baseline hazard function relating the hazard rate $h_t(X_{it})$ at the tth interval to the spell duration (Jenkins 1995).

This model can be extended to account for unobserved but systematic differences among firms. Suppose that unobserved heterogeneity is described by a random variable μ_i independent of X_{it}. The proportional hazards form with unobserved heterogeneity can be written as:

$$h_t(X_{it}) \equiv 1 - \exp\{-\exp(X_{it}'\beta + \theta(t)) + \mu_i\} \tag{5.6}$$

where μ_i is an unobserved individual-specific error term with zero mean, uncorrelated with the X s. Model (5.6) can be estimated using standard random effects panel data methods for a binary dependent variable, under the assumption that some distribution is provided for the unobserved term. In this paper, we assume that μ_i is distributed Normal.[10] Also, we perform a likelihood ratio (LR) test for the unrestricted (with unobserved heterogeneity) and the restricted models (without unobserved heterogeneity). The reported estimates are chosen from the LR test.

We expect the hazard of exit to depend primarily on firm performance. We define firm performance in terms of profitability and productivity. We define profitability as the ratio of operating cash flow over assets.[11] Because operating cash flow can be negative, and values in log will be entered as regressors, we transform the variable by adding to it its minimum value plus one. Next, we control for negative profits by adding to the vector of independent variables, a dummy variable set to unity if the firm witness negative profitability, and 0 otherwise.[12] We expect profitability to be the main explanation for firm survival, and to impact negatively on the hazard of exit. The reason for this is that profitability is the most ideal condition and the chief objective if firms are to survive, and expand their activities. Productivity should play a similar role, albeit in a more subtle way. Productivity impacts on profitability: higher productive efficiency means lower unit costs, positively boosting firm operating income in the short run. Thus the inclusion of both profitability P and productivity as explanatory variables in estimating firm survival, dictates that both be independent. In order to account for this we extract the profitability residual of P as follows:

$$\ln P_{it}^{u|tfp} = \ln P_{it} - \ln \hat{P}_{it} \qquad (5.7)$$

where

$$\ln \hat{P}_{it} = E[\ln P_{it} \mid \ln TFP_{it}] = \hat{\beta} \times \ln TFP_{it}$$

and

$$\hat{\beta} \equiv [\ln P_{it} - (\alpha + \sum_{jt} \delta_{jt} \times (S_j \cdot D_t) + \mu_i + \varepsilon_{it})] / \ln TFP_{it}$$

where P_{it} is the profitability of firm i at time t, and is defined as the ratio of operating income over assets, and both S_j and D_t are indicator variables for sector S and year D, respectively. Depending on their age, we do not expect all performance variables to have a similar effect. As documented earlier, entrants suffer from significantly higher hazard rates. The reasons could be related to firm-level characteristics, such as smaller sizes of young firms, structure of ownership (Audretsch and Mahmood 1995) or access to financial resources (Aghion et al. 2006), or to industry characteristics such as Minimum Efficient Scale (MSE), nature of the technological regime (Audretsch 1991) and stage in the industry life cycle (Agarwal and Audretsch

1999). Therefore, we expect productivity to deter exit for incumbents, i.e. to boost firm survival, whereas we expect no particular effect for entrants.

We follow Mata and Portugal (1994) and Mata et al. (1995) and include variables controlling for market structures and turbulence that may steer firm exit beyond and above the presumably chief role of firm performance. To do so, we define the industries at the three-digit level, decomposing French manufacturing into 53 classes. The reason for not using broader classes is to define markets around more homogeneous product classes. Although this remains far from a fully sketched product definition, as in Klepper (2002b) for example, this finer level of industry definition should prove more satisfactory than the two-digit level. We define market structures by measuring market size (computed as the sum of sales for firms belonging to the four-digit industry) and the Herfindahl concentration index (defined as the sum of the squared market shares). Interpreting these measures as an indirect measure of industry maturity, we expect both to relate negatively to firm exit. We also provide an *ex ante* measure of barriers to entry by computing the Minimum Efficient Scale – following the methodology defined by Lyons (1980).[13] The characteristics of industry dynamics indicate the turbulence of an industry. We define market growth as the growth rate in the industry sales, assuming that higher growth rates should equate with more frequent market opportunities. We also control for the number and average size of entrants. First, entry represents a threat – an increase in competition – for incumbents; therefore, in industries with high entry rates, we expect firm lifetimes to be shorter, i.e. we expect a positive sign on firm exit. The average size of entrants indicates demand attributable to entrants.[14] We expect a negative sign for the average size of entrants on young firm hazard rates.

Table 5.5   Persistency in variables

	β	N	R^2
Profitability (ln)	0.769	174,416	0.57
Residual of Profitability (ln)	0.773	174,416	0.58
TFP (ln)	0.764	174,416	0.57
Labour Productivity (ln)	0.912	174,416	0.83
Herfindahl (ln)	0.869	583	0.83
Minimum Efficient Scale – MES (ln)	0.607	583	0.37
Market Size (ln)	1.011	583	0.99
Market Growth (ln)	0.158	583	0.03
Mean Size of Entrants (ln)	0.374	583	0.14
Number of Entrants (ln)	0.873	538	0.75

Note: Ordinary Least Squares on the value of variables lagged one year.

Before discussing the results, we look at the persistency of all variables by regressing the explanatory variables on themselves. In order for a firm to decide to withdraw from the market, observation of their current performance must provide them with reliable information on the stream of expected future profits. In order for these variables to be economically meaningful, we start by revealing their persistency (Table 5.5). We see that the variables characterizing firm performance are all very persistent, notably $\ln P_{it}^{u|tfp}$ and TFP. In fact, we can expect high persistency in firm productivity, since productivity is conditional on the firm's workforce, capital stock and a vector of unobserved but persistent characteristics such as the organization of productive tasks, the presence of a labour union and management practices.

Results

Table 5.6 reports the results for different specifications, introducing all explanatory variables sequentially. All models initially control for unobserved heterogeneity as specified above. Looking at the LR test for $\rho = 0$, the unrestricted model accounting for unobserved heterogeneity is preferred over the restricted specification without unobserved heterogeneity. For the sake of clarity, we report marginal effects computed in three steps. In the first step, we compute the mean probability of exit (mean hazard rate h^x for the average, i.e. representative, firm of mean age and for the mean year). In the second step, we measure a second probability of exit adding one standard deviation to the average value of the considered explanatory variable $h^{x+\sigma_x}$, holding all other explanatory variables at their average value. Lastly, we compute the difference in percentages between probability $(h^{x+\sigma_x} - h^x)/h^x \times 100$. For the qualitative variable indicating negative profits (Profit < 0), the difference is computed between probabilities with null or positive profit and negative profit.

We start by introducing profitability as the sole explanatory variable, together with the indicator variable pointing firms recording a negative operating income. We find that profitability boosts firm survival in two ways. First, profitable firms are more likely to remain in the market (–0.137). In terms of marginal effect, a negative departure of one standard deviation from the sample mean of profitability raises the probability of exit by a considerable 40%. Most importantly, we also find the probability of exit rises significantly if profits are negative (+0.660), increasing the probability of exit by 88% relative to firms with positive operating cash flows. Looking at the full specification (fifth column of Table 5.6), the marginal effect reaches 134%. Hence profitability significantly affects the hazard rate of exit in the expected direction and magnitude.

Table 5.6 Sequential regressions for firm hazard rates

	(1)	(2)	(3)	(4)	(5)
Profit (ln)	-0.137 (0.025)	-0.101 (0.025)			
Profit < 0 (dummy)	0.660 (0.018)	0.633 (0.018)	0.881 (0.071)	0.891 (0.071)	0.895 (0.071)
TFP (ln)		-0.396 (0.058)	-0.577 (0.063)	-0.543 (0.064)	-0.498 (0.064)
Res. of Profit (ln) (> 0)			-0.061 (0.026)**	-0.058 (0.026)**	-0.045 (0.026)*
Res. of Profit (ln) (< 0)			-0.319 (0.069)	-0.323 (0.069)	-0.322 (0.069)
Herfindahl (ln)				-0.019 (0.007)	0.056 (0.011)
MES (ln)				-0.141 (0.017)	-0.100 (0.018)
Market size (ln)				-0.046 (0.012)	-0.086 (0.014)
Market growth (ln)					-0.723 (0.151)
Mean size of entrant (ln)					-0.095 (0.011)
Number of entrants (ln)					0.114 (0.014)
Observations	209,005	209,005	209,005	209,005	208,535
Number of firms	34,589	34,589	34,589	34,589	34,585
Likelihood (ln)	-57,825.3	-57,802.0	-57,797.3	-57,755.3	-57,543.2
LR test [a]	1807.4 [b]	46.6	9.4	84.0	424.3
ρ	0.066	0.066	0.066	0.065	0.061
LR test for $\rho = 0$	57.5	60.4	60.5	59.8	53.9

Notes:

Link function: complementary log-log with unobserved heterogeneity. Non-parametric baseline hazard function. All models include a full vector of time dummies, year dummies, age at entry, and an indicator variable for the firm's presence in the database starting year 1984. Standard errors in parentheses. All coefficients are significant at the 1% level apart from those with marks '***'/'**'/'*' that are significant at 5%/10% respectively.

[a] LR test on previous column. All LR tests are significant at the 1% level.
[b] LR test on model without profitability variables.

In the column (2), we introduce TFP as a supplementary explanatory variable. The inclusion of productivity adds significant information, as shown in the LR test. We find all variables to be significant, with productivity negatively affecting the hazard rate of exit. Textbooks in economics tells us that this is to be expected, since the implication is that more efficient firms are more likely to survive and remain on the market. However, as stressed earlier, the introduction of both profitability and productivity makes it difficult to separate the effects of productive efficiency and profitability, irrespective of TFP. Therefore, in column (3), we amend the model in two ways. First, we introduce profitability net of the contribution of TFP, as specified in Equation (5.7). Second, we distinguish between positive and negative profitability (net of TFP) by interacting the indicator variable on negative profits with $\ln P_{it}^{\mu|tfp}$. We do this to account for possible non-linearities in the influence on the hazard rate of exit. Whereas we would expect negative profitability to depend largely on 'how negative they are', the effect of positive profitability on firm survival should be less strict as once profits are positive, the remuneration of all production factors is secured.

From column (3) we can see that the new specification adds significant information (LR = 9.4) and all variables are significant. TFP influences negatively the probability of exit (–0.577), implying that markets select against less efficient firms. A one standard deviation move above the representative firm decreases the probability of exit by 7.5%. Interestingly, we find the effect of negative profits to be far more dramatic than that of positive ones. One standard deviation below the average value of negative profit is associated with a 13% increase in the probability of exit, whereas one standard deviation above the average value of positive profit is associated with a 3.5% decrease in the probability of exit.[15] Altogether, it appears that the overall effect of profitability is far larger than that of productivity, the overall effect of negative profit being to increase the probability of firm exit by 143%. These results should come as no surprise: profitable firms ought to remain in the market, whereas variations in firm profitability due to micro-, meso- and macro-economic shocks may have dramatic consequences for firm survival. These results hold strongly across alternative specifications displayed in subsequent columns.

Column (4) includes all the variables describing market structures: (the Neperian logarithm of) the size of the industry; of the Herfindahl index and of the MES. First with a versatile sign in both columns (4) and (5), the role of market concentration (Herfindahl) is hard to grasp. In fact, concentrated industries, in a traditional sense, are imperfect markets, which should boost the survival of incumbents with strong market power, and increase the probability of exit for firms with weak market power. Thus the effect of market concentration mitigates these two opposing forces, which may in turn produces instability in the role of concentration. Second, we find that MES boosts the survival of incumbent firms (–0.141): in industries where MES is one standard deviation higher than the representative industry, the probability of firm exit decreases by a significant 6%. In fact, as a measure of barriers to entry, MES must be a hindrance to the threat of new firms to incumbents.

Industry size has a similar effect (–0.046), implying that in industries with a total industry sales value one standard deviation higher than the representative industry, the probability of firm exit decreases by a significant 3%. There are two alternative, perhaps opposite, interpretations. First, large sectors (in terms of sales) offer a wide range of unexplored and unexploited, but available market opportunities. This allows all types of firms to benefit from first mover advantage in these unexplored niches. It is not clear whether incumbents or entrants are better able to seize such opportunities as this depends on initial sunk costs, barriers to entry, minimum efficient scale and the technological competencies needed to enter these niches. Second, industry size acts as a proxy for the maturity of industry. With little or no room for additional entrants, all incumbent firms operate near or at equilibrium, such that the rate of industry turnover is low. Thus the observed coefficient could also indicate industry maturity. It is not easy to say which effect dominates, and we will come back to this issue when we investigate the stability of selection mechanisms by distinguishing entrants from mature firms. Note that the impact of industry size doubles in our preferred specification, where the probability of exit diminishes by almost 6%.

To further our analysis of the influence of industry characteristics on market selection, we include in column (5) variables to describe industry turbulence in terms of market growth rate, and number and mean size of entrants. Rapidly expanding industries offer numerous niche opportunities, which in turn increases firm survival. One standard deviation above the average market growth rate decreases the probability of exit by 4.7%. Large entrants are also associated with a lower probability of exit of 6.8%. The largest marginal effect is found for number of entrants (+11%): industries with numerous entrants have equally numerous firm exits. This result confirms other findings that entry and exit rates are tightly correlated (Caves 1998). Note that the effect of the Herfindahl index on the hazard of exit is both significant and positive. This suggests that concentrated industries boost the selection of firms. This should be expected: industrial concentration processes translate into a lower number of firms by boosting firm exit.

Taken together, our results suggest that the chief factor in firm selection is profitability. If firms are profitable to the point where they can remunerate their production factors, they will enjoy significantly higher chances of survival. If we look only at the role of productivity, we find that markets select according to what the theory tells us, i.e. markets select out less efficient firms. Market structures and industry turbulence also have an effect. Imperfect markets in terms of industry size and barriers to entry equate with higher firm survival for incumbents. Industry growth and firm entry also influence the hazard rate of exit, albeit in opposite directions. Lastly, we find that the effect of market concentration depends on the econometric specification. Notably, the fact that control for industry turbulence modifies its effect is suggestive that market concentration has a differentiated effect on firms, depending on their market power. Firms with high market power should benefit from concentration in terms of survival. Firms with a low market power, typically young firms, should suffer from market concentration, which will reduce their probability of making it to the next period.

To address this issue directly, we decompose the population of firms into age classes: from age 1 to 3, from age 4 to 9, and 10 years or more in order to investigate whether market selection forces operate equally over different age classes. Table 5.7 displays the results for the whole population of firms (column (5), replicated from Table 5.6) and for different age classes. Because it is hard to compare the parameter estimates per se, we computed the marginal effects of each variable on the hazard rate of exit, which are displayed in Table 5.8.

First we looked at the effects of firm performance on the hazard of exit. The most immediate observation is that the chief reason for firm exit, across all types of firms, is a negative operating cash flow. On average, a negative operating cash flow more than doubles the probability of exit (+134.0%, which equates with a multiplication of the probability of exit by a factor of 2.34). Importantly, this effect becomes more dramatic with firm age. Whereas the fact of having negative profit almost doubles the hazard rate for young firms (+86.1%), it triples the rate for old firms (+200.8%). These figures may seem unduly large, but their economic meaning is crystal clear. The decision to exit is first and foremost determined by the capacity of firms to generate profit, and this condition becomes more critical as firms grow. The second observation is that if global manufacturing markets screen out less efficient firms, the consequence of a negative productive efficiency gap on firm survival increases with age. For old firms, productivity is negatively associated with the hazard of exit, suggesting that a move away from productive efficiency is particularly painful and may translate into lower profitability, and eventually into exit from the market. For young firms, TFP has no particular effect.

These results suggest that firm performance, in terms of either profitability or productivity, becomes gradually more critical for firm survival as the firm grows. We can interpret this in two ways. First, it reflects the opportunity costs of remaining in the market, that is, the difference between the economic

Table 5.7 *Market selection along the firm life cycle*[a]

	(5) All	(6) [1, 3]	(7) [4, 9]	(8) [10, +]
Profit < 0 (dummy)	0.895 (0.071)	0.682 (0.108)	0.861 (0.117)	1.145 (0.150)
TFP (ln)	−0.498 (0.064)		−0.573 (0.104)	−0.974 (0.135)
Res. of Profit (ln) (> 0)	−0.045 (0.026)*			−0.116 (0.055)**
Res. of Profit (ln) (< 0)	−0.322 (0.069)	−0.252 (0.104)**	−0.283 (0.114)**	−0.560 (0.148)
Herfindahl (ln)	0.056 (0.011)	0.068 (0.018)	0.070 (0.019)	
MES (ln)	−0.100 (0.018)	−0.122 (0.030)	−0.105 (0.030)	
Market size (ln)	−0.086 (0.014)	−0.111 (0.023)	−0.111 (0.022)	−0.057 (0.031)*
Market growth (ln)	−0.723 (0.151)	−0.987 (0.251)		
Mean size of entrant (ln)	−0.095 (0.011)	−0.108 (0.019)	−0.082 (0.018)	−1.205 (0.321)
Number of entrants (ln)	0.114 (0.014)	0.170 (0.025)	0.124 (0.023)	−0.072 (0.022)
Observations	208,535	43,364	84,244	80,927
Number of firms	34,585	20,217	24,905	13,887
Likelihood (ln)	−57,543.2	−17,662.4	−19,833.2	−17,000.7
ρ	0.061	0.044	0.017	0.041
LR test for $\rho = 0$	53.9	114.7	5401.3	114.6

Note:

[a] See previous table footnote. We did not report coefficients not significantly different from zero.

definition of profit, which includes opportunity costs, and the accounting definition of profits. Clearly, our results suggest that the opportunity costs of remaining in the market grow with firm age, moving the cursor from the minimum level of profitability to the right of the distribution. Second, the difference simply reflects the fact that young firms are more exposed to market selection, so that the relationship between firm performance and survival becomes looser. In other words, the micro-economic determinants of markets selection of young firms lie elsewhere, perhaps in firm size (Audretsch and Mahmood 1995) and, again, credit constraints (Aghion et al., 2006).

Turning to the effects of market structure on firm survival, there are two main results. Overall, we find that market structures impact mainly on young firms rather than on mature firms. Market concentration impacts positively on the probability of young and middle-aged firms exiting. Old firms are immune to it. This reflects both the positive correlation between firm age and firm size, and the positive association between firm size and survival rates. Since older firms are generally larger, they contribute positively to industry concentration, while they are hard to market contest. The puzzle lies in the minimum efficient scale. We would expect MES to have a negative influence on the survival rates of young firms. Such newly established companies generally operate at suboptimal scale, dragging profitability downwards. This somewhat surprising result is reminiscent of Audretsch's (1991) study, which argues that since high-MES industries are usually associated with high price–cost margins, firms operating at the optimal scale of production may in the short-run benefit from them. Finally, industry size is negatively associated with the hazard rate of exit of young firms. This argues in favour of the idea that large sectors offer a wide range of unexplored market opportunities principally for entrants, boosting their survival rate.

Second, the most important effect of industry characteristics on firm survival lies not in the static dimensions (concentration, scale and size), but in the dynamic features. The greatest effect is observed for 'Number of entrants', where one standard deviation above the average value for this variable increases the probability of exit of young firms by 16% and for middle-aged firms by 12%. Large firms are not statistically influenced by the number of entrants. In fact, this result echoes the observation that entry and exit rates are highly correlated. Thus, young and middle-aged firms, but not old firms, find it hard to survive in turbulent industries. High market growth exerts a positive influence on young and old firms, but not on middle aged ones. If age and market opportunities can be considered acceptable proxies for firm size and technological opportunity respectively, this result may be a replication of the Schumpeterian debate on the inverted U-shape relationship between firm size and innovation. In our case, young firms benefit from flexibility and reactivity, allowing them to occupy strategic niches, whereas large firms may enjoy some size advantage in terms of higher internal economies of variety. This suggests that both young and old firms succeed in seizing market opportunities, but in rapidly growing industries, the critical age remains a grey area where firms need to scale up their operations without the benefit of either flexibility or economies of variety.

Table 5.8　Marginal effects of firm performance and industry structure on the hazard rate of exit*

Age	All	[1, 3]	[4, 9]	[10, +)
Profit < 0 (dummy)	134.0	86.1	126.6	200.8
TFP	–6.5	*–1.7*	–7.4	–12.0
Res. of Profit. (> 0)	*–2.5*	*–2.4*	*–2.5*	–6.4
Res. of Profit. (< 0)	–11.8	–9.4	–10.4	–19.8
Herfindahl	6.2	7.6	7.9	2.8
MES	–4.2	–4.7	–4.2	–2.7
Market Size	–5.7	–6.8	–7.1	*–0.7*
Market Growth	–4.5	–6.1	*–0.7*	–6.7
Mean size of entrants	–6.8	–7.3	–5.7	–5.5
Number of entrants	11.6	16.3	12.6	*3.3*

Note: Percent change in the probability of exit. Figures in italics mean non-significance at 5% level. See text for computational details.

These findings suggest the existence of a two-tier market structure. The first layer is comprised of rather stable large firms, i.e. incumbents, for which competition is mainly based on price competition, implying that a departure from productive efficiency may be harmful. Such firms are not very sensitive to market structures because they themselves define the bulk of the industry. This first stable layer differs from the second, more turbulent, layer where entrants are subjugated to market structures. With the exception of number of entrants, all industry characteristics have a significant effect on firm exit.

Our findings suggest that more than one game is being played out on the same court, and that selection mechanisms differ depending on firm age. The first game involved incumbents competing with each other. It relies heavily on productive efficiency, profitability and competition, and the players are fairly stable and well identified. In this case, market selection operates according to economics textbooks, and less efficient firms are driven out of the market. The second game involves both incumbents and new entrants. It is unbalanced with failing entrants on average being more efficient than surviving incumbents. On the whole, entrants are significantly more affected by market structures.

CONCLUSION

In this paper we analysed market selection in French manufacturing markets for the period 1990–2002. Our investigation was based on the hypothesis that the competitive challenges that firms have to face may change along their life cycles. Our empirical investigation led to the following results. First, that conditional on survival, firms experience continuous productivity gains throughout their life cycles. In the first few years of existence, the productivity growth of surviving firms is higher than that of the industry average but then decreases continuously to finally vanish completely. This militates for a model of industry dynamics in which a learning effect dominates when firms are young and a vintage effect dominates when firms become mature. Second, profitability is by far the chief reason for firm exit, since firms with negative profit are twice as likely to exit the industry. Third, firm performance, in terms of either profitability or productivity, becomes gradually more critical for firm survival over time. Conversely, the selection effect of industry characteristics – both in terms of industry concentration and turbulence – is much larger for young than for old firms. These findings suggest the existence of a two-tier market structure, where old and rather stable firms compete in productive efficiency and profitability while young firms evolve in a more turbulent environment where productive efficiency has less influence on selection. The micro-economic determinants of market selection for young firms lie in aspects such as a size disadvantage or access to financial resources.

These findings support the recent theoretical industrial dynamics literature in that, on the whole, exiting firms display below-average productivity levels and are smaller than their surviving counterparts. Thus, micro data on French manufacturing industries show an average behaviour consistent with the common view that market selection favours the most efficient firms. Our results also point to a need for a deeper examination of the institutional differences among countries, which could explain why market selection processes may impact differently on firms of different ages, within a given industry. The French case suggests that the effect of institutions that help markets to operate this selection process appropriately, could be more severe on young firms than more mature ones. Young firms are challenged not because of their relative efficiency (they reveal themselves more efficient than old firms) but in terms of industry concentration and turbulence. This is not to say that mature firms are free from competition. Rather, mature firms face the challenge to continuously renew their productive efficiency and economic profitability, since those that fail to do so will eventually be forced to quit the market.

NOTES

1. This article is reproduced with the kind permission of Oxford University Press. It originally appeared as Bellone et al. (2008), 'Market selection along the firm life cycle.', *Industrial and Corporate Change*, **17** (4), 753–777.
2. Evidence of this market selection mechanism has been found in a large variety of countries. A non-exhaustive list of contributions includes Baily et al. (1992), Haltiwanger (1997), Foster et al. (2001) for the United States, Griliches and Regev (1995) for Israel, Aw et al. (2001) for South Korea and Taiwan, among others. A notable exception is the paper by Nishimura et al. (2005) which advocates that selection mechanisms no longer work in severe recessions. The authors show that over a decade of a recessive Japanese economy, mature unproductive Japanese firms remained in the market while younger efficient ones exited.
3. For instance, Scarpetta et al (2002) argue that, on average, firms tend to exit with better relative productivity levels in periods of downturn and in mature and/or restructuring industries. Aw et al. (2001) compare data for Taiwan and South Korea from 1983 to 1993, a period of rapid economic expansion for both those economies. They conclude that institutions in Taiwan were more effective at supporting the market selection process acting against unproductive firms.
4. By focusing on the distinction between young and mature firms, we are aligning more with the literature that emphasizes the distinction between small and large firms (Audretsch et al. 1999).
5. While this total of 23,000 firms represents 25% of all manufacturing firms in France, it accounts for 75% of employment and 80% of value added in French manufacturing.
6. A firm may decide to close a plant for reasons other than relative efficiency or pure selection. The decision will draw primarily on the ability of the firm to restructure and monitor its scope of activities across several plants.
7. In the EAE data source, an acquisition results in the disappearance of the identifying number of the acquired unit, but survival of the identifying number of the acquiring unit. A merger can result either in the disappearance of the identifying numbers of both firms and creation of a new one, or the disappearance of one of the identifying numbers and the survival of the other.
8. Note that Figures 5.1 and 5.2 and Table 5.4 report mean differences expressed as percentages.
9. The persistence of year 3 as the peak year is very puzzling. The fact that the learning effect is bounded to such a short period of time suggests that firms learn to use a vintage technology without updating it. Obviously, this question is beyond the scope of this paper.
10. See Chapters 17 and 18 of Cameron and Trivedi (2005) for a discussion on the appropriate choice of distribution for the parameter of unobserved heterogeneity.
11. Operating cash flow is defined as earnings before interest, taxes, depreciation and amortization, derived from the company's income statement. Firm assets are defined as a company's common stock equity, i.e. total assets, from which are subtracted liabilities, preferred stock, and intangible assets.
12. To do this, we do not set the threshold value of profits to its accounting value, in other words, operating cash flow must be above zero. We define the indicator variable on negative profit to be equal to unity if the operating cash flow does not outweigh the interest charged on debts, and 0 otherwise. This dummy variable is designed to grasp more accurately the short-run, break-even condition that price covers average variable costs.
13. In simple terms, MES is defined as the logarithm of one-half of the average size of the firms that, on average, operate 1.5 establishments within an industry.
14. Note that inclusion of both number and average size of entrants is tantamount to jointly introducing the number and total size of entrants and to adding a constraint to the parameter estimate associated with the number of entrants.
15. Note that as we introduce more explanatory variables into subsequent regressions, the parameter estimate for positive profitability becomes decreasingly significant.

REFERENCES

Aghion, P., T. Fally and S. Scarpetta (2006), 'Credit constraints as a barrier to the entry and post-entry growth of firms: lessons from firm-level cross country panel data', mimeo, 23 pages.
Agarwal, R. and D. Audretsch (1999), 'The two views of small firms in industry dynamics: A reconciliation', *Economics Letters*, **62** (2), 245–251.
Asplund, M. and V. Nocke (2003), 'Imperfect competition, market size and firm turnover', CEPR. Discussion Paper DP 2625, Centre for Economic Policy Research.
Audretsch, D. (1991), 'New-firm survival and the technological regime', *Review of Economics and Statistics*, **73** (3), 441–450.
Audretsch, D. and T. Mahmood (1995), 'New firm survival: New results using a hazard function', *Review of Economics and Statistics*, **77** (1), 97–103.
Audretsch, D., Prince, Y. and A. Thurik (1999), 'Do small firms compete with large firms?', *Atlantic Economic Journal*, **27** (2), 201–209.
Aw, B., Chen, X. and M. Roberts (2001), 'Firm-level evidence on productivity differentials and turnover in taiwanese manufacturing', *Journal of Development Economics*, **66** (1), 51–86.
Baily, M., Hulten, C. and D. Campbell (1992), 'Productivity dynamics in manufacturing plants', *Brookings Papers on Economic Activity*, Microeconomics Series, 187–249.
Baldwin, J. and M. Rafiquzzaman (1995), 'Selection versus evolutionary adaptation: Learning and post-entry performance', *International Journal of Industrial Organization*, **13** (4), 501–22.
Bartelsman, E., J. Haltiwanger and S. Scarpetta (2004), 'Microeconomic evidence of creative destruction in industrial and developing countries', The World Bank, Policy Research Working Paper Series, (3464).
Bartelsman, E., Scarpetta, S. and F. Schivardi (2005), 'Comparative analysis of firm demographics and survival: Evidence from micro-level sources in OECD countries', *Industrial and Corporate Change*, **14** (3), 365–391.
Cameron, Adrian and Pravin Trivedi (2005), *Microeconometrics: Methods and Applications*, Cambridge: Cambridge University Press.
Caves, R. (1998), 'Industrial organization and new findings on the turnover and mobility of firms', *Journal of Economic Literature*, **36** (4) 1947–1982.
Caves, D., L. Christensen and W. Diewert (1982), 'Multilateral comparisons of output, input, and productivity using superlative index numbers', *Economic Journal*, **92** (365), 73–86.
Ericson, R. and A. Pakes (1995), 'Markov-perfect industry dynamics: a framework for empirical work', *Review of Economic Studies*, **62** (1), 53–82.
Foster, Lucia, John Haltiwanger, C. Krizan, Charles Hulten, Edwin Dean and Michael Harper (2001), Aggregate productivity growth: lessons from microeconomic evidence, in 'New developments in productivity analysis', *NBER Studies in Income and Wealth*, **63**, Chicago and London: University of Chicago Press, pp. 303–363.
Good, David, Nadiri, Ishaq and Robin Sickles (1997), *Handbook of Applied Econometrics: Microeconometrics*, 'Index number and factor demand approaches to the estimation of productivity', Blackwell, Oxford.
Gort, M. and S. Klepper (1982), 'Time paths in the diffusion of product innovations', *Economic Journal*, **92** (367), 630–653.

Griliches, Z. and H. Regev (1995), 'Firm productivity in Israeli industry 1979–1988', *Journal of Econometrics*, **65** (1), 175–203.

Hall, R. (1988), 'The relation between Price and Marginal Cost in U.S. Industry', *Journal of Political Economy*, **96** (5), 921–947.

Haltiwanger, J. (1997), 'Measuring and analyzing aggregate fluctuations: the importance of building from microeconomic evidence', *Federal Reserve Bank of St. Louis Review*, May, 55–77.

Hopenhayn, H. (1992), 'Entry, exit, and firm dynamics in long run equilibrium', *Econometrica*, **60** (5), 1127–1150.

Jenkins, S. (1995), 'Easy ways to estimate discrete time duration models', *Oxford Bulletin of Economics and Statistics*, **57** (1)129–138.

Jovanovic, B. (1982), 'Selection and the evolution of industry', *Econometrica*, **50** (3), 649–670.

Jovanovic, B. and C.-Y. Tse (2006), 'Creative destruction in industries', Mimeo.

Klepper, S. (1996), 'Entry, exit, growth, and innovation over the product life cycle', American Economic Review, **86** (3), 562–583.

Klepper, S. (2002a), 'The capabilities of new firms and the evolution of the us automobile industry', *Industrial and Corporate Change*, **11** (4), 645–666.

Klepper, S. (2002b), 'Firm survival and the evolution of oligopoly', *Rand Journal of Economics*, **33** (1), 37–61.

Klepper, S. and K. Simmons (2005), 'Industry shakeouts and technological change', *International Journal of Industrial Organization*, **23** (1), 23–43.

Lyons, B. (1980), 'A new measure of minimum efficient plant size in UK manufacturing industry', *Economica*, **47** (185), 19–34.

Mata, J. and P. Portugal (1994), 'Life duration of new firms', *The Journal of Industrial Economics*, **42** (3), 227–245.

Mata, J., Portugal, P. and P. Guimaraes (1995), 'The survival of new plants: Start-up conditions and post-entry evolution', *International Journal of Industrial Organization*, **13** (4), 469–481.

Nishimura, K., Nakajima, T. and K. Kiyota (2005), 'Does the natural selection mechanism still work in severe recessions? Examination of the Japanese economy in the 1990s', *Journal of Economic Behavior and Organization*, **67** (2), 53–78.

Prentice, R. and L. Gloeckler (1978), 'Regression analysis of grouped survival data with application to breast cancer data', *Biometrics*, **34** (1), 57–67.

Scarpetta, S., P. Hemmings, T. Tressel and J. Woo (2002), 'The role of policy and institutions for productivity and firm dynamics: Evidence from micro and industry data', OECD Economic Department Working Paper, No. 329, 61 pages.

APPENDIX

Main Variables Used in TFP Computation

All nominal output and inputs variables are available at firm level. Industry level data are used for price indexes, hours worked and depreciation rates.

Output
Gross output deflated using sectoral price indexes published by INSEE (French System of National Accounts).

Labour
Labour input is obtained by multiplying the number of effective workers (i.e. number of employees plus number of outsourced workers minus workers taken from other firms) by the average hours worked. The annual series for hours worked are available at the 2-digit industry level and provided by INSEE. Note that a large drop in hours worked occurs between 1999 and 2000 because of the specific 'French 35 hours policy' (on average, worked hours fell from 38.39 in 1999 to 36.87 in 2000).

Capital input
Capital stocks are computed from investment and book values of tangible assets following the traditional perpetual inventory method (hereafter, PIM):

$$K_t = (1 - \delta_{t-1}) K_{t-1} + I_t$$

where δ_t is the depreciation rate and I_t is real investment (deflated nominal investment). Both investment price indexes and depreciation rates are available at the 2-digit industrial classification from INSEE data series.

Intermediate inputs
Intermediate inputs are defined as purchases of materials and merchandise, transport and travel, and miscellaneous expenses. They are deflated using sectoral price indexes for intermediate inputs published by INSEE.

Input cost shares
With w, c and m representing respectively wage rate, user cost of capital and price index for intermediate inputs $CT_{kt} = w_{kt} L_{kt} + c_{It} K_{kt} + m_{It} M_{kt}$ represents the total cost of production of firm k at time t. Labour, capital and intermediate inputs cost shares are then respectively given by

$$s_{Lkt} \equiv \frac{w_{kt} L_{kt}}{CT_{kt}} ; s_{Kkt} \equiv \frac{c_{It} K_{kt}}{CT_{kt}} ; s_{Mkt} \equiv \frac{m_{It} M_{kt}}{CT_{kt}}$$

To compute labour cost share, we rely on the variable 'labour compensation' in the EAE survey. This value includes total wages paid to salaries plus income tax withholding, and is used to approximate the theoretical variable $w_{kt} L_{kt}$. To compute the intermediate inputs cost share, we use variables for intermediate goods consumption in the EAE survey and the price index for intermediate inputs in industry I provided by INSEE.

We computed the user cost of capital using Hall's (1988) methodology in which the user cost of capital (i.e. the rental price of capital) in the presence of a proportional tax on business income and of a fiscal depreciation formula, is given by

$$c_{It} \equiv (r_t + \delta_{It} - \pi_t^e) \left(\frac{1 - \tau_t z_I}{1 - \tau_t} \right) p_{IKt}$$

where π_t^e is the expected inflation rate for investment computed as a 3 periods moving average of the past inflation rate in investment price index. τ_t is the business income tax in period t and z_I denotes the present value of the depreciation deduction on one nominal unit investment in industry I.

Complex depreciation formulae can be employed for tax purposes in France. To simplify this, we chose to rely on the following depreciation formula

$$z_I \equiv \sum_{t=1}^{n} \frac{(1 - \overline{\delta}_I)^{t-1} \delta}{(1 + \overline{r})^{t-1}}$$

where $\overline{\delta}_I$ is a mean of the industrial depreciation rates for the period 1984–2002 and $\overline{r}$ is the mean of the nominal interest rate on the period 1990–2002.

6. A Test of the Schumpeterian Hypothesis in a Panel of European Electric Utilities[1]

Evens Salies

INTRODUCTION

Electric utilities are urged to increase both the thermal efficiency of their existing plants, and the substitution of renewable energy resources for fossil fuel in electricity production. In the meantime, they must manage to stabilize future costs by reducing the dependence vis-à-vis oil and gas, the prices of which have shown sharp fluctuations since year 2000. As it is progressively deregulated, the internal energy market is characterized by tremendous institutional changes that have been shaping the industrial structure of the electricity industry. There is now clear evidence that more market forms of mechanisms used between the unbundled system operators, generators and retailers for decision making (governance) have significantly influenced the R&D policy of electric utilities in developed economies. Markard et al. (2004) showed for a sample of several European countries (Germany, Switzerland and the Netherlands) that liberalization induced changes in the selection of innovations by electric utilities produced by equipment builders and themselves. In addition, increased liberalization of the European electricity industry has created new opportunities for further internationalization of already big electric utilities, with the consequence that some electric utilities decided to increase their debts to extend their scope of activities abroad through acquisitions rather than to fund R&D projects. This restructuring gives birth to a more concentrated European oligopoly of electric utilities fringed by smaller entrants, which raises the question whether large firms would have an advantage to achieve the aforementioned objectives.[2] The bottom line is that the EU may not meet its ambitious environmental goal to reduce greenhouse gas emissions by at least 20% by 2020 (Commission of the European Communities 2007), for it may not have created a sufficiently stable environment that is yet necessary for promoting renewable energy resources.

This chapter studies the determinants of R&D expenditures. To understand the drivers of R&D in the case of the European electricity industry, I follow previous authors and focus on an input albeit imperfect measure of innovation in the electricity industry, namely research and development expenditures (hereafter, R&D). Figure 6.1 shows the evolution of total R&D expenditures over the period 1980 through to 2007 for a sample of nineteen major European electric utilities.

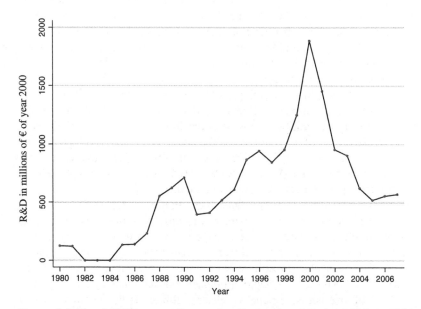

Figure 6.1 Total R&D expenditures for European electric utilities, 1980–2007

We observe a striking similarity with the trend reversion reported in Sanyal and Cohen (2008) and Sanyal (2007) in the case of U.S. firms, yet the reversion period occurs later for European firms. In the U.S.A., the maximum national value is achieved about 1993, whereas here the peak is in 2000. This dramatic decline was reported for both total R&D (Sanyal and Cohen 2008) and environmental R&D (Sanyal 2007) expenses by electric utilities.

Which factors stand behind this decline? The determinants of R&D within the electricity industry in Europe drew the attention of economists following its decline from the early 1980s in the U.S.A. and the U.K. The main reasons advocated by several authors are the higher competition expected from the deregulation of the utilities which increases uncertainty in the value of future revenues (Sanyal and Cohen 2008; Sanyal 2007; Margolis and Kammen

1999). Hence deregulation would act as a disincentive to undertake research activities. A further reason in the U.S.A. was an overall reduction in federal and state funding, more particularly in nuclear, fossil fuels and biological and environmental R&D (see GAO 1996, p. 5). Interestingly, this literature suggests it is not deregulation per se that matters but its expected consequences. Sanyal argues that utilities anticipating further deregulation may have cut back on environmental research following the first sign of change. Therefore, actual restructuring, when it happens, would have little impact.[3] More recently, Jamasb and Pollitt (2008) reach the same conclusion on the role of markets liberalization in explaining the decline in R&D efforts in several European countries. Sanyal (2007, p. 337) suggests that increased competition will lead electric utilities to cut back on R&D, in particular when R&D spending are more directed towards social goals and 'public interest' (e.g. research on global warming), because such research does not confer short-term cost reduction or efficiency enhancement that would bring private benefits to electric utilities. This negative influence on R&D of expected competitive pressures is reinforced by the public good nature of innovation in electricity due to the negative external effects characterising most environmental problems (Horbach 2008, p. 165). This tends to limit the scope of private involvement as spillovers reduce the returns from R&D expenditure to private investors (Jamasb and Pollitt 2008, p. 998).

The purpose of the present chapter is to provide applied evidence of the combined effect of size and reforms on innovative activity by electric utilities, through a test of the 'Schumpeterian hypothesis', for a sample of twenty European electric utilities with annual observations for the period 1980 to 2007. To our knowledge a pioneer contribution analysing the effect on R&D of size across a panel of electric utilities is the seminal paper of Wilder and Stansell (1974). Their main results, which are stable over the period 1968 through to 1970, are that R&D intensity increases with firm size and that electric utilities perform more R&D associated with electric operations than with other operations. This led them to the conclusion that '. . . increasing [electric utility] size, either through a merger or internal growth, would have a favourable effect on R&D outlays.' Since the earliest work of Wilder and Stansell (1974), there is a limited number of econometric studies on this general issue as noticed by Jamasb and Pollitt (2008; see also references therein). Sanyal (2007) and Sanyal and Cohen (2008) are the most recently published works on this issue in the case U.S. electric utilities. From their and a couple of previous econometric studies, the elasticity of R&D spending with respect to size lies in the interval 0.84–1.61 with an everage value of 1.24.

These results suggest a positive concentration effect on R&D. Quoting Jamasb and Pollitt (2008, p. 999), '[s]ince vertical unbundling and horizontal splitting of utilities reduce the size of utilities significantly, these results imply that following restructuring, large reductions in utility R&D spending are possible.'

A statement of the advantage of large firms is given in Cohen and Klepper (1996) and is referred to as 'the R&D cost spreading advantage' (hereafter we shall refer indifferently to their model or to the cost spreading advantage by using the abbreviation 'CSA') thereby the larger the firm then the greater the level of output over which it can apply the fruits and average the costs of its R&D. Apart from Jamasb and Pollitt's (2008, p. 999) assertion that '[i]t is conceivable that large utilities were better positioned to benefit from the scale factor that new technologies offered', what we know about the relevance of the CSA in the case of European electric utilities is still opened to question.[4]

The main contribution of the present paper is to test a 'weak version' of this hypothesis in the case of European electric utilities. We shall not only analyse the determinants of R&D, with size as the primary variable of interest, but also the effect of factors likely to be responsible for the decrease in aggregated R&D efforts. The next section describes the theoretical framework underlying the CSA hypothesis suggested by Cohen and Klepper, and its relevance for application to electric utilities. We then present the data and the econometric model before estimating the relationship between firm R&D efforts and size conditional on other factors. Several hypotheses are tested in the present paper, of which two are classical in the literature on the economics of innovation. First, the Schumpeterian hypothesis thereby R&D intensity increases with firm size. The second and stronger hypothesis can be termed the 'threshold size hypothesis' (see Symeonidis 1996). According to this latter hypothesis the amount of R&D expenditures is independent of or declines proportionally with size beyond a certain level of size. This latter test is motivated by the work of Wilder and Stansell (1974) who had not found such threshold size in a panel of more than 200 electric utilities in the late 1960s. These hypotheses can be tested through the theoretical framework of the CSA model applied to electric utilities. We also consider the role of firm's characteristics including financial variables and the differential effects of some characteristics of the country to which they belong. Finally, we summarize the results and provide policy recommendations pertaining to the electricity industry.

THE MODEL

Cohen and Klepper (1996) provided a theoretical and directly estimable model of the close relationship often estimated between firm R&D effort and firm size at the business unit level, that is to say at the level of a firm's activity within a given product market. One consequence of the CSA hypothesis is that R&D efforts should rise proportionally with size at the business unit level. The simple version of the CSA model relies on two assumptions/conditions (our working assumptions):

- The firm exploits almost all its innovation through its own output;
- The firm does not innovate to grow rapidly (at the time of innovation).

In a nutshell, R&D would rise more than proportionally to sales in larger firms as they have more incentive to exploit their innovations chiefly through their own output and to do so at the time they conduct R&D. This implies that due to cost spreading, the consolidation of two or more firms can lead them to undertake R&D projects that were not previously profitable, thereby increasing the industry's rate of innovation (Cohen and Klepper 1996, p.947).

The second condition means that the firm expects that its innovation will diffuse among its current level of output or a closely related value of it. This is what Cohen and Klepper term as '*ex-ante* output' or the output at the time the firm conducts R&D. The higher this output, then the greater the firm incentive to conduct R&D. The CSA also predicts that returns to R&D should depend more on firms size than if the firm could sell their innovation in disembodied form due to product innovation (Cohen and Klepper, p. 927): '... if firms could reap the full rents from their innovation via licensing, there would be no [CSA] of large size and (*ex ante*) firm size would not condition the returns to R&D.' (Cohen and Klepper 1996, p. 947). These assumptions are the roots of the 'strong form' of the CSA hypothesis. As we work at the corporate level, we must focus on the prediction of the CSA model for this level of aggregation, which we call the 'weak form' of the CSA hypothesis. As noted by the authors, the prospect of appropriating a fraction of the returns of innovation obviously depend, among other things on patents application and the market structure, this latter being related to firm size.

The CSA Model and Electric Utilities

Testing the CSA is particularly difficult however, given the evolution of aggregated R&D efforts shown in Figure 6.1. Moreover, as suggested previously paragraph, changes in the market structure are likely to have influenced the appropriation of returns to innovation, an issue not explicitly modelled by Cohen and Klepper. More crucial, data limitation does not permit us to consider R&D at the level of business units. Therefore, if we find a close and positive (possibly more than proportional) relationship between R&D and size at the corporate level may not be evidence of the validity of the CSA hypothesis at the business unit level. Still, we believe the assumptions underlying their model are relevant for our understanding of the behaviour of electric utilities with respect to R&D effort, however.

By the CSA hypothesis, if there is a close relationship between R&D and size observed at the corporate level, it reflects an aggregation of such relationships at the business unit level. Other correlates of overall firm size can also account for that relationship at the corporate level (see Cohen and Klepper 1996, p. 935–36; Symeonidis 1996, p. 16). To mention a few, corporations have greater:

- Willingness to incur the risks associated with R&D (risk pooling);
- Access to finance (liquidity);
- Ability to internalize R&D spillovers due to greater diversification (scope economies);
- Likelihood to possess the complementary capabilities (e.g. marketing) necessary to exploit innovations.

Beyond the aforementioned correlates, the relationship between R&D and size should be strong in electricity for several reasons. First of all electricity research is very specific to the electric industry, with little scope for redeployment. Therefore, electric utilities have more incentives than firms from other industries to incorporate their process innovation in their own output.

Moreover, several incentives must have induced electric utilities to exploiting their innovation mainly through their own output rather than by selling them in disembodied form to competitors.[5] A first incentive is related to the high degree of concentration that we observe in the electricity industry. Over most of the period covered by our data several electric utilities were vertically integrated from generation to retail. Some were regional or national incumbents (a single or a few firms were enfranchised and deemed natural monopolies). Therefore, as incumbents they used to have a sort of pre-emption right on the use of innovations provided by domestic equipment builders. They feared less imitation from competitors, gained more scale economies associated with innovations (Horbach 2008, p. 165) and the possibility of replication was restricted to the regional monopoly area of each utility. Second, for a homogenous good like electricity, the number of product markets is small (the good is essentially differentiated over time). This nature of electricity implies that electric utilities used to increase their margins in particular by reducing costs through process R&D.[6] The CSA model encompasses process R&D (see Cohen and Klepper, paragraph 2, p.931) whose principal purpose is to lower the average cost of production of the firm's entire output. Unlike product R&D, process R&D should have as consequence that '. . .the expected returns to process innovation will be conditioned to some degree by the firm's ex ante output.' (Cohen and Klepper 1996, p. 943).[7] The third incentive is an assumption at the heart of Cohen and Klepper's model whereby firms that have a CSA are granted with some market power over their products, which allows them to increase their margin once process innovation has reduced their cost of production. This is an appropriate assumption for electric utilities, the consumers of which have very high costs to switch them (see Salies 2008 and the references therein). Customers generally have high switching costs even several years after retails markets are opened up to competition, which makes incumbents willing to incur the risks associated with sunk R&D outlays. Electricité de France (hereafter, EdF) is a case in point given its position as ex-incumbent electricity retailer to almost 29 millions residential consumers. A fourth reason is that the incentive to increase margins by reducing costs is reinforced by the fact that retail electricity rates are heavily regulated (although to a lesser extent since the wave of electricity markets liberalization). To put it briefly, rate regulation ensured some revenue to the firm, but induced it to raise margins through cost reduction. For example, in the case of the U.K., the Office for Gas and Electricity Markets reported that the effect of price cap regulation in distribution businesses turnover and operating income had as consequence lower revenues to electric utilities.

The Formal Model

In the CSA model firms differ with respect to their R&D expenditures R_{ict} ($i = 1,...,N$ in country $c = 1,...,C$ at year $t = 1,...,T$). Given sales and other variables, all firms face the same price–cost margin schedule M_{ict} given by the following function:

$$O_{ct}(1-1/\beta)^{-1}(R_{ict}^{1-1/\beta} -1) \tag{6.1}$$

where $R_{ict} > 0$, $\beta \geq 1$ and O_{ct} represents an index of industry technological opportunities, which affects firms in country c equally and is allowed to vary over time. Therefore M_{ict} is an increasing but concave function of R_{ict} (process R&D in power plants diminishes production cost, regardless of the level of consumer prices). The derivative of M_{ict} with respect to R_{ict} is what Cohen and Klepper (1996, p. 932) term as the marginal return from R&D (or marginal R&D productivity schedule). Firms are assumed to differ with respect to the productivity of their R&D efforts (as M is increasing in R, there is an advantage of being large as an innovator). When $1/\beta$ approaches 1, the l'Hôpital's rule leads to the margin schedule given in Cohen and Klepper (1996): $M_{ict} \rightarrow O_{ct}\ln(R_{ict})$ and the marginal R&D productivity schedule is equal to O_{ct}/R_{ict} . When $1/\beta < 1$ then the marginal R&D

productivity schedule falls less rapidly than O_{ct} / R_{ict}. This is exactly the situation where R&D will rise more than proportionally with firm size, which will be reinforced in firms benefiting from higher O. Following Cohen and Klepper (1996), our price–cost margin functional allows for the case where $1 / \beta \neq 1$. There is also a difference with respect to Cohen and Klepper's (1996) model in that in their paper, O is a fixed parameter. Here, O are country-specific to capture the influence of scientific capacity and the general propensity of countries to patent over time, in a single industry, namely electricity.

Let us denote Q_{ict} the level of output at the time the firm conducts its R&D. Cohen and Klepper assume firms earn rents from their R&D for one period that is the length of time before R&D is imitated, which they formalize as gQ_{ict}, that is the fraction of output embodying the firm's innovation. Besides, since innovation does not influence current output they relate the amount of R&D to sales lagged one year.[8] Thus Q_{ict-1} is substituted for Q_{ict} in the theoretical model. Firm i chooses R_{ict} to privately maximize profits $M_{ict}(R_{ict})N_i \, gQ_{ict-1} - R_{ict} - F$, which we denote by Π_{ict} subject to the constraint that Π_{ict} is non-negative. N_i denotes the productivity level of firm i's R&D and F denotes a fixed cost required to carry out R&D programmes. On introducing N_i, the authors allow smaller firms to have greater R&D productivity to cover F, which accommodates departure from proportionality. Substituting (6.1) into Π_{ict} then maximizing, one obtains the following expression for R&D:

$$
R_{cit} = \begin{cases} (gO_{ct}N_i Q_{ict-1})^{\beta} & \text{if } \Pi_{ict} \geq 0 \\ 0 & \text{if } \Pi_{ict} < 0 \end{cases}. \tag{6.2}
$$

Note that Eq. (6.2) which relates R&D expenditures of one firm only to its own output, its technical opportunities and returns to R&D implies electric utilities make 'independent R&D decisions'. The possibility that firms acquire another innovative one involved in complementary R&D activities is, perhaps, an argument against the independence assumption. I will look at the correlation structure of our model to test for the independence between all cross-section units over time.

THE DATA

Data on R&D and other variables of company's accounts listed below are from Thomson Financial (Datastream). We collected data on 22 major floated electric utilities operating mainly in Europe for the year 1980 through to 2007. We discarded equipment builders such as Areva and Alstom (France) or Siemens (Germany). This is left for future research (see our conclusion section). When several firms merged, we only consider the merged entity. Apart from Electrabel, the acquisition of which by Suez is recent, affiliates are not considered as separate individuals in our sample. Furthermore, we focus on those particular firms that achieve a ratio of at least 50% of their sales in electricity in the year 2004 (see footnote 1 of Table 6.1). We therefore discarded British Gas, Gaz de France and Suez to avoid the consequence on our statistical results of heterogeneity across firms due to the presence of multi-utilities. Note this does not imply that the fraction of R&D expenditures devoted to electricity is at least 50%. Wilder and Stansell (1974) follow a similar approach to differentiate electric utility operations from other types of utility activities.[9] In their model, the ratio of electric to total operating revenue is inserted in the set of right-hand side variables. They avoided criticism of the lack of such ratio for R&D by presuming that revenues derived from activities such as gas distribution involve static technologies. In the present paper we were unable to find that ratio for all years of observation due to data limitation. Furthermore, this fraction has certainly changed over time as a result of acquisition of other firms.

Our panel is unbalanced for several obvious reasons. For example, some firms can be traced back longer than others. More crucial, there are missing values for the R&D variable with a few firms that never report R&D expenditures. For example, Iberdrola has missing R&D values from 1981 to 1990. We do not know whether this latter type of incompleteness is due to randomly missing observations. We are in the 'ignorable selection rule' as described in Baltagi (2005 p. 220). One obvious reason might be that certain firms refuse to report R&D, which should be controlled for. Another reason could be that according to their accounting standard some countries give firms the possibility to capitalize their R&D expenses, under certain conditions however (over most of the period covered in the present analysis, our firms were not subject to report R&D expenditures).

Firm's Characteristics

A brief discussion of innovation in the electricity sector will be given in the following paragraphs,[10] with our choice of potential determinants of R&D in our sample of European electric utilities.

Electric utilities R&D
Our input innovation variable is total electric utilities R&D (their subsidiaries' R&D inclusive). It represents all direct and indirect costs related to the creation and development of new processes, techniques,

applications and products with commercial possibilities. These costs can be categorized as basic research and applied research.[11] Electric utilities do not dedicate large sums to R&D (three out of our 22 utilities have no R&D expenditure and one firm reports only one value). They spend about 2% of their sales in R&D in the most favourable years (EdF, Edison, Enel, E.ON, International Power, RWE, Verbund), compared with equipment builders such as Areva (about 3.5%) and Vestas (2%). Compared to manufacturing firms in other industries (drugs and medical instruments, information and communication technologies, aircraft and aerospace), these figures are not big, neither for equipment manufacturers. A possible reason is that as we do not consider capitalized R&D expenses that are included in intangible assets (this is left for future researches), we may miss a significant fraction of realised R&D. More important, according to Deufeilley and Furtado (2000), the problem of electric utilities is that of adopting the right innovative technology, in particular in generation, than creating those technologies, which remains the role of equipment builders. As a consequence electric utilities dedicate fewer funds to researches that are more specific to equipment builders. This was conjectured by GAO (1996, p. 9) that suggested that electric equipment manufacturers may take on the development of new products.

The electricity industry as a whole favours the development of incremental technologies aimed at improving energy efficiency of existing plants from existing ones (small hydro plants, clean coal plants), notably in responses to movements in the price of energy resources (Defeuilley and Furtado 2000, pp. 2–4). As emphasized by Jamasb and Pollitt (2008, p. 1005), '[g]iven the slow rate of growth in demand for electricity, it is less likely that utilities will engage in long-term and path breaking research'. As an example, researches on clean coal technologies (e.g. Topping Cycle technology in England and Wales) were neglected in favour of combined cycle-thermal gas plants during the period known as 'dash for gas'. We notice political influence was a powerful driver for major innovations like the introduction of nuclear power (Markard et al. 2004, p. 210). Let us note that organizational innovations as well resulted from market liberalization (Markard et al. 2004). Many electric utilities have for example undergone a phase of organizational restructuring, which includes the spinoff of research units (for example, EdF Energies Nouvelles is a 100% subsidiary of EdF corporation). As suggested in Markard et al. (2004), on founding subsidiaries to pursue a very progressive innovation strategy, the parent company can avoid frictions with the established business.

R&D in electricity can be split between environmental and non-environmental projects. We point out this distinction because, as regards to the U.S. experience, it is environmental R&D that decreased significantly following electricity markets deregulation. According to many utility R&D managers in the U.S.A., their companies shifted the focus of their R&D away from long-term advanced-technology R&D to short-term projects that would provide a competitive edge in the near term (GAO 1996, p. 11). This paragraph also gives us an opportunity to be more explicit about R&D activity by electric utilities. Environmental R&D covers the full range of upstream and downstream issues relating to electricity. It is the R&D directed towards public-interest projects such as research on global warming. Environmental innovation in particular consists of new or modified processes, techniques, systems and products to avoid or reduce environmental damage (see Horbach 2008, p. 163 and the references therein which suggest that it is difficult to agree on a definition of 'environmental innovation'). Long-term environmental researches are on micro-cogeneration, fuel cell batteries, tidal turbine systems, new solar energy technologies, and biomass gasification (Gulli 1995). They also include researches on the local impact of climate change, biodiversity and water quality through studies on storage of radioactive wastes. From a short-run perspective its aim is to make more efficient uses of energy, to improve or develop coal plants with carbon dioxide capture, plants fed with renewable energy resources and energy saving appliances oriented towards small and large consumers, to contract out smart network management to allow better integration of centralized generation and distribution of energy, to improve the performance of heat pumps (high temperature), electric vehicles and hybrid vehicles in partnership with the automotive industry.

Nonetheless, the distinction between environmental and non-environmental R&D is not trivial. Companies like EdF consider researches on future generation reactors as belonging to the former type.[12] Although several R&D and test facilities have been closed in the past decade in Europe (WEC 2007, pp. 79–80), France and other countries of the EU maintain active researches in nuclear fission (e.g. fast neutron reactor) and fusion both to meet more demanding safety criteria and maintain the EU's technological lead for a technology facing competition from the U.S. and several far-Eastern countries.[13] In fact many big electric utilities conduct both types of researches. It is important to emphasize that unlike Sanyal (2007) who employs 'environmental R&D', we are unable to make that distinction over the period covered by our data (our sample spans 28 years).[14] Patents turn out to be a more relevant variable to overcome that problem (see the concluding section of the present paper).

Table 6.1 shows that apart from four out of 18 firms (British Energy, Endesa, Iberdrola and Vattenfall), R&D intensity decreased following the first piece of legislation. Iberdrola increased its expenditure in R&D per Euro of assets size three years before the Spanish act in 1994 and three years after.

No R&D data have been reported since 1997 inclusive. The 46% increase in R&D intensity of British Energy must be considered with caution as this firm reported R&D for only a three-year period, 2005–2007. Similarly, the drop of –53% of Verbund corresponds to a short period, 1998–2001. The evolution of R&D intensity for firms like EdF and E.ON is typical of results found in the literature: the change in R&D intensity is positive or small and negative before the first piece of legislation then it decreases significantly after (nearly –10% for EdF and –25% for E.ON).

Table 6.1   Changes in R&D intensity before and after liberalization

Firm	Share[1] Energy/Electricity	Year of first piece of legislation	ΔIntensity (%) before legislation[2]	ΔIntensity (%) after legislation
Atel	100/100	2002	NA	NA
British E.	100/100	1989	NA	46.58
CEZ	100/92.6	2000	NA	–17.44
EdF	96/93	2000	29.48	–9.84
Edison	95/70.5	1999	–7.81	–28.63
EDP	95.5/90.7	1995	NA	NA
Electrabel	91/73[4]	1999	NA	0[5]
Endesa	98.6/95	1994	NA	27.89
Enel	82/69	1999	1.30	–18.78
E.ON	97.8/55	1998	–2.05	–24.47
Iberdrola	95.7/92	1994	17.00	10.57
Inter. Power	NA[3]	1989	NA	–13.59
MVV Energie	95/52[4]	1998	NA	–12.38
RWE	82.6/56	1998	–0.96	–19.78
SSE	95/70	1989	NA	–1.01
U. Fenosa	86.4/80.9	1994	NA	NA
Vattenfall	93.4/87.2	1995	NA	49.59
Verbund	98.5/98.5	1998	NA	–53.08

Notes:

1. For some firms, the column includes the share of electricity in total sales in 2004 (Eurostaf 2005, p. 81). We consider firms whose the share of electricity in total sales or revenues is at least 50%. For firms not present in the 2005's Eurostaf document, we checked in Datastream. The year is that before the firm merged or was acquired. When Datastream reports that the firm operates in the 'electricity sector' but the share of electricity sales in total sales is not available we went to visit firms' corporate website. We retain firms whose annual report in 2007 explicitly mentions that most sales are derived from owning and operating power plants.
2. The date of liberalization varies across countries, but is not reported here.
3. 'NA' stands for 'Not Available' as there was no R&D data reported for that period.
4. Figures for Electrabel and MVV Energie are observed in 2005 and 2008, respectively.
5. '0' means the firm reported one value for R&D.

To show the significance of these results, it is important to emphasize that following the national energy acts, firms associated with a decrease in R&D intensity have also reduced the level of their R&D expenditures. There is one exception, namely SSE.

Size

The choice between sales and assets as a proxy of size is not obvious, more particularly in the energy sector. Wilder and Stansell (1974) and Sanyal and Cohen (2008) employ annual total utility operating revenues as the size variable whilst Dhrymes and Kurz (1964) used sales. As in Sanyal (2007) we use total assets. Del Monte and Papagni (2003) recommended using sales as a proxy for size, as this has merit in avoiding problems of revaluation of capital during periods of inflation. On the other hand, changes in the price of fossil fuels may be responsible for significant changes in sales through changes in the wholesale price of electricity. This may reinforce the potential endogeneity of sales as a size variable. For these reasons, we prefer to use assets.[15]

Network activities

A distinction between firms owning regulated networks and others is important as shown in Bourgade (2008) from a sample of firms operating in electricity. It is crucial to differentiate electric utilities with respect to network business owning, for price regulation of network activities provides vertically integrated utilities with highly predictable and recurrent cash flows (Bourgade 2008, p. 2): revenues from distribution are partially guaranteed as regulators control distribution prices which are typically set a year ahead. As a consequence the acquisition of distribution businesses can be more attractive than acquisition of generation assets since revenues from generation activities fluctuate with the intensity of competition and the volatility of the price of energy resources, thus the less productive firms may experience some intermittent losses when retail rates are capped low. Whereas supply activities will have to face lower profitability for firms exposed to CO_2 prices and emission schemes (Bourgade 2008), cash flows related to network activities bring stable revenues which could be used to fund R&D projects.

A dummy for the existence of network activities will be inserted. The expected influence of the 'network' dummy variable is ambiguous, however. Network activities are a source of predictable cash flows likely to finance innovation in vertically integrated utilities, certainly, but network businesses have less incentive to spend in environmental R&D than supply businesses. Sanyal (2007) does not consider electricity distributors as innovators compared to power producers and equipment builders. Unlike generators and retailers, network businesses do not contract directly with consumers thus have little scope to competing for consumers outside their local network. In fact, they are more the subject of acquisitions by other firms.

M&A operations

The issue here is whether for those firms that acquired others, innovating activities are different. We remind the reader that we selected firms that have not been subject to acquisitions by others. Therefore, financial reports of all firms are available until 2007 that is the latest year in our sample. One exception is Electrabel, the financial report of which dropped in 2007. M&A operations are favourable events to test for the Schumpeterian hypothesis as they have a systematic effect of increasing the size and impact several variables of the balance sheet. They may therefore have a positive effect on internal R&D in regards to the CSA model as the output over which to spread the cost of R&D increases. M&A operations can also influence positively the amount spent in R&D, for merged entities find complementarities in research outputs that are favourable to each individually (technological transfer, etc). They would increase their control over the diffusion and use of their innovation. On the other hand intense domestic and more particularly cross-border merger operations can have the effect of reducing the variety in innovative activities by electric utilities (Markard et al. 2004, p. 212). M&A operations can indeed be motivated by the acquisition of external technical knowledge, or firms would acquire others to substitute their R&D skills for their own (Bertrand and Zuniga 2006; Brouwer and Kleinknecht 1996, p. 193), so that M&A operations influence negatively the amount of R&D per unit of size.

Sanyal and Cohen (2008, pp. 25, 46) controlled for pending mergers through a dummy that takes the value 1 from the time mergers are announced till the date they are consumed and found a negative influence on R&D. We choose a different approach. Given R&D reorganization requires time, to test the hypothesis that mergers reduce duplication of R&D expenditures (the coefficient multiplying the M&A variable should be negative or zero), we follow Bertrand and Zuniga (2006) who used as a measure of M&A intensity the past cumulated number of M&A over a period of three years with a year lag to account for the delayed repercussion of industrial restructuring on R&D. The different kind of operations (full purchase, merger and increase in shareholding) are not distinguished. Thus a non-significant coefficient could reflect the aforementioned opposite influences.

Financial policy

Little is known about the link between electric utilities' corporate financial policy and R&D funding in the economic literature. There are at least two reasons. Papers that address this issue did so for U.S. electric utilities and without going into details (Sanyal 2007 and Guerard 2005 who report the study on electric utilities of a famous Modigliani and Miller paper from 1958; Wilder and Stansell 1974). Other works on electric utilities' finance did not consider R&D (Blacconière et al. 2000; Dhrymes and Kurz 1964). Recent acquisitions by European electric utilities however suggest these firms are willing to use a large portion of their financial resources for foreign investment, notably cross-border acquisitions and purchases of shares in companies' stock. In fact, acquisitions can increase debt to such an extent that *The Financial Times* recently reported financial analysts were expecting EdF to be cash-flow negative at the operating level in 2009 and 2010 (Hollinger 2009).

The financial policy of electric utilities
Wilder and Stansell (1974) and Sanyal (2007) considered a profitability variable among the determinants of R&D. The usual argument about the profitability-R&D link is if firm margins rise, then managers become more optimistic about their firms' fate and raise R&D spending (Mahlich and Roediger-Schluga 2006, p 154). Though, Wilder and Stansell found an inelastic response of R&D suggesting that an increase in the regulated rate of return would not be an effective way to increase utility R&D outlays. Conversely, Sanyal found a strong positive impact which she interpreted as electric utilities with more spare resources spend more in environmental R&D. These opposite results, notwithstanding they relate to different sample periods, do now allow us to predict the expected effect of profitability on R&D for European electric utilities.

Related papers on the financial policy of electric utilities are that of Dhrymes and Kurz (1964) who considered the determinants of the dividend policy of electric utilities before the U.S. electricity industry was deregulated, and Blacconière et al. (2000) who considered the role of deregulation on the value relevance of earnings. Dhrymes and Kurz found that payout ratios were characterized by a considerable degree of inertia with significant differences across firms, however. They interpreted a significantly positive influence of sales on the payout ratio and on dividends per dollar of sales as evidence that small electric utilities tend to retain a higher portion of their profits (distribute less dividends) than the larger ones. From this and other results they suggested as an explanation that size is also an indication of ease of access to the capital market with smaller firms that are 'compelled' to finance a relatively larger portion of their investment programme by internal means. Blacconière et al. found that U.S. electric utilities were more able to earn abnormal rents (or incur abnormal losses) following deregulation in 1992 (the U.S. Energy Act). As mentioned previously, under rate regulation, utility shareholders are virtually assured a rate of return on 'stranded assets'.[16] In a deregulated environment, the eventual recovery of these costs depends more closely on future prices of energy, regulatory interventions (Blacconière et al. 2000, p. 238) and perhaps the toughness of competition policies. The main reason that is also their main conclusion is that earnings have become more important in the valuation of electric utilities (Blacconière et al. 2000, p.234). Unlike a sample of capital intensive firms in manufacturing (used as control group), the value of electric utilities' earnings became more relevant than book value. They also found results consistent with utilities being valued differently than non-utilities prior to deregulation and more similarly to non-utilities following deregulation (Blacconière et al. 2000, p. 247).

Given the small number of papers about the influence of financial policy on R&D funding by European electric utilities, we find logical to draw on studies about the interdependencies of financial policy and R&D efforts outside the electricity industry. Initially, we briefly review recent empirical papers on R&D funding by small and large firms in manufacturing, before turning to the peculiarities of electric utilities with regards to financial constraint. Then we list the financial policy variables considered for our sample of electric utilities.

R&D and financial policy in manufacturing
A way to consider the role of financial policy on R&D funding is through testing for the presence of liquidity constraints, or excess sensitivity to cash-flow shocks that are not signals of future demand increases. This literature has mainly looked at the cost implication of debt versus equity financing (Casson et al. 2008, p. 210). If a firm uses some of its additional cash for R&D, then it is said to be financially constrained in the sense that it must have had some unexploited investment opportunities that were not profitable using more costly external finance (Hall 2002, pp. 41–43). Empirical evidence typically shows a positive association between R&D spending and cash flow, indicating a gap between the external and the internal costs of capital (Mahlich and Roediger-Schluga 2006, p. 147). However debt is usually serviced from cash flow (debt requires a stable source of cash flow), which reduces the amount available to sustain a productive R&D programme. This literature also concludes however that the existence of financial constraints on innovation decreases with firm size, and depends on sectors. But the use of cash flow can be misleading. Mohnen et al. (2008) report a study where cash flow was not informative about the flow of R&D for panels of U.K. and German firms. There is also some agreement in the literature that cash flow sensitivity of investments need not identify liquidity constraints but rather is indicative of high demand and expectations of future profits (see Mohnen et al. 2008; Musso and Schiavo 2007). As a consequence, we can't

be sure whether the absence of a significant relationship between R&D and cash flows is indicative of an absence of financial constraints. To overcome that problem we will insert real GDP per capita in our regression equations to isolate cash-flow shocks that are not signals of future demand increases (see our paragraph on countries' characteristics).

The relationship between financial policy and R&D is also studied through the role of dividend policies in imperfect markets. In perfect financial markets R&D decisions should be independent of the firm's financing decision. New debt is issued to finance R&D while new capital issues raise funds from which R&D is undertaken too. The existence of a negative relationship between R&D expenditures and dividend paid is a standard result of the hypothesis of imperfect financial market. 'Given that dividends and investment are alternative uses of funds, as dividends increase is an imperfect market one would expect investment to fall.' (Guerard et al. 1987, p. 1421). Guerard et al. find evidence of this as the effect of dividends on R&D is either non-significant or significantly negative in a sample of manufacturing firms in the U.S.A., which suggests that research is an alternative use of funds to paying dividends.

It also turns out from this literature that R&D-intensive firms use a different financial policy to fund R&D projects. In a panel excluding utilities, Bah and Dumontier (2001, p. 675) suggest that non-R&D intensive firms (firms which exhibit an R&D-to-sales ratio lower than 5% in their paper) should exhibit a higher dividend payments and lower proportion of cash than R&D-intensive firms. R&D-intensive firms on the other hand prefer equity financing/short-term debts and less dividend payments/more cash reserves to finance their R&D investments. For a panel of large and medium-sized firms in the U.K., Casson et al. (2008, pp. 215–17) find that '[f]irms with positive R&D tend to use more debt [total debt as a share of total assets] than firms with zero R&D, but among the R&D performing sub-sample the use of debt declines with R&D intensity.' This is consistent with firms that report positive but low R&D use more debt finance than firms that report no R&D. Hall (2002, p. 40) also emphasizes that large firms do prefer internal funds for financing investment in R&D while small and startup R&D-intensive firms are either unable or reluctant to use debt finance for R&D investment.

A general conclusion from this literature is that most R&D is funded internally as markets for financing R&D tend to be incomplete (investors outside the firm have difficulty distinguishing good projects from bad when the projects are long-term R&D investment). A corollary to that statement is that if firms have ready access to relatively cheap and long-term external funds, then R&D investment decisions is less dependent on internally generated cash flow (Mahlich and Roediger-Schluga 2006, pp. 152–3; Hall 2002, p. 38). Casson et al. (2008, p. 211) summarise the debt-equity tradeoffs by asserting that 'Although firms may prefer internal funding ... [they] are faced with fluctuations in profitability and have dividend policies with target dividend payout ratios, limiting the availability of funds for investment. In doing so, debt is the preferred form.'

Given the limited number of papers on the R&D-financial policy by electric utilities and since these latter have their own peculiarities, it is important to emphasize some of their characteristics that guided our choice of financial variables.

The peculiarities of electric utilities in regard to financial constraint
Firstly, it is important to highlight the influence of regulation and deregulation. We previously provided elements which suggest that financial policy may have changed following the deregulation of electricity markets. In this respect Dhrymes and Kurz (1964, p. 81) asserted how delicate it is undertaking a statistical study of the financial policy of electric utilities, '... since there are many *semipolitical* factors that enter into the decision making and since differences in the controlling power of local regulatory commissions may affect the financial policy of the firms.' Rate regulation, which protects the firm against the risk of large losses, plays certainly a role but also denies above normal profits which could result from innovative activity (Wilder and Stansell 1974, p. 647). Above all, the essential role played by the electricity industry in the growth of nations is such that investments by electric utilities were largely oriented by governments' energy policies, more particularly before the deregulation of electricity markets. Note as well a low 'investability' (or openness to foreign equity investors) of many European electric utilities: state-controlled electric utilities like EdF (85% belongs to the French state) may not have the freedom to call on shareholders for more funds, which stretches their financial flexibility.

The liberalisation of electricity markets has, as expected by electric utilities themselves (GAO 1996), induced higher requirements on return on capital (WEC 2007, p. 65). Markard et al. (2004), for example, conducted an empirical survey which revealed the minor role played by financial returns in electric utilities before market liberalization in Germany, The Netherlands and Switzerland. Since financial requirements are becoming high in the business of electric utilities, it has also been suggested (Bourgade 2008, p. 2) that a favourable financial profile will stand as a valuable and competitive asset for some firms, in particular where the categorization of certain liabilities is at stake: 'Moderately leveraged firms, with solid debt servicing ratios can better benefit from profitable growth opportunities than firms suffering from more aggressive financial profiles,. . .' As electric utilities started being privatized and engaged in cross-border mergers with other utilities, the role of financial policy as a signal to investors became more crucial (see our previous discussion on the higher relevance of earnings in the valuation of electric utilities). Electric utilities would tend to resemble smaller, not-established firms in manufacturing to which retained earnings in the R&D investment decision play an important role, independent of their value as a signal of future profitability (Hall 2002, p. 41). It is thus expected that positive cash flow (internal finance) will play an increasing role for R&D than for ordinary investment.

In addition to the differential effect of changes in market structure due to the reforms, the slow turnover of physical assets and the specificity of power plants should be another key factor behind the choice of financial policy by electric utilities. Indeed, the long term is the timeframe that should be used to judge electric utilities more particularly in the nuclear sector (Hollinger 2009). Though R&D expenses can reduce short-term profitability, they are viewed as a long-run investment, more particularly for upstream firms where the turnover time for current power generation infrastructure is slow (Margolis and Kammen 1999). This long-run nature of investments is likely to favour debt financing of R&D projects. Bourgade (2008, p. 13) also concludes that the structure of liabilities is not a key determinant of firms market capitalization, which reflects the long-term nature of investment projects in the electric industry too.

In addition to the stability or increases of cash flows, the composition of electric utilities' assets should be a main factor influencing their financial structure. Hall (2002) reports that banks and debt-holders prefer to use physical assets to secure loans and are reluctant to lend when the project involves substantial R&D investment rather than investment in plant and equipment. On the other hand, assets that are not very redeployable are less suited to the governance structures associated with debt (asset specificity à la O. Williamson). Electric utilities are a case in point; they invest in large, capital-intensive production plants that have very few alternative uses (see Jolink and Niesten 2008). But, non-redeployment is precisely a characteristic of R&D-intensive firms who invest in highly specialized research. Electric utilities are not R&D-intensive, however as we already showed. These seemingly contradictory results suggest that electric utilities' financial policy could be similar to that of both R&D-intensive firms and non R&D-intensive firms (e.g. in manufacturing) in particular as regards indebtedness. Our opinion is that as most electric utilities are still regional or national incumbents, clearly protected against bankruptcy, they enjoy a particular situation which enables them to carry a high proportion of liabilities.

We shall now list the variables we considered to control for the influence of financial policy on R&D funding by electric utilities. As in Bah and Dumontier (2001) we name these variables by using the Thomson Financial's

Worldscope numerical classification. This will help comparison with future research on the role of corporate financial policy on electric utilities' R&D funding. We also use some abbreviations used in the financial economics literature.

Electric utilities' financial variables
To measure indebtedness we use long-term debts (3251). Regarding profitability, we follow Bah and Dumontier (2001) and Wilder and Stansell (1974) who use returns on equity (ROE) that is earnings before extraordinary items (1551) divided by total equity (3501). Note that Sanyal (2007) uses the so-called EBITDA (earnings before interest, taxes, depreciation and amortization) divided by total assets. We use one measure of dividend policy, namely the total common and preferred dividends paid to shareholders of the company (4551). Finally, for our measure of budget constraints we use one measure of the level of cash at the disposal of the firm (2001). If the coefficient multiplying the cash flow variable is not significantly different from zero then firms are not subject to any external financial constraint whilst if it is significantly positive, the firm faces some contraint (see Mahlich and Roediger-Schluga 2006, for an application to the pharmaceutical industry).

Country's Characteristics

We follow Sanyal (2007) and use country-level data to capture market structure changes due to restructuring and the pace of deregulation. Besides, as a corporate may be located in or have its main activities in a geographical area which may be more or less conducive of innovation, we control for the possible contributions of upstream suppliers' innovation and the general influence on R&D decisions of national propensities to innovate. Furthermore, we control for the mix in generation capacities held by electric utilities. We motivate the choice of these three factors in the following paragraphs.

Deregulation and competition
As suggested in the literature, institutional changes (deregulation, full market liberalization) are of importance on R&D efforts, more particularly as regards electricity generation where competition often is greatest. Since a fraction of R&D is connected to generation activity, the divesture of generation assets that generally follows market deregulation should have a negative impact on R&D. As suggested by Jolink and Niesten (2008), 'The unbundling and the introduction of competition into the industry have increased the importance of the dedicated investments [henceforth R&D] and uncertainty for the electricity generators as they have lost their relatively stable customer base'.

For example, vertical integration provided a safeguard for the generators against opportunism by the network operators. The link between upward competition and technology development was emphasized even earlier by the International Energy Agency (Skeer 1996, p. 9). According to the Agency,

> As generators are unsure of which customers they will be servicing at the expiration of short-term generation contracts, there is little or no incentive for them to engage in R&D efforts which aim to reduce the cost or raise the efficiency of generating technologies over the long-term, even where there would be clear ... benefits for society.

It would be interesting to use some annual values of a concentration variable at the firm level. Unfortunately, generation data at the firm level is not available over the whole period covered in the present analysis. More important, such a variable is not appropriate because electric utilities were not competing for market shares abroad before market liberalization which occurred at different dates across countries. Differences in the configuration of the electricity industry at the time of market liberalization across countries could also be of importance. As an example, in England, as more firms started competing at the time where regions opened up to entry of firms from foreign regions and foreign countries, potential competition was subsequently higher. But for a similar reason than that just given, changes in the number of players is available and only partially since the deregulation of electricity markets. A further interesting variable is the toughness of price regulation over time. We have only found that variable for European electric utilities for the year 2005, however. In the case where a more complete variable would be available, it would be necessary to isolate an unregulated control group in the industry to see the particular effect of price regulation. But, all our firms were subject to rate or revenue regulation for most of the years spanned by our data. This problem is similar to that in Wilder and Stansell (1974) whose sample included more than 90% of regulated firms thus could not find a net effect of regulation on R&D outlays.

For these reasons, we capture the effect on R&D of deregulation and competition through a variable that takes a value equal to 1 since the year of the first piece of legislation, and a variable that measures the number of years since countries fully opened their retail markets to competition. The choice of the former variable is motivated by the work of Sanyal (2007) who found that passing an order for retail competition has more effect on *environmental* research than implementing legislation for retail access. That variable also captures the change from regulated to deregulated utilities. It is an appealing candidate to capture the trend reversion that we observed in R&D. Nonetheless, it is important to allow for a differential effect of deregulation and competition, which motivates our choice of a potential 'retail competition effect'. We do not use the same variable as in Sanyal (2007) who classifies U.S. states according to the stage of deregulation they reached in 1996 (the year that showed wide spread deregulation activity). We assume that that variable, the value of which can vary across firms but is constant over time for each firm, should capture similar influence than the variables used in Sanyal (2007), however: we expect the later the year of retail market opening, the lower should be the decrease in R&D.

Technological opportunities

In addition to our previous variables, we include a variable of technological opportunities to control for differences between firms with respect to their propensity to patent the results of inventive activity (we borrow this idea from Johnstone et al. 2008; see p. 5 of their paper). The rationale behind this assertion can also be found in details in Nelson and Wolff (1997, p. 207) who assert that the richer the technological opportunities, the more R&D it is profitable for firms to fund (efforts in R&D are more productive). We follow Johnstone et al. (2008) who capture differences in both scientific capacity and the propensity to patent across countries and time through the use of patent applications to the European Patent Office by priority year at the national level divided by nominal gross domestic product. This variable is influenced by national innovation policies and cultural factors. It may also capture differences in environmental regulation due to difference in environmental policy instruments which unfortunately are not available over the entire period covered by our dataset. This variable is also a rough measure for the contributions of upstream suppliers' innovation which is made by equipment and research equipment suppliers from industries outside electricity (chemistry, metallurgy, mechanical engineering and so on).

Technological opportunities should be positively related to R&D efforts, for at least two reasons. It is expected that a firm in a country with a persistent higher level of technological opportunities than that in other countries, will benefit from higher R&D spillovers. Second, as this variable takes values that also change over time, in countries with increasing technological opportunities, R&D at the level of firms should increase too. Obviously as Nelson and Wolff (1997, p. 213) point out, R&D done upstream can pre-empt or be a substitute for R&D in the electricity industry (the more of the work that is done upstream, the less is done in-house), thus diminishing the role played by this variable.[17]

Fuel mix

The consideration of the fuel mix in each country is motivated by the work of Sanyal (2007) who finds a positive influence of a 'coal heavy state dummy' on environmental R&D spending. This is supported by the study of Markard et al. (2004) at the firm level that shows evidence that in case of green power, existing resources and assets like hydro power plants '. . . represented a strong incentive to launch a green power product whereas a long tradition in nuclear or fossil fuel based power generation rather represented a barrier.' It is therefore likely that in firms like EdF, which produces electricity essentially from nuclear and hydro plants, these variables will have opposite effects on R&D. We can't use the share of coal at the firm level, due to data limitation. We use a time-varying variable that is available at the country level from the International Energy Agency, namely the share of conventional net thermal generation (electricity generated from oil, coal and gas) of country c in year t divided by net generation in that year from hydro and renewable resources (net generation excludes the energy consumed by the generating units).

Demand side factor

We finally consider proxies for growth opportunities. P. Sanyal uses gross state product to see if richer states conduct more environmental research, asserting that '... environmental preferences and ability to take collective actions is greater in richer areas than poorer ones and this translates into differential environmental strategies adopted by [electric utilities]...' (Sanyal 2007, p. 349). Our variable is gross domestic product (GDP hereafter), at market price per capita. We thus expect that that variable will have a positive effect on R&D.

Currencies from countries outside the European Monetary Union were converted to euro. R&D, size, GDP and other monetary variables are measured in real terms by using the GDP deflator. The data on national patent applications to the European Patent Office by priority year are from the Eurostat website. Patent applications at the firm-level were collected from the European Patent Office's Espace Access data base. Finally, information on M&A operations are from Lévêque and Monturus (2008). We checked and completed them by using other online resources.

THE ECONOMETRIC MODEL AND RESULTS

The Model Specification

Unlike Cohen and Klepper (1996) we estimate the multiplicative form of marginal returns to R&D schedule, which will involev taking the logarithm of the variables:

$$R_{ict} = (gO_{ct}N_{it,s}Q_{ict-1})^{\beta} e^{V_{it}} \tag{6.3}$$

We take the Napier logarithm of Eq. (6.3), which gives:

$$\ln R_{ict} = \beta_1 + \beta \ln(O_{ct}) + \beta \ln(N_{it,s}) + \beta \ln Q_{ict-1} + V_{it} \qquad (6.4)$$

where $\beta_1 \equiv \beta \ln g$. Throughout productivity $N_{it,s}$ is approximated by corporate past growth rate:

$$(Q_{ict} / Q_{ics})^{1/(t-s)}, \; s < t. \qquad (6.5)$$

where unlike t, s is fixed. Since accounting data are available later than 1980 for some firms, we start with a value for s such that $s = \min\{1990, t : Q_{ict} > 0\}$. Note that unlike Cohen and Klepper (1996), we consider neither technological opportunities nor R&D productivity as fixed parameters.[18] Therefore there is no reason why the coefficients multiplying these variable should take the same value in the population. Besides, they must be sensitive to the proxy we choose for measuring technological opportunities (O_{ct}) and the proxy for productivity ($N_{it,s}$).We thus relax the constrain on the βs in (6.4) and offer a more general specification including firm-effects and our control variables stacked in the vector x_{ict}:

$$\ln R_{ict} = \beta_1 + \beta_2 \ln Q_{ict} + \beta_3 \ln(O_{ct}) + \beta_4 \ln(N_{it,s}) + x_{ict}' \beta_5 + \sum_{j=1}^{N} M_j d_{ij} + W_{it} \quad (6.6)$$

where $d_{ij} = 1$ if $j = i$ and 0 otherwise, $r_{i,t-s}$ is the average exponential growth rate of sales for firm i and period $[s,t]$ (when this rate is small, $\ln(N_{it,s}) \cong r_{i,t-s}$), and V_{it} contains the firm-specific effects plus an error W_{it}.

The Results

As in most empirical studies of the R&D–firm size relationship, we employ data at the corporate level. Unlike Cohen and Klepper (1996 p. 937), it is thus impossible to test for the effect of corporate size on business unit R&D and therefore the 'strong' form of the CSA hypothesis can not be tested (see Cohen and Klepper 1996, p. 936). However, when aggregated across firms the existence of a proportional R&D − firm size relationship at the level of business units must produce a close relationship between corporate R&D and corporate sales. The analysis of the CSA hypothesis at the business unit for electric utilities is left for future research.[19] Our main hypothesis (the 'weak' form of the CSA) is $H_0^1 : \beta_2 \leq 1$, against $H_1^1 : \beta_2 > 1$. If the null is rejected, or the estimate of β_2 is greater than one, this will lead to acceptance of the Schumpeterian hypothesis and rejection of the threshold side hypothesis.

As in Sanyal (2007) our objective is to estimate a random effect model which would be an appropriate way of proceeding here as our sample in hand may not be sufficiently representative of the underlying population. Our sample is indeed drawn from of a larger population that includes more than two hundred firms including multi-utilities which have significant activities in electricity, and we did not consider separately the affiliates from our firms. There are three other crucial issues we have to address before we start to provide estimates for the coefficient of the variables supposed to determine R&D. One is related to the *poolability* of the data, the second is the *endogeneity* of size over our sample period, and the third is *sample selection.*

Poolability

We use the Roy–Zellner version of the test for poolability. As the number of variables of our model approaches that of firms we restricted the model by excluding the control variables (x_{ict}) to avoid collinearity between subsets of the regressors. The model is estimated with random-firm effects by using the Swamy–Arora estimator (see Baltagi 2005, p. 70). It includes our three explanatory variables plus their interaction with firm dummies. We dropped some interaction variables as the model estimation was not very satisfying, possibly due to collinearity. The test statistic is equal to 194.25. It is distributed as a $\chi^2(32) = 46.19$ which leads us to reject poolability.

The first column in Table 6.2 reports results for the basic model. From this model, the Student statistics associated with $H_0^1 : \beta_2 \leq 1$ is 0.639, that is lower than the 5 or 10% critical value thus we reject the hypothesis from this model. As we shall show, this model specification is too simple and omits several of the key variables introduced in the previous section.

Table 6.2   The basic model

	Model 1		Model 2	
Size	1.064	***	1.159	***
	(0.100)		(0.095)	
Productivity	−4.471	***	−2.412	***
	(1.536)		(0.537)	
Tech. Opportunity	0.073	*	0.126	***
	(0.042)		(0.044)	
Constant	−7.523	***	−9.931	***
	(1.885)		(1.684)	
No. observations	104		59	
R^2 overall	0.69		0.73	

Notes:

The models have random-firm effects. The coefficients are estimated by GLS. Standard errors are robust. '***', '**', '*' denote significance at the 1%, 5% and 10% level, respectively. Model 1 assumes $s = 1990$ in the formula for $N_{i,t-s}$ whilst $s = 1998$ in Model 2.

Table 6.3　Full model

	Model 3		Model 4		Model 5	
Size	1.538	***	2.083	***	2.249	***
	(0.508)		(0.324)		(0.210)	
Productivity	2.324	*	0.876		0.132	
	(1.372)		(1.107)		(0.764)	
Tech. Opportunity	0.093					
	(0.149)					
Distribution Network	dropped					
M&A	0.825					
	(0.068)					
Debt	−0.525	***	−0.715	***	−0.765	***
	(0.174)		(0.130)		(0.117)	
Cash	0.119					
	(0.132)					
Profitability (ROE)	−0.114					
	(0.299)					
Dividend	-6.35×10^{-7}	***	-4.18×10^{-7} ***		-4.10×10^{-7}***	
	(1.75×10^{-7})		(1.16×10^{-7})		(1.08×10^{-7})	
Electricity Act	−0.569	**	−0.211		−0.337	**
	(0.279)		(0.191)		(0.169)	
Retail liberalization	dropped					
Fuel Mix	0.120	***	0.078	***	0.058	***
	(0.032)		(0.021)		(0.017)	
GDP	1.586					
	(1.098)					
Constant	−26.178	***	−15.720		−17.478	***
	(11.169)		(4.690)		(2.827)	
Inverse Mills Ratio			1.809	***	1.895	***
			(0.317)		(0.283)	
No. observations	108		126		292	
R^2 overall	0.28		0.55			

Notes:

'***', '**', '*' denote significance at the 1%, 5% and 10% level, respectively. 'Model 3' has fixed-firm effects. The coefficients are estimated by OLS. A test for the equality of the fixed effects produces an f-statistic of 5.11 that is greater than the tabulated value ($\cong 1.8$). 'Model 4' has fixed-firm effects corrected from sample selection. The hypothesis for the equality of the fixed effects is also rejected in this model. 'Model 5' is a Tobit with left-censoring at zero. To scale the results, the model includes a dummy that is equal to one for each observation associated with a zero R&D value.

Endogeneity

As we already emphasized firm size is more likely to respond to domestic electricity demand, due to obligation of services. Therefore, size is likely to be exogenous. As emphasized by Cohen and Klepper (1996, footnote 26, p.939) however, 'R&D is expected to affect growth with a considerable lag due to the time it takes to generate, develop and commercialise innovations'. But, our sample period covers 28 years, which is exactly the situation in which we should care about a possible effect of R&D on Size, an issue not addressed in Sanyal and Cohen (2008) and Sanyal (2007). Cohen and Klepper (1996) suggested an indirect test of this endogeneity bias, which consists in checking if different values for s in $N_{it,s}$ affect significantly the result of the overall model estimation. We thus test for the possibility that R&D determines firm's size by varying s in $N_{it,s}$. We compare the previous result with $s = \min\{1998, t : Q_{ict} > 0\}$. The model is reported in the second column of Table 6.2. The coefficients seem to change significantly for both size and productivity, showing evidence of endogeneity. Note that the number of observations is reduced dramatically due to the restriction imposed on the productivity variable. Besides, the sub-period from which we estimate the model corresponds to the deregulation of the electricity industry in several countries, with an average of 5 years per firm. The coefficient estimates are thus less subject to the trend reversion in R&D. From this model, the Student statistics associated with $H_0^1 : \beta_2 \leq 1$ is 1.670 that is surprisingly equal to the 5% critical value and greater than the 10% critical value of 1.9. We thus reject the hypothesis of an advantage of small firms in R&D in favour of the Schumpeterian hypothesis. We also ran the classical Hausman procedure to test for exogeneity of the size variable in the panel from the results of a model with firm-fixed effects.

Since endogeneity was detected with the previous procedure, we decide to include all the variables presented in the previous section as this omission may be the source of the endogeneity problem. To have a larger sample size as possible, for each firm we use $s = \min\{1980, t : Q_{ict} > 0\}$. The test statistic is equal to 52.40 that is distributed as a $\chi^2(10) = 18.31$ which leads to rejection of the null hypothesis and also to adoption of the model with firm-fixed effects. The results for the estimated coefficients of this model are reported in the first column of Table 6.3. The coefficient on 'Productivity' is more consistent with the predictions of the CSA model and results found elsewhere in the literature: '... the larger the past growth rate of the firm ... then the greater the future output of the firm over which it can apply its R&D, thereby providing it with a greater incentive to conduct R&D' (Cohen and Klepper 1996, footnote 35, p. 942). Although the estimated coefficient on the size variable takes a larger value than in the previous model, its precision has reduced. The problem here is that of sample size bias.

Before interpreting the results we must try to overcome the loss of degrees of freedom due to the large number of reported zero R&D values. A quick-and-easy way would be to estimate a Tobit model with left censoring. In fact, in our case, with nearly 68% missing empty R&D observations, the Tobit is definitely justified. Following Sanyal (2007) we try first to find evidence of sample selection.

Sample selection

Sanyal (2007) uses a random effect Tobit specification with the lower bound at zero since she did not find evidence of selection. Sanyal and Cohen (2008) find evidence of selection, however.[20] The rationale for sample selection is justified as follows. Our R&D (dependent) variable contains a considerable amount of zeros, however. For example Union Fenosa does not report R&D at all. It is difficult to know whether no reporting of R&D is a randomly missing process or an endogenous decision (see Bound et al. 1984, pp. 22–25): 'An important issue is whether the fact that [some] firms do not report R&D expenditure will bias results based only on firms which do.' Sanyal and Cohen (2008) and Sanyal (2007) formulated the problem of sample selection as one where electric utilities' investment in R&D is a two-step process. First, electric utility i decides whether it invests in R&D or not in year t, a decision which depends on the firm's expected future benefits from R&D. If this latter expectation is above some threshold then it decides the amount it wants to spend (the structure of the formal econometric model can be found in Sanyal and Cohen 2008).

This approach is consistent with the condition that the profit maximizing level must be non-negative (see Eq. (6.2)), which en passant suggests that the firm's profit can be considered as a selection variable. It turns out that this description relies on accounting practices in the U.S.A. where firms must claim R&D expense as they are incurred (capitalization is not allowed in the U.S.A. with a few exceptions; see Oswald and Zarowin 2007) whereas in Europe, companies have more discretion regarding the possibility to capitalize their R&D expenses. We must therefore admit that as some if not all of our firms have the choice to claim or capitalize their R&D efforts, the factors behind missing R&D expenditures are less obvious to understand.

We estimated a pooled regression model on the whole data. Our choice of variable is crucial but limited by the small number of firms in our sample and the overrepresented amount of zeros for R&D for most of them. We selected the following variables: firm size, intangible assets (intangible assets include capitalized R&D) divided by size, profitability, indebtedness divided by size, deregulation (see the 'DATA' section for their definition). As in Sanyal and Cohen (2008) we find that the size of electric utilities matters in the decision to report R&D, or bigger firms are more likely to engage in R&D than smaller firms. Apart from profitability and capitalization, all variables are significant at the 5% level. The estimate of the coefficient multiplying debts has a negative sign which suggests that electric utilities may decide or not to report R&D to have some control over their indebtedness.

The next step consists in re-estimating the equation for R&D in level and correcting for sample selection. We estimate that model after removing the variables that were non significant in 'Model 3'. The results are reported in the second column of Table 6.3 ('Model 4').

Further results
We interpret the results from 'Model 5' which by considering the entire set of observations seem to produce more precise results. The coefficient on the firm size variable is largely in favour of the Schumpeterian hypothesis. The Student statistics associated with $H_0^1 : \beta_2 \leq 1$ is equal to 5.937 which is largely above the critical value. We thus reject the hypothesis of proportionality and of an advantage of small firms in R&D in favour of the Schumpeterian hypothesis. We also estimated the Tobit model with sales net of R&D rather than assets as the size variable to avoid the criticism pointed out in Hall et al. (2007) that there is a simple accounting correlation between size and R&D. This correlation should imply a one–for–one relationship between R&D and size. With sales net of R&D we still find a significantly positive coefficient that is not statistically different to 1 at the 5% level (0.917). But since its value is lower than unity we must reject a higher than proportional relationship between R&D and net sales whereas we accept assets as the size variable. The bottom line is that proportionality characterizes electric utilities, which lends credence to Cohen and Klepper's CSA hypothesis for electric utilities.

The financial variables (debt and dividends) are negatively related to R&D. This result for the former variable supports the behaviour of electric utilities during the past ten years by which they spent considerable funds to make domestic and cross-border M&A operations. An increase of 100,000 euros in dividends is associated with a 4.1 percentage points decrease in R&D. Thought the M&A variable itself was not significant throughout the regressions, indebtedness was. The result for dividends is more politically sensible as it would suggest that research is an alternative use of funds to paying dividends, or the higher the money paid to investors, notably private investors, the lower is the amount spent in R&D. The non-significance of the cash variable in all our regressions would suggest that electric utilities are not financially constrained. As we mentioned earlier, cash–flow sensitivity of R&D investment need not identify liquidity constraints but rather is indicative of high demand and expectations of future profits. We controlled for that by considering a measure of domestic wealth at the country level, namely GDP. Perhaps that a more precise measure of the demand addressed to the electric utilities would lead to a different result, which is left for a future version of the present paper.

The coefficient on the effect of deregulation is still negative and significant. As the variable is a dummy and R&D is measured in logarithm, we deduce the percentage impact of the deregulation variable on R&D from the formula given for example in Sanyal and Cohen (2008, footnote 44). We find a negative impact of 135% which is considerable but fully consistent with the figures of decrease in R&D and hence R&D intensity for some firms.

The variable of fuel mix that is the ratio of thermal to renewable electricity generation also has the expected sign: firms in countries with a relatively higher share of clean energy need to spend less in R&D. To put it differently, our result suggests that firms that produce electricity from energy resources that are detrimental to the environment are also those that spend more in R&D, everything else being equal.

CONCLUSION

The present paper aims to provide a better understanding of the effect of reforms on R&D by electric utilities. Following previous works done for U.S. electric utilities, we expect that it will contribute to the formulation of more effective energy R&D policies, a claim made by Jamasb and Pollitt (2008) very recently. Our results have some implication regarding the consequence of merger policies on innovation. The most obvious is that by preventing consolidation of the larger firms, competition commissions may impede increases in total industry R&D efforts.

While special attention was given to firm size, the present paper provided insights into a larger number of factors behind innovation input. Overall, these results also suggest that the management of activities associated with discovering new knowledge and applying it to new products is likely to be different in the electricity sector to other industries. The main reason is that electric utilities are subject to specific regulations and obligations. As we have shown, these peculiarities are such that electric utilities were and still seem not subject to financial constraint. But, it turns out that the entry of new investors, following the privatization of electric utilities, are creating some competition for funds, notably at the expense of R&D.

Further analyses are left for future researches. First of all, it would be interesting to increase the number of firms so as to be able to estimate less misspecified models and consider more variables, notably, to have a clearer control on the influence of the decision by firms not to report R&D. Regarding other measures of innovation, a complementary research would be to see whether large electric utilities generate more or less innovations per euro of R&D. As this research contributes to the more general question of what is the profile of electric utilities that are more likely to spend in research and development, and since these firms are necessarily those more likely to 'survive' in an environment under competitive pressures, a deep analysis of the determinants of M&A operations would be very valuable too.

As suggested in Hall (2002), there can also be an important role for policy based on the existence of significant spillovers and externalities, rather than on the financing-gap argument, in particular for large established firms. The electricity industry is a case in point. This is perhaps more important an argument than those based on the existence of financial constraints which are a much more crucial consideration for small and startup firms in R&D-intensive industries.

NOTES

1. This research is funded by the French Energy Council under contract CFE – 52. I am grateful to Emmanuelle Fortune, Jean-Luc Gaffard and all participants to the OFCE-I2C seminar given on 02/25/2008 where a preliminary work on this paper was presented. I also thank Samira Demaria and Jean-Christophe Vidal who drew my attention to accounting choices regarding R&D capitalization. This chapter also benefited from comments and technical advises by Lionel Nesta, Paoma Sanyal and text revision by Adam Cutforth. Research assistance from Jean-Marie l'Allemain and more particularly Benoît Bourné is greatly acknowledged too. The usual disclaimer remains.
2. This issue is becoming of practical interest to competition commissioners who should base their decision to cancel or not a merger on the basis of the consequences a more concentrated liberalized market would have on the propensity of the candidates to the merger to innovate.
3. To fully understand this argument, it is worth noticing wholesale market deregulation is always followed by a progressive opening up of retail markets to competition.
4. Margolis and Kammen (1999) noticed the little work done on return on investment s in R&D in the energy sector. A possible reason of the lack of such analyses could be that the capital structure of electric utilities still remains, to a significant extent, in the hands of regulators and administration, although this dependence varies across countries and over time, depending on the degree of market liberalization, firms' privatization and divesture. This introduces some heterogeneity which can't simply be controlled for by including firm or industry effects. As a consequence, the behaviour of electric utilities and utilities in general, is analysed in papers specific to this category of firms.
5. A private discussion with an employee involved in R&D activities at Electricité de France (the firm has been floated since November 2005) revealed that R&D expenditures aimed to increase energy saving by consumers is more strategic than ever before.
6. Obviously, some innovation is more specific to a type of power plant. As an example, operating costs in nuclear energy are directly related to incidents, the occurrence of which can be reduced from organizational (process) innovations which can give to the firm a competitive advantage (see Roux-Dufort and Metais 1999 who address this issue in the case of the nuclear power producer, Electricité de France; the firm changed its way of managing nuclear risks by introducing in 1982 an organizational innovation known as the 'Human Factor' policy).

7. Baumol (2002, p. 154) defines product innovation as one innovation that shifts the demand curve for the affected final product to the right, while a process innovation shifts the pertinent cost curves downward. If successful, process innovation can expand output and reduce product price. If, by converse, marginal cost rises, this is accepted in returns for a large cut in fixed costs. The distinction between product and process innovation is not clear in the field of environmental researches, however '... because significant improvements of environmental conditions may be attained by both types of innovations.' (Horbach 2008, p.169).

8. This is a consequence of the second condition of the CSA, that at any given moment, electric utilities are not expected to grow rapidly due to innovation. Furthermore, R&D expenditures are usually budgeted several months before they are spent (Cohen and Klepper 1996, pp. 926, 937)

9. Unlike Wilder and Sansell (1974) we do not have the ratio of electric to total operating revenue for all years of our sample of observation.

10. See Jamasb and Pollitt (2008, 2009), Johnstone et al. (2008), Sanyal and Cohen (2008) and Sanyal (2007) for more details on innovation by electric utilities.

11. A more documented definition can be found in Datastream. Note that it excludes government sponsored research, contributions by government, customers, partnerships or other corporations to the company's research and development expense.

12. In 2008 it spent about one fourth of its R&D budget to environmental projects (EdF 2008, p. 185).

13. Defeuilley and Furtado (2000) report a change from £201 million in 1998 to £40–50 million in the 1990s of researches aimed at nuclear energy.

14. There are studies with less gross measures of R&D. As an example Sanyal (2007) uses environmental R&D whereas Sanyal and Cohen (2008) use total R&D expenditures that include all internal and external R&D expenditures by the utility. Within internal there are expenditure of generation, transmission, distribution and environmental projects. The external R&D is contributions to the research institutes. I thank Paoma Sanyal for pointing out this distinction to me.

15. A pooled regression of total assets on sales and a constant leads to a n R^2 equal to 0.98; the coefficient which multiplies the constant is not significantly different from zero at the 1% level of significance whereas the coefficient multiplying sales equals 1.71 with a standard error of 0.041.

16. Relatively high-cost generating facilities, and more generally costs that are not expected to be recovered in a competitive wholesale power market (Blacconière et al. 2000).

17. Upstream firms traditionally used to undertake research projects in collaboration with electric utilities as evidenced e.g. through the EdF/Areva and E.ON/Alstom/Siemens established partnerships. In the case of electricity industrial policies prompt cooperative research which allows electric utilities and equipment builders to share the cost of some R&D project, e.g. the joint EdF-Areva project for construction of a pressurized water reactor, the EPR.

18. In their paper, O_{ct} is constant and as such it enters the intercept. Regarding productivity it is calculated once for all in their paper as they transformed their panel data to a cross-section by averaging over their annual observations. This specification allows marginal returns to R&D to vary across firms according to the value of β provided we assume that that parameter varies across firms (Cohen and Klepper 1996 allow that parameter to vary across industries). We keep that parameter constant and consider O and N as alternative factors likely to influence the R&D-size relationship.

19. This would be possible by analysing corporate websites which are available at most for the last two to five years for most firms.

20. In a private discussion the author gave as justification that since in her 2007 s paper R&D is just environmental, the selection equation there was whether the firm first decides whether to conduct environmental R&D or not, thus suggesting that the larger selection decision would be at the aggregated R&D level as supported in Sanyal and Cohen (2008).

REFERENCES

Al-Sunaidy, A. and R. Green (2006), 'Electricity deregulation in OECD (Organisation for Economic Co-operation and Development) countries', *Energy*, **31** (6-7), 769–787.

AMECO,
http://ec.europa.eu/economy_finance/db_indicators/db_indicators8646_en.htm.

Bah, R. and P. Dumontier (2001), R&D intensity and corporate financial policy: some international evidence, *Journal of Business Finance & Accounting*, **28** (5–6), 671–692.

Baltagi, B. (2005), *Econometric Analysis of Panel Data*, John Wiley & Sons, 3rd edition.

Baumol, W.J. (2002), *The Free-Market Innovation Machine – Analyzing the Growth Miracle of Capitalism*, Princeton, NJ: Princeton University Press.

Bertrand, O. and P. Zuniga (2006), 'R&D and M&A: are cross-border M&A different? An investigation on OECD countries', *International of Industrial Organization*, **24** (2), 401–423.

Blacconière, W.G., M.F. Johnson and M.S. Johnson (2000), 'Market valuation and deregulation of electric utilities', *Journal of Accounting and Economics*, **29** (2), 231–260.

Bound, J., C. Cummins, Z. Griliches, B.H. Hall and A. Jaffe (1984), 'Who does R&D and who patents? in NBER (ed.), *R&D, Patents and Productivity*, The University of Chicago Press, pp. 21–54.

Bourgade, M. (2008), 'Comparaison des structures de passif des principaux groupes énergétiques européens', October, Master Dissertation, Sciences Po.

Brouwer, E. and A. Kleinknecht (1996), 'Firm size, small business presence and sales of innovative products: a micro-econometric analysis', *Small Business Economics*, **8** (3), 189–201.

Casson, P.D., R. Martin and T.M. Nisar (2008), 'The financing decisions of innovative firms', *Research in International Business and Finance*, **22** (2), 208–221.

Cohen, W. and S. Klepper (1996), 'A reprise of size and R&D', *Economic Journal*, **106** (437), 925–951.

Commission of the European Communities (2007), 'Mid-term review of industrial policy: a contribution to the EU's growth and jobs strategy', COM(2007)374, 4th July 2007,
http://eur-lex.europa.eu/LexUriServ/site/en/com/2007/com2007_0374en01.pdf.

Defeuilley, C. and A.T. Furtado (2000), 'Impacts de l'ouverture à la concurrence sur la R&D dans le secteur électrique', *Annals of Public and Cooperative Economics*, **71** (1), 5–28.

Del Monte, A. and F. Papagni (2003), 'R&D and the growth of firms: empirical analysis of a panel of Italian firms', *Research Policy*, **32** (6), 1003–1014.

Dhrymes, P.J. and M. Kurz (1964), 'On the dividend policy of electric utilities', *The Review of Economics and Statistics*, **46** (1), 76–81.

EdF (2008), 'Edf Group: 2008's reference document', http://www.edf.com.

Europa (2007), 'Commission launches public consultation on sustainable consumption and production and sustainable industrial policy', Press Releases IP/07/1215,
http://europa.eu/rapid/pressReleasesAction.do?reference=IP/07/1215&format=HTML&aged=0&language=EN&guiLanguage=en, accessed October 27, 2008.

Eurostaf (2005) 'Les strategies de développement des compagnies européennes d'électricité', Vol. 1, Analyses et Conclusions, Collection Perspectives stratégiques et financiers.

General Accounting Office (1996), 'Changes in electricity-related R&D funding', GAO/RCED-96-203 Federal Research.

Guerard, J.B. (2005), *Corporate Financial Policy and R&D Management*, 2nd ed., NJ: John Wiley & Sons.

Guerard, J.B. A.S. Bean and S. Andrews (1987), 'R&D management and corporate financial policy', *Management Science*, **33** (11), 1419–1427.

Gulli, F. (1995), 'Product and process innovation in the energy industry: the development of integrated tar gasification combined cycle plants (ITGCC), *Energy Policy*, **23** (8), 647–658.

Hall, B., D. Foray and J. Mairesse (2007), 'Pitfalls in estimating the returns to corporate R&D using accounting data', paper presented at the First Conference on Knowledge for Growth, October 8–9, 16 pp.

Hall, B.H. (2002), 'The financing of research and development', *Oxford Review of Economic Policy*, **18** (1), pp. 35—51.

Hollinger, P. (2009), 'Acquisitions have led to balance sheet pressure', *The Financial Times*, 11/05/2009.

Horbach, J. (2008), 'Determinants of environmental innovation – New evidence from German panel data sources', *Research Policy*, **37** (1), 163–173.

Jaffe, A.B. (1986), 'Technological opportunity and spillovers of R&D: evidence from firms' patents, profits, and market value', *American Economic Review*, **76** (5), 984–1001.

Jamasb, T. and M. Pollitt (2009), 'Electricity sector liberalisation and innovation: an analysis of the UK patenting activities', *Cambridge Working Paper in Economics*, 0902 and *EPRG Working Paper* 0901.

Jamasb, T. and M. Pollitt (2008), 'Liberalisation and R&D in network industries: the case of the electricity industry', *Research Policy*, **37** (6–7), 995–1008.

Johnstone, N., I. Hascic and D. Popp (2008), 'Renewable energy policies and technological innovation: evidence on patent counts', *NBER Working Paper Series*, No. 13760.

Jolink, A. and E. Niesten (2008), 'Governance transformations through regulations in the electricity sector: the Dutch case', *International Review of Applied Economics*, **22** (4), 499–508.

Lévêque, F. and R. Monturus (2008), 'Mergers and acquisitions within the European power and gas sectors – Cases and patterns', CERNA.

Mahlich, J.C. and T. Roediger-Schluga (2006), 'The determinants of pharmaceutical R&D expenditures: evidence from Japan', *Review of Industrial Organization*, **28** (2), 145–164.

Margolis, R.M. and D.M. Kammen (1999), 'Underinvestment: the energy technology and R&D policy challenge', *Science*, **285**, 690–692.

Markard, J., B. Truffer and D.M. Imboden (2004), 'The impacts of market liberalization on innovation processes in the electricity sector', *Energy and Environment*, **15** (2), 201–214.

Mohnen, P., F.C. Palm, S. Schim van der Loeff and A. Tiwari (2008), 'Financial constraints and other obstacles: are they a threat to innovation activity?' *United Nations University Working Paper Series*, 2008-06.

Musso, P. and S. Schiavo (2007), 'The impact of financial constraints on firms survival and growth', *OFCE Working Paper Series*, 2007-37.

Nelson, R.R. and E.N. Wolff (1997), 'Factors behind cross-industry differences in technical progress', *Structural Change and Economic Dynamics*, **8** (2), 205–220.

Oswald, D. and P. Zarowin (2007), 'Capitalisation of R&D and the informativeness of stock prices', *European Accounting Review*, **16** (4), 703–26.

PricewaterhouseCoopers (2008, January), 'Power deals – Annual Review', http://www.pwc.fr/power_deals_2007.html, accessed February 8, 2008.

Roux-Dufort, C. and E. Metais (1999), 'Building core competencies in crisis management through organizatioal learning – The case of the French nuclear power producer', *Technological Forecasting and Social Change*, **60** (2), 113—127.

Salies, E. (2008), 'Mergers in the GB electricity market: effects on retail charges', *Applied Economics*, **14** (11), 1483–1490.

Sanyal, P. (2007), 'The effect of deregulation on environmental research by electric utilities', *Journal of Regulatory Economics*, **31** (3), 335–353.

Sanyal, P. and L.R. Cohen (2008), 'R&D choice in restructured industries: in-house v/s collaborative research in the US electricity industry, http://people.brandeis.edu/~psanyal/Elec_Restruc_RD_Int_Ext.pdf.

Skeer, J. (1996), 'How is electric power technology development affected by growing power sector competition?', A summary of discussion at the 10th Meeting of the CERT Group of Experts on Electricity Power Technologies, International Energy Agency Headquarters, Paris 26th–27th October 1995.

Symeonidis, G. (1996), 'Innovation, firm size and market structure: Schumpetarian hypotheses and some new themes', Economics Department Working Papers, No. 161, OCDE/GD(96)58.

Wilder, R.P. and S.R. Stansell (1974), 'Determinants of research and development activity by electric utilities', *The Bell Journal of Economics and Management Science*, **5** (1), 646–650.

World Energy Council (2007), *The role of nuclear power in Europe*, www.worldenergy.org/documents/wec_nuclear_full_report.pdf, January, London.

PART III

Firms' Performance and Industrial Dynamics

7.   Jack of all Trades or Master of One? The Specialization–Flexibility Trade-off

Rodolphe Dos Santos Ferreira and Ehud Zuscovitch

INTRODUCTION[1]

The decision to specialize, i.e. to focus on specific skills or characteristics in the production of goods and services, is motivated by the greater economic efficiency that stems from the improved technical performance of the selected attribute. At the same time specialization narrows the general (or wider) ability of the skilled worker, the production team or the firm, to adapt to changes in the environment like when different product configurations are needed. In '*The Limits of Organization*', Arrow (1974) stressed this simple fact that often eluded theorists of technology and growth even in their more recent models. Specialization entails a loss of flexibility.

Many areas in economics are affected by problems related to this specialization-flexibility trade-off. The issue can be traced back to putty-clay analysis of investment in fixed capital, and to a more recent concern with 'lock-in' effects in technological competition (Arthur 1988). In the industrial organization literature, the specialization–flexibility trade-off (hereafter SFT) appears in various forms. It sheds light on the respective roles of scale economies and of economies of scope (Chandler 1990) whose impact on market structures underlies much empirical and theoretical work in industrial economics. Scale economies depend on significant cost reductions through the mass production of standardised products, each representing a single point in the characteristics space. The benefits of scope are important in the context of diversity and multi-product manufacturing. These are clearly SFT issues. Models of monopolistic competition in relation to optimal product differentiation (Lancaster 1975; Dixit and Stiglitz 1977) are yet another branch of the literature where SFT is a critical consideration within the context of variety vs. efficiency.

When one looks carefully, SFT issues are everywhere in business and everyday life. Business journals are full of accounts on corporate decisions of successful diversification, just as they are abundant with stories about the benefits of refocusing on the firm's 'core competencies'. In the chemical industry the most radical transformation since World War II was the shift from commodities to specialties after the second oil shock, whereas in mechanical automation one usually compares in cost/benefit terms the performance of dedicated capital goods with the flexible equipment alternative. In fact, this distinction between the specialized and the flexible is so rooted in our life that often they practically become institutionalised. As consumers of services we certainly take SFT into consideration when we decide whether to consult a generalist or a specialized physician, or when we sequentially take education decisions involving both duration decisions and choice of institutions and programmes.

Real world simple observations lead us to formulate two 'stylized facts' that we feel an analytical model of SFT should be able to generate. The first is that various economic sectors exhibit different market configurations: some areas are typically symmetric and firms are either all narrowly focused or all broader in their scope. In other industries and service sectors asymmetric behaviour is the rule and highly specialized firms coexist with more general-purpose ones. The second stylized fact is that firms, whether small businesses or corporate giants, quite frequently shift from one type of behaviour towards the other: at times they expand their scope of product lines, looking for higher flexibility, while at other times they suddenly decide to re-centre and deepen traditional capabilities.

We have decided to treat SFT as a matter of technological choice because it deals with the very way in which economic agents decide to solve problems and this 'how' dimension is fundamentally a choice of technology. Another reason for the technology choice setting is that competition among concrete technologies often underlies investment and diversification decisions. More often than not, several technologies compete for alternative uses and there again, during different stages in their development, a different SFT is available. Greater diversity and flexibility are found in the beginning of the development process, whereas later, standardization of the way by which technical problems are tackled brings about cost reduction for some key features but limits flexibility to change.[2]

Finally there is a very important reason for dealing with SFT issues in a technological choice setting. This has to do with the massive diffusion of information technologies. While the incorporation of microprocessors is revolutionizing all aspects of our lives in terms of both work and leisure, the importance of this phenomenon has not been fully realised by economists. With the exception of early works on multi-product firms, e.g. within the industrial organization approach of contestable markets (Baumol et al. 1982) or in the technological innovation strategic approach of Teece (1982), the mainstream of industrial organization rarely considered the impact of increased flexibility on product differentiation. More recently, few noticeable exceptions have appeared under the heading of economies of flexible manufacturing: emphasizing complementarities and non-convexities like Milgrom and Roberts (1990) or, closer to our point, stressing the role of flexibility in promoting concentration through increased product diversity, like Eaton and Schmitt (1994). Yet, the phenomenon is both larger and deeper. Larger, because the issue is by far wider than the one of flexible manufacturing and concerns the evolution of the economy towards information-intensive production systems (Willinger and Zuscovitch 1988); deeper, because the issue is not only diversity as such, but the diversity potential in relation to efficiency, as depicted by the SFT frontier.

The just mentioned Eaton and Schmitt (1994) paper approaches competition among firms endowed with flexible technologies with essentially the same spatial model as the one we use. But their focus is on entry and ultimately on the consequences of (exogenous) flexibility on market structure. The conditions of a specialization–flexibility trade-off and indeed the implications of its existence itself are however an essential part of the story, which is missing in their paper.

This trade-off is by contrast taken into account by von Ungern-Sternberg (1988), using a similar model of spatial competition[3] between firms which supply more or less general-purpose products. His paper wants to reconsider the question of the optimal degree of product differentiation; accordingly, entry is again emphasized and asymmetric outcomes are ignored. The observed coexistence of special and general-purpose products is conjectured to depend upon heterogeneity of consumers' tastes, very much in contrast with our own conclusions, suggesting that it can be ascribed to moderately decreasing returns to specialization.

Another contribution by von Ungern-Sternberg (1988) comes closer to these conclusions, pointing to the asymmetry of equilibrium outcomes. But the analysis is there performed in a framework involving perfect competition, whereas our results, at least the possible multiplicity of equilibria, one symmetric and the others not, rely on oligopolistic competition. Also, heterogeneity of firms at equilibrium is attributed by von Ungern-Sternberg to a fundamental non-convexity in the SFT, whereas we only need a not too high degree of convexity in order to get the same result.

We can now briefly present our own analytical framework. As the first two above-mentioned papers, we use a variant of the conventional Hotelling model of spatial competition. The transportation cost can be understood in this context as the cost the firm has to incur in order to adapt its product, by moving from the point of the characteristics space on which it has chosen to focus to the point now requested by the consumers. Contrary to these two papers, we wish however to concentrate on the basic specialization–flexibility trade-off under strategic interaction. We shall therefore abstract from entry considerations and remain in the pure duopoly case. Each of the competing firms may adopt technologies which are flexible in Stigler's sense, with relatively high average unit costs but with a strong ability to change product characteristics; it may on the contrary prefer specialized technologies, more efficient in terms of unit costs, but more rigid in terms of product design. In spite of what this opposition might suggest, our analysis will not be restricted to a binary choice between two technological configurations; we shall instead refer to a continuum of technological options.

The strategic implications of the technological choice will be examined by looking at the subgame perfect equilibria of a three-stage game in which firms first choose technologies, then determine locations in the characteristics space, and finally compete in prices à la Bertrand. It is quite well-known that equilibrium outcomes of multi-stage games may be very sensitive to the particular sequential ordering of strategic choices. It is however natural to give priority to specialization choices (encompassing both degree and focus) over pricing decisions, since a greater degree of irreversibility or commitment is involved in the former. Unlike the adjustment to fashion and tastes, the attitude with respect to the SFT and, although somewhat less so, the selection of a basic product type cannot be modified everyday for obvious cost reasons, so that technological decisions are primary determinants of the domain of opportunities. Hence, the same rationale leading to a sequential ordering of first location and then pricing in the two-stage spatial competition models is applied here to the three-stage setting of technology, location and price competition. The decision not to allow firms to simultaneously decide on cost and location characteristics in a first stage may seem more questionable. But taking this alternative two-stage approach would be roughly equivalent (as shown in the sixth section) to modelling the centralized decision of a social planner or of a cartel. We would then somewhat miss the effectiveness of strategic interaction.[4]

The paper will be organized as follows. After presenting the model in the next section we reduce subgame perfect equilibria of the original three-stage game to equilibria of a symmetric game in strategic form. We then consider the implication of different degrees of convexity of the SFT frontier. Concavity of this frontier (non-decreasing returns to specialization or non-increasing costs of flexibility), the case examined in a fourth section, induces either extremely specialized or extremely flexible technological choices, which may coincide for both firms (in a symmetric equilibrium) or instead diverge in a highly asymmetric one. A relatively high convexity of the SFT frontier (significantly decreasing returns to specialization or increasing costs of flexibility), the case examined in the fifth section, leads by contrast to non-necessarily extreme technological choices at a symmetric equilibrium that may well coexist with other, more or less asymmetric, equilibria. As we have already mentioned by referring to the two stylized facts we wanted to reproduce, we feel that greater attention should be given to both asymmetry and multiplicity, because they convey in a meaningful way the characteristics of many real world situations where various flexible and specialized firms coexist and where shifts in strategic behaviour are frequent. Finally, we consider optimality issues and show that more specialization than the one achieved through competition would in general be required. Then we conclude.

THE MODEL

Two firms compete to sell one good, located in a one-dimensional characteristics space. This competition is described by a three-stage game, in which firms choose first technologies, then locations and finally prices.[5]

The model has (at least) two different although closely related interpretations. Hotelling (1929) assumed that a continuum of heterogeneous customers is uniformly distributed in the characteristics space, each customer buying one unit of the good from the firm whose product has the lowest delivered price, equal to the sum of the mill price set by the firm plus a linear transportation cost paid by the customer. As already suggested by Hotelling, spatial competition need not be understood in a geographical sense. The transportation cost may indeed be seen as the disutility resulting for the customer from the discrepancy between his preferred characteristic and the one displayed by the purchased product. We follow Hotelling but, unlike him, we assume delivered pricing: the transportation cost is borne by the seller, who is thus able to price discriminate among differently located customers. The transportation cost may then be viewed either as the cost incurred by the firm to adapt his product and bring it into conformity with each customer's tastes, or as a discount granted to the buyer in order to compensate him for the difference between the product characteristic and his preferred one. In contrast to the assumption of uniform mill pricing with linear transportation costs, the assumption of delivered pricing has the advantage of ensuring existence of a price equilibrium for any location pair (see Hoover 1937; Eaton and Lipsey 1979; Lederer and Hurter 1986; MacLeod et al. 1988).

Again unlike Hotelling, but in accordance with his predecessor Launhardt (1885), we also allow different transportation rates for the two products. Launhardt himself considered the difference in transportation rates as a difference in quality, thus taking into account vertical as well as horizontal differentiation, as shown by Dos Santos Ferreira and Thisse (1996). Here we may see it as a difference in product versatility, i.e. as a more or less 'general purposeness' of the two products (von Ungern-Sternberg 1988). As should be expected, we assume that the price paid by the firm for getting more versatility is a higher production cost.

There is an alternative interpretation of the model, to which we shall essentially refer from now on (the reader will readily translate into the traditional understanding of the spatial competition model any interpretative statement formulated in the following). We assume homogeneous customers concentrated, at any given moment, in just one point of the characteristics space. Location is now a uniformly distributed random variable, the realization of which is only revealed at the third stage of the game, a stage supposed to be repeated very often. Thus, the two firms must choose their own locations at the second stage so as to maximise the mathematical expectation of their profits, preparing to transform their products (or to adapt their equipments) in order to meet the demand once the customers' location is revealed. When choosing their technologies at the first stage, they face a trade-off between production and transformation costs: they can opt for flexibility (in a sense akin to Stigler 1939), with a low (linear) transformation cost at the expense of a high production cost, or prefer the reverse choice, specialization, leading to cheap production balanced against the threat of a later expensive transformation.

More precisely, at the first stage of the game, each firm $i \in \{1,2\}$ chooses a technology (t_i, c_i), characterized by the 'transformation rate' t_i (such that the cost of transforming one unit of product of characteristic a_i in one unit of good of characteristic α is $t_i |a_i - \alpha|$) and by the 'unit production cost' c_i (the cost of producing one unit of the good, whatever its characteristic). Since choices can be restricted to the efficient (lower) frontier of the technology set, described by the function C, firm i controls the strategic variable t_i at this stage, implicitly selecting $c_i = C(t_i)$ at the same time (see Figure 7.1). The function C is a decreasing function, so that the firm is confronted with a 'technological trade-off', apart from strategic considerations to be analysed in the following. We assume that C is twice-differentiable and defined on the non-empty compact interval $T \subset R_+$. By normalization of costs (and given that we assume a rigid demand), we may take $T = [\theta, 1]$ (with $\theta \in [0,1)$) and $C(1) = 0$.

At the second stage, each firm i chooses the characteristic $a_i \in [0,1]$ of the good to produce, just knowing the probability distribution of the characteristic α that will be demanded. This distribution has a unit mass and is uniform over the characteristics space $[0,1]$. Finally, at the third stage, the characteristic α is revealed, and the two firms compete in prices. The firm i which can offer the lowest (delivered) price p_i meets the whole demand, after producing one unit of good at cost $c_i + t_i |a_i - \alpha|$, including the cost of transforming it (or adapting the corresponding equipment) from characteristic a_i into characteristic α. This stage is in principle repeated many times.

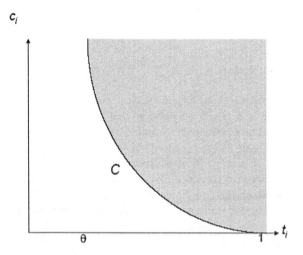

Figure 7.1 The technological trade-off

THE EQUILIBRIA

We are interested in subgame perfect equilibria of this three-stage game, which can be found by backward induction.

Prices

At the third stage, firm i is able to sell one unit of type α at the total (production plus transformation) cost $c_i + t_i |a_i - \alpha|$ if its price p_i is lower than the price set by its competitor. The equilibrium of this pricing game is the so-called *Bertrand equilibrium*: both firms set the same price, equal to the highest total cost. The firm with the cost advantage undercuts the lowest possible price of its rival by an amount that is just sufficient to attract the whole demand (for characteristic α). By neglecting this amount, we obtain the following equilibrium profit of firm i:

$$\pi_i\left(t_1,t_2,a_1,a_2,\alpha\right)=\max\left\{0,C\left(t_j\right)+t_j\left|a_j-\alpha\right|-C\left(t_i\right)-t_i\left|a_i-\alpha\right|\right\} \quad (7.1)$$

for $i\in\{1,2\}$ and $j\in\{1,2\}\setminus\{i\}$. Notice that production and transformation costs are borne only by the winning firm.

Locations

At the second stage, firm i's payoff is the mathematical expectation of its profit:

$$\hat{\pi}_i\left(t_1,t_2,a_1,a_2\right)=\int_0^1\pi_i\left(t_1,t_2,a_1,a_2,\alpha\right)d\alpha \quad (7.2)$$

In order to determine the equilibrium locations, we now assume, without loss of generality, that $t_1\le t_2$ (by convention) and that $a_1\le a_2$ (by symmetry). Two regimes must be considered, according to the existence of, respectively, a cost disadvantage or a cost advantage of firm 1 at its own location. In the former case, the lowest position of the product characteristic that can be supplied at the same cost by both firms is x, to the left of firm 1 (see Figure 7.2). It is y, between the two firms, in the latter case (see Figure 7.3). We denote by z the highest product characteristic equalizing both total costs. We show in the first part of the appendix that the case of Figure 7.2 cannot correspond to an equilibrium regime. Neither can the case of Figure 7.3, once z is smaller than 1. In both cases, one at least of the two firms has an incentive to move away from the other.

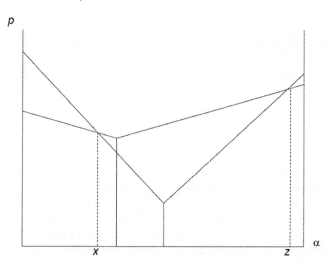

Figure 7.2 Firm 1 has a cost disadvantage at its own location

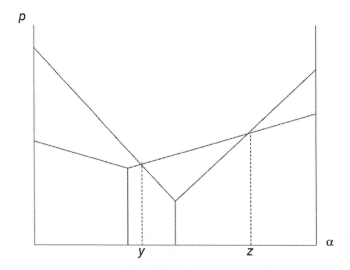

Figure 7.3 Firm 1 has a cost advantage *at its own location*

We are thus left with the case in which firms 1 and 2 have a cost advantage in their respective (connected) market areas $[0, y)$ and $(y, 1]$, with

$$y = \frac{t_1 a_1 + t_2 a_2 - (c_1 - c_2)}{t_1 + t_2} \tag{7.3}$$

The mathematical expectation of firm 1 profit is then

$$\hat{\pi}_1(t_1, t_2, a_1, a_2) = \int_0^y \left[c_2 + t_2 (a_2 - \alpha) - c_1 - t_1 |a_1 - \alpha| \right] d\alpha \tag{7.4}$$

so that the first order condition for a maximum is

$$\frac{\partial \hat{\pi}_1(t_1, t_2, a_1, a_2)}{\partial a_1} = t_1 (y - 2a_1) = 0 \tag{7.5}$$

Similarly,

$$\hat{\pi}_2(t_1, t_2, a_1, a_2) = \int_y^1 \left[c_1 + t_1 (\alpha - a_1) - c_2 - t_2 |a_2 - \alpha| \right] d\alpha, \tag{7.6}$$

leading to

$$\frac{\partial \hat{\pi}_2(t_1, t_2, a_1, a_2)}{\partial a_2} = t_2 (y + 1 - 2a_2) = 0 \tag{7.7}$$

Notice that, by the two first-order conditions (7.5) and (7.7), each firm is located at the centre of its market area. Using these conditions, we finally obtain the following equilibrium locations in the characteristics space:

$$a_1^* = \frac{t_2/2 - (c_1 - c_2)}{t_1 + t_2} \quad \text{and} \quad a_2^* = \frac{t_1/2 + t_2 - (c_1 - c_2)}{t_1 + t_2} \tag{7.8}$$

with the corresponding equilibrium expected profits

$$\hat{\pi}_1(t_1, t_2, a_1^*, a_2^*) = (t_1 + 2t_2) a_1^{*2} \quad \text{and} \quad \hat{\pi}_2(t_1, t_2, a_1^*, a_2^*) = (2t_1 + t_2)(1 - a_2^*)^2 \tag{7.9}$$

Technologies

By a simple inspection of equations (7.8) and (7.9), we see that these equilibrium expected profits, the payoffs at the first stage of the game, can be expressed for each of the two firms by the same function of the technological choices. Thus, looking for subgame perfect equilibria of the original three-stage game ultimately amounts to investigate the equilibria of a symmetric two-person game in strategic form, where each player, say firm $i \in \{1,2\}$, given the strategy t_i of the other player, chooses a strategy t_i in the set $T = [\theta, 1]$ on the basis of the payoff function

$$\Pi(t_i, t_j) = (t_i + 2t_j) \left(\frac{t_j/2 - C(t_i) + C(t_j)}{t_i + t_j} \right)^2 \tag{7.10}$$

if $C(t_i) - C(t_j) \leq t_j/2$, and $\Pi(t_i, t_j) = 0$ otherwise.[6] Any such equilibrium is a pair $(t_1^*, t_2^*) \in T^2$ such that t_i^* maximizes $\Pi(\cdot, t_j^*)$ over T, for each $i \in \{1,2\}$ and $j \in \{1,2\} \setminus \{i\}$.

The necessary first order condition for a maximum over $(\theta, 1)$ of $\Pi(\cdot, t_j)$ is:[7]

$$\partial_1 \Pi(t_i, t_j) = -\Pi(t_i, t_j) \left[\frac{t_i + 3t_j}{(t_i + 2t_j)(t_i + t_j)} + \frac{2C'(t_i)}{t_j/2 - C(t_i) + C(t_j)} \right] = 0 \tag{7.11}$$

Of course, in order to decide if the payoff function has a maximum at some critical point, we must check the sign of the second derivative at point $\partial_1 \Pi(t_i, t_j) = 0$:

$$\partial_{11}^2 \Pi(t_i, t_j) = \frac{\Pi(t_i, t_j)}{t_i} \frac{t_i + 3t_j}{(t_i + 2t_j)(t_i + t_j)} \left[\frac{(t_i + 5t_j)t_i}{2(t_i + 2t_j)(t_i + 3t_j)} + \frac{C''(t_i)t_i}{C'(t_i)} \right]. \tag{7.12}$$

The first term in the brackets is positive but not larger than $1/2$, so that the sign of the second derivative is necessarily negative at any critical point whenever $-C''(t_i)t_i/C'(t_i) > 1/2$ for any $t_i \in (\theta, 1)$. In other words, the payoff function is strictly quasi-concave in this case, as it has either a unique critical point, which must be a maximum, or no critical point at all. By a symmetric argument, the payoff function is strictly quasi-convex if $-C''(t_i)t_i/C'(t_i) \leq 0$, that is, if C is concave. As one may easily figure out, and as we are going to see in more detail, the curvature of the technological frontier, as measured by the elasticity of its slope, plays a crucial role in determining the different possible equilibrium configurations. To keep things simple, we restrict our analysis to the two mentioned cases where the curvature leads either to quasi-concavity or to quasi-convexity of the payoff function.

To be thorough, we must keep in mind that an optimal choice is not necessarily an interior point of the strategy space; therefore, the first order conditions characterising corner solutions cannot be ignored:

$$\partial_1 \Pi(t_i, t_j) \leq 0 \text{ for } t_i = \theta \text{ and } \partial_1 \Pi(t_i, t_j) \geq 0 \text{ for } t_i = 1 \qquad (7.13)$$

NON-DECREASING RETURNS TO SPECIALIZATION

Let us first consider the case of a concave technological frontier, meaning that returns to specialization are non-decreasing (or, equivalently, that the cost of flexibility is non-increasing). We have seen that the payoff function is strictly quasi-convex in that case. As a consequence, optimal strategies cannot be interior to the strategy set $T = [\theta, 1]$, so that we may restrict our analysis to the boundary $\{\theta, 1\}$ of T.

Two kinds of symmetric equilibria are then possible: an equilibrium (θ, θ) with extreme flexibility, if $\Pi(\theta, \theta) \geq \Pi(1, \theta)$, and an equilibrium $(1,1)$ with extreme specialization, if $\Pi(1,1) \geq \Pi(\theta, 1)$. Clearly, a pair of extremely asymmetric equilibria $(\theta, 1)$ and $(1, \theta)$ exists, if both inequalities are reversed.

By (7.10), the condition for existence of a *symmetric equilibrium with flexibility* (recalling that $C(1) = 0$) is:

$$\frac{3\theta}{16} \geq \frac{1 + 2\theta}{4} \left(\frac{\theta + 2C(\theta)}{1 + \theta} \right)^2$$

or equivalently

$$C(\theta) \leq \frac{1 + \theta}{4} \sqrt{\frac{3\theta}{1 + 2\theta}} - \frac{\theta}{2} \qquad (7.14)$$

Similarly, the condition for existence of a *symmetric equilibrium with specialization* is:

$$\frac{3}{16} \geq \frac{2+\theta}{4} \left(\frac{1-2C(\theta)}{1+\theta}\right)^2$$

or equivalently

$$C(\theta) \geq \frac{1}{2} - \frac{1+\theta}{4} \sqrt{\frac{3}{2+\theta}}. \qquad (7.15)$$

Since the right-hand side of inequality (7.14) is smaller than the right-hand side of inequality (7.15), the two conditions are incompatible. Also, existence of an 'asymmetric equilibrium' is thereby possible under the condition:

$$\frac{1+\theta}{4} \sqrt{\frac{3\theta}{1+2\theta}} - \frac{\theta}{2} \leq C(\theta) \leq \frac{1}{2} - \frac{1+\theta}{4} \sqrt{\frac{3}{2+\theta}} \qquad (7.16)$$

Notice that the flexible firm has an advantage over the specialized firm at an asymmetric equilibrium. Its market share is indeed $y^* = (1 - 2C(\theta))/(1+\theta)$, which by (7.16) is larger than 1/2 for a value of $C(\theta)$ leading to this type of equilibrium. Its profit, according to (7.9), is correspondingly larger than the profit of the specialized firm. Still, by the very definition of equilibrium, the latter firm prefers to specialize given the opposite choice of its competitor. As both firms have access to the same technology, this asymmetry is a good illustration of the fact that there is more in the specialization-flexibility trade-off than its purely technological dimension.

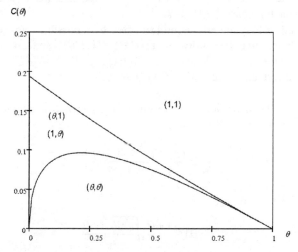

Figure 7.4 Equilibrium types for non-decreasing returns to specialization

The conclusion of the preceding analysis is that an equilibrium always exists and that uniqueness is ensured, at least generically, when returns to specialization are non-decreasing. Both firms specialize (resp. go flexible) when the cost of flexibility $C(\theta)$ is high (resp. low). But, for intermediate values of $C(\theta)$, when the cost of flexibility (or the return to specialization) is only moderate, the equilibrium is *necessarily* asymmetric. Also, the range of values of $C(\theta)$ leading to asymmetry increases significantly (at the expense of those entailing widespread flexibility) with the scope of the trade-off (that is, as θ decreases towards zero). We represented in Figure 7.4 the boundaries of the regions corresponding to each one of the three equilibrium types in the parameter space.

DECREASING RETURNS TO SPECIALIZATION

We next consider convex technological frontiers, meaning decreasing returns to specialization or, equivalently, increasing costs of flexibility. We further assume that the degree of convexity of the frontier is high enough to ensure strict quasi-concavity of the payoff function: $-C''(t)t/C'(t) > 1/2$ for any $t \in (\theta,1)$. The solution to the firm maximising problem is then unique whatever the strategy chosen by the other firm (a solution always exists, since the payoff function is continuous and defined on a non-empty compact set). As a consequence, there exists a continuous best-reply function for firm i:

$$f(t_j) = \arg\max_{t_i \in T} \Pi(t_i, t_j). \qquad (7.17)$$

This function is entirely characterized by the first order necessary conditions (7.11) and (7.13), which are sufficient for a global maximum in this case.

Symmetric Equilibria

In a symmetric equilibrium (t^*, t^*), t^* is a fixed point of the best-reply function which must satisfy by conditions (7.11) and (7.13):

$$C'(t^*) = -1/6, \text{ or} \qquad (7.18)$$

$$t^* = \theta \text{ if } \lim_{t \to \theta} C'(t) \geq -1/6,$$

$$t^* = 1 \text{ if } \lim_{t \to 1} C'(t) \leq -1/6$$

Clearly, since C' is an increasing function, these three cases cover all possible situations, and there always exists a unique symmetric equilibrium.[8]

For simplicity and explicitness of further results, we will refer from now on to a specification of the technological frontier with a constant degree of convexity $-C''(t)t/C'(t) = \rho$ for any $t \in T$:

$$C(t) = \gamma\left(1 - t^{1-\rho}\right), \tag{7.19}$$

with $\gamma > 0$, $1/2 < \rho < 1$, and $0 \leq t \leq 1$. In order to concentrate on only two parameters, we have taken $\theta = 0$, that is, $T = [0,1]$. Thus, $C(\theta) = \gamma$ in the following. Finally, notice that taking a non-positive ρ would lead us to the case of a concave technological frontier examined in the preceding section, and that the restriction $\rho > 1/2$ ensures strict quasi-concavity of the payoff function, as already established.

Coexistence of Symmetric and Asymmetric Equilibria

With the function C specified as above, extreme flexibility is never an optimal choice, since $\lim_{t \to 0} C'(t) = -\infty$, implying $\lim_{t_i \to 0} \partial_1 \Pi(t_i, t_j)/\Pi(t_i, t_j) = \infty$ for any t_j. Thus, we are left with only two types of (unique) symmetric equilibria: $t^* = (6\gamma(1-\rho))^{1/\rho} \in (0,1)$ if $\gamma < 1/6(1-\rho)$, and $t^* = 1$ otherwise. Asymmetric equilibria are also of two types, either involving both firms in solutions which are interior to the technology set T, or having one firm with extreme specialization. Conditions for existence of such equilibria are discussed in the second part of the Appendix.

Here, we directly represent in Figure 7.5 the regions in the space $\rho \times \gamma$ where the parameter values are compatible with the different types of symmetric and asymmetric equilibria. The increasing boundary (which can be extended to values of ρ larger than 0.54) separates the region of *symmetric* equilibria $(1,1)$ with *extreme* specialization (SE) from the region of *symmetric* equilibria (t^*, t^*) with *intermediate* technological solutions (SI), interior to the technology set T. As the cost of flexibility (or the benefit of specialization) $C(0) = \gamma$ decreases towards 0, these intermediate solutions become more and more flexible, tending to extreme flexibility.

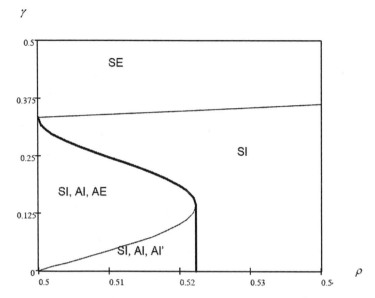

Figure 7.5 Equilibrium types for decreasing returns to specialization

For a small degree of convexity of the technological frontier ($\rho < \hat{\rho} \approx 0.5223$) and for a small cost of flexibility (below the thick decreasing curve), there exists, in addition to the symmetric interior equilibrium (SI), a pair[9] of *asymmetric interior* equilibria (AI), and yet another pair with higher asymmetry, which can be either interior (AI'), for very low values of the cost of flexibility, or have one firm choosing extreme specialization (AE), for intermediate values of that cost. For any given value of ρ, a decrease in the cost γ of flexibility naturally induces more flexible technological solutions across asymmetric equilibria: of both firms (while keeping constant the ratio t_i/t_j) if the equilibria are interior, or of the sole flexible firm (by diminishing the ratio $t_i/t_j = t_i/1$) if the equilibria involve extreme specialization of one firm.

The following example shows that the same parameter values may lead to quite different equilibrium configurations, with varying degrees of asymmetry, when multiplicity prevails. For $\rho = 0.51$ and $\gamma = 1/6$, we have indeed three types of equilibria:

$$\text{(SI)} \quad t_i = t_j \approx 0.247$$
$$\text{(AI)} \quad t_i = 0.153, \ t_j = 0.461$$
$$\text{(AE)} \quad t_i = 0.104, \ t_j = 1$$

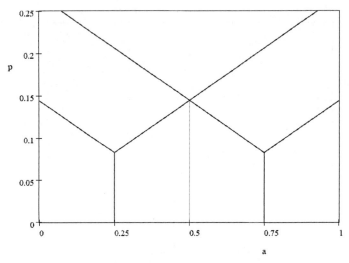

Figure 7.6 Equilibrium of type SI

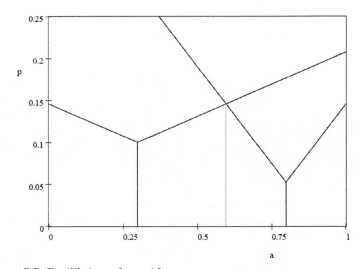

Figure 7.7 Equilibrium of type AI

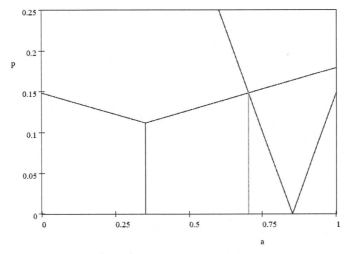

Figure 7.8 Equilibrium of type AE

These equilibria are represented in Figures 7.6, 7.7 and 7.8, respectively, showing that the market share of the flexible firm increases with the degree of asymmetry. The equilibrium profits correspondingly increase with flexibility:

$$\Pi(1, 0.104) = 0.027, \quad \Pi(0.461, 0.153) = 0.031$$
$$\Pi(0.247, 0.247) = 0.046$$
$$\Pi(0.153, 0.461) = 0.095, \quad \Pi(0.104, 1) = 0.26$$

We see that a significant technological asymmetry, inducing a high asymmetry in market shares, is quite profitable for the flexible firm, while only mildly disadvantageous to the specialized firm.

OPTIMALITY

The Criterion

To assess equilibrium optimality, we assume existence of an arbitrarily high reservation price. By referring to this price, it is then possible to evaluate either the social surplus (the sum of profits plus consumers' surplus), or the collusive profit that would result from the appropriation of this surplus by the two firms.

The optimality criterion is the same in both cases, differing only in the way total surplus is shared, namely the maximization of social surplus (or, in the present case, the minimization of total expected costs) under the constraint that exactly two production units are located in the characteristics space. Proceeding in two stages, and considering first the choice of locations, it is easy to realize that the equilibrium locations a_1^* and a_2^* in (7.8), conditional on the technological choice $(c_i, t_i)_{i=1,2}$ at the first stage, are socially optimal. Indeed, the expected profit function of firm i, given by (7.1) and (7.2), can be equivalently expressed as the sum of two terms:

$$\hat{\pi}_i(t_1, t_2, a_1, a_2) = \int_0^1 \left[C(t_j) + t_j |a_j - \alpha| \right] d\alpha \qquad (7.20)$$

$$-\int_0^1 \min \left\{ C(t_j) + t_j |a_j - \alpha|, C(t_i) + t_i |a_i - \alpha| \right\} d\alpha,$$

with $i \in \{1,2\}$ and $j \in \{1,2\} \setminus \{i\}$. The first term does not depend upon firm i decision to locate at a_i, so that the second term

$$-g(t_1, t_2, a_1, a_2) = -\int_0^1 \min \left\{ C(t_j) + t_j |a_j - \alpha|, C(t_i) + t_i |a_i - \alpha| \right\} d\alpha \quad (7.21)$$

can be used alone as the payoff function of the location game without changing the equilibrium locations, as already shown by Lederer and Hurter (1986). Thus, both firms face in fact the same *expected total cost* function $g(t_1, t_2, \cdot, \cdot)$, which must be minimized over $[0,1]^2$ at the unique equilibrium locations (a_1^*, a_2^*).

This argument can be extended to technological choices. Indeed, should technologies and locations be *simultaneously* chosen at the first stage of a two-stage game, it would still be irrelevant to take as the payoff function of, say, firm 1 the expected profit $\hat{\pi}_1(\cdot, t_2, \cdot, a_2)$ or (by neglecting the first, constant, term of (7.20)) the function $-g(\cdot, t_2, \cdot, a_2)$. It follows that at least one of the subgame perfect equilibria of the two-stage game would minimize the total expected cost (equilibrium uniqueness consequently entailing optimality). By contrast, the first term of the right-hand side of equation (7.20) cannot be taken as independent of the technological choice of firm i in the three-stage game we have adopted, since the equilibrium value of a_j^* at the second stage depends by (7.8) upon the choice of t_i at the first stage. Profit maximization hence ceases to be equivalent to total cost minimisation in this context, and equilibrium optimality is upset.

Let us now consider the technological choice (t_1, t_2) that minimizes the expected total cost at the optimal locations:

$$g(t_1, t_2, a_1^*, a_2^*) = \min_{(a_1, a_2) \in [0,1]^2} g(t_1, t_2, a_1, a_2) \qquad (7.22)$$

$$= \int_0^{y^*} \left[C(t_1) + t_1 \left| a_1^* - \alpha \right| \right] d\alpha + \int_{y^*}^1 \left[C(t_2) + t_2 \left| a_2^* - \alpha \right| \right] d\alpha$$

with y^* given by (7.3) and such that $y^* = 2a_1^* = 2a_2^* - 1$ (by the first-order conditions (7.5) and (7.7)). Thus, we may introduce the function:

$$G(t_1,t_2) = g\left(t_1, t_2, y^*/2, (1+y^*)/2 \right) \tag{7.23}$$

$$= \left(C(t_1) + t_1 y^*/4 \right) y^* + \left(C(t_2) + t_2 (1-y^*)/4 \right)(1-y^*)$$

with

$$y^* = \frac{t_2 - 2\left(C(t_1) - C(t_2) \right)}{t_1 + t_2} \tag{7.24}$$

The first order conditions for an interior minimum of G with respect to t_1 and t_2 (taking into account the fact that the partial derivatives of g with respect to the two last arguments are equal to zero for optimal locations) are

$$\partial_1 G(t_1,t_2) = \left(C'(t_1) + y^*/4 \right) y^* = 0 \tag{7.25}$$

and a corresponding equation for $\partial_2 G(t_1,t_2)$, obtained by reversing the index of t and replacing y^* by $1 - y^*$.

The second partial derivative of $\partial_1 G(t_1,t_2)$ with respect to t_1 given (7.25) is

$$\partial_{11}^2 G(t_1,t_2) \Big|_{\partial_1 G(t_1,t_2) = 0} = \left(C''(t_1) + \frac{1}{4} \frac{\partial y^*}{\partial t_1} \right) y^* \tag{7.26}$$

$$= \left(\frac{C''(t_1) t_1}{C'(t_1)} + \frac{1}{2} \frac{t_1}{t_1 + t_2} \right) \frac{C'(t_1)}{t_1} y^*$$

with a corresponding equation for the second partial derivative with respect to t_2. Hence, the second partial derivatives with respect to each one of the technological variables are negative at any critical point of G if the technological frontier is concave. This function is then strictly quasi-concave in both arguments, and consequently minimized at values of t_1 and t_2 belonging to the boundary of the technology set. By contrast, and by a symmetric argument, the function G is strictly quasi-convex in both arguments if the technological frontier displays a degree of convexity $-C''(t)t/C'(t) > 1/2$ for any value of t.

Non-Decreasing Returns to Specialization

As just stated, the expected total cost function G can have no interior minimum with respect to t_1 or t_2 when the technological frontier is concave, that is, when returns to specialization are non-decreasing. In this case we should only consider the values taken by G on the boundary $\{0,1\}^2$ of T, that is, by (7.23) and (7.24),

$$G(\theta,\theta) = C(\theta) + \theta/8, \ G(1,1) = 1/8$$

$$G(\theta,1) = G(1,\theta) = \frac{1}{4}\left(1 - \frac{(1-2C(\theta))^2}{1+\theta}\right) \tag{7.27}$$

Optimality of the all flexible solution results from the inequality $G(\theta,\theta) \le \min\{G(1,1),G(\theta,1)\}$, which is equivalent to

$$C(\theta) \le \min\left\{\frac{1-\theta}{8}, \frac{\sqrt{\theta(1+\theta)/2}-\theta}{2}\right\} = \frac{\sqrt{\theta(1+\theta)/2}-\theta}{2} \tag{7.28}$$

Similarly, it is optimal to choose specialization for both firms if $G(1,1) \le \min\{G(\theta,\theta),G(\theta,1)\}$, or

$$C(\theta) \ge \max\left\{\frac{1-\theta}{8}, \frac{1-\sqrt{(1+\theta)/2}}{2}\right\} = \frac{1-\sqrt{(1+\theta)/2}}{2} \tag{7.29}$$

Finally, the pair of asymmetric solutions is optimal in the complementary case $G(\theta,1) \le \min\{G(\theta,\theta),G(1,1)\}$, or

$$\frac{\sqrt{\theta(1+\theta)/2}-\theta}{2} \le C(\theta) \le \frac{1-\sqrt{(1+\theta)/2}}{2} \tag{7.30}$$

We represent in the following Figure 7.9 the regions of parameter values in the space $\theta \times C(\theta)$ that lead to the three different types of optimal solutions. The boundaries separating these regions are represented by thick curves, to be compared with the thin curves separating the corresponding regions in our duopoly model (the same as in Figure 7.4). We see that the boundaries are now lower: an equilibrium choice of flexibility, by one or both of the firms may thus be sub-optimal. Thus, technological choices resulting from competition exhibit a bias in favour of flexibility as compared with the solutions preferred by a social planner or by a cartel. This bias is of course linked to the sequential choice of strategies (first technologies, then locations) in the three-stage game we have been studying, and would disappear should technologies and locations be chosen simultaneously.

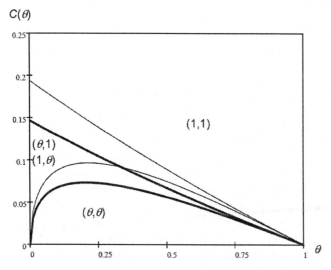

Figure 7.9 Optimal solutions for non-decreasing returns to specialization

Decreasing Returns to Specialization

We have seen that the total cost function G is strictly quasi-convex in each one of its arguments if $-C''(t)t/C'(t) > 1/2$ for any t. Given $t_j \in [\theta,1]$, it is then possible to determine the unique value of t_i that minimizes $G(\cdot,t_j)$,

$$\phi(t_j) = \arg\min_{t_i \in [\theta,1]} G(t_i,t_j), \qquad (7.31)$$

by referring to the first order condition, which is sufficient in the present case. Clearly, a local minimum of G must occur at some point (t_i,t_j) such that $t_i = \phi(t_j)$ and $t_j = \phi(t_i)$, so that $t_i = \phi \circ \phi(t_i)$. By continuity of ϕ, this local minimum must be unique if the graph of $\phi \circ \phi$ can only cut the first diagonal from above, that is, if at any fixed point $t_i \in [\theta,1]$ of $\phi \circ \phi$, the derivative of this function is smaller than 1: $\phi'(\phi(t_i))\phi'(t_i) < 1$ (an argument which is equivalent to establishing strict quasi-convexity of the function G). We show in the third part of the Appendix that this is indeed true in the case of a degree of convexity of the technological frontier larger than $1/2$.

Now, G is symmetric with respect to its arguments, so that the optimal solution, if unique, must itself be symmetric: $t_i = t_j = \hat{t}$. If this solution is interior, it must satisfy (by the first order condition (7.25), with $y^* = 1/2$) $C'(\hat{t}) = -1/8$. Otherwise, G is minimised either at $\hat{t} = \theta$ if $\lim_{t \to \theta} C'(t) \geq -1/8$ or at $\hat{t} = 1$ if $\lim_{t \to 1} C'(t) \leq -1/8$. Comparing with the condition $C'(t^*) = -1/6$ for an equilibrium, and since C' is increasing, we conclude (as in the case of concavity of the technological frontier) that competition between the two firms leads to an outcome displaying too much flexibility from the social or from the collusive point of view. This conclusion agrees with the corresponding result of von Ungern-Sternberg (1988). However, as already emphasized, our conclusion depends upon the sequential character of the strategic choices (technological decisions preceding location decisions), whereas von Ungern-Sternberg's result is related to his assumption of uniform mill pricing.[10]

As a matter of fact, we have seen that competition between firms with sequential choices favours not only flexibility, but also (at least when the technological frontier is only mildly convex) multiplicity of equilibria, whereas optimal solutions are generically unique up to the numbering of the two firms. Moreover, equilibrium choices, in this mild convexity case, can be asymmetric, whereas optimal solutions are necessarily symmetric within the same range of parameter values.[11]

Before concluding, let us recall the example at the end of the last section, and rank the different equilibria according to the criterion of the social planner (or of the cartel):

$$\text{(SI)} \quad G(0.247, 0.247) = 0.11354$$
$$\text{(AI)} \quad G(0.153, 0.461) = 0.1134$$
$$\text{(AE)} \quad G(0.104, 1) = 0.11342$$

We see that the different equilibria lead to quite similar total costs, with a slight advantage to the weakly asymmetric equilibrium outcome. The minimum total cost, at $\hat{t} = 0.434$ for both firms, is however more neatly smaller, equal to 0.11. Hence, at least in this example, inefficiency is the consequence of the non-cooperative character of competition, rather than of a failure to coordinate on the good equilibrium.

CONCLUSION

This paper dealt with a central, yet rather neglected issue. The decision whether to specialize, by developing highly specific skills, or to remain flexible, thus preserving a wider set of options, can be found in all realms of economic activity, and applies more generally to many aspects of everyday life which are not necessarily considered as pertaining to economics proper. The decision itself is however economic in its very essence, since it involves a trade-off: specialization improves performance, but at the cost of making it more difficult to respond to a changing environment; conversely, in order to preserve flexibility, one has to renounce to part of the benefits of a precise matching with the current characteristics of the environment. We have modelled this specialization–flexibility trade-off by referring to the decreasing efficient frontier of the set of all admissible combinations of two kinds of costs: the cost of producing a differentiated good and the cost of adapting it, once produced, in order to fit changing customers' tastes.

Clearly, the extent of specialization is partly determined by the technological conditions of the trade-off, more precisely by the shape (slope and curvature) of the specialization–flexibility frontier: a high cost of flexibility in terms of production costs naturally favours specialization and, perhaps more significantly, non-decreasing returns to specialization determine extreme decisions (either strong specialization or wide flexibility), whereas decreasing returns typically lead to compromising solutions. By introducing two firms (or production units) we have also shown that optimal configurations are not necessarily symmetric with respect to the extent of specialization and to the location in the space of characteristics.

We were however principally interested in the effects of competition on the outcomes of the specialization-flexibility trade-off, and used accordingly a sequential game with two firms supplying a product located in a one-dimensional characteristics space, and taking successively technological, 'locational' and pricing decisions. This ordering conveys in particular the claim that there is a greater commitment to the extent of one's specialization than to the specific orientation of that specialization, and is in accord with our basic intuition regarding the irreversibility of technological choices. Moreover, because of the Bertrand competition assumed at the final stage, merging technological and locational decisions in one single preliminary stage would determine the same outcome as the one of a centralized decision process. We have shown that competition leads on the contrary in our context to excessive flexibility, sought by each one of the two competitors because of its positive effect on the market share. Also, multiple equilibria may easily emerge, so that a simple change in each competitor's conjecture about the rival's behaviour can trigger a complete reversal of strategy regarding the specialization–flexibility trade-off. Such behavioural shifts are often observed, with firms, once strongly diversified, suddenly re-focusing on their core competencies.

NOTES

1. This paper developed from an idea formulated by Ehud Zuscovitch into a complete version, first presented at the 20th Conference of the EARIE (Tel Aviv, 4–7 September 1993). A revised version was circulated as a BETA Working Paper, dated December 1995. The process of revising and resubmitting has alas been stopped, three years after, by the long disease that would finally take Ehud away from us. The present version is quite close to the BETA WP, and has only been slightly modified in order to improve the exposition of some technical developments. No attempt has been made to update the references. An exception is Boyer and Moreaux (1997), with the same emphasiz as ours on asymmetric equilibria and excessive flexibility, although in a different context where firms choose capacities rather than locations. Moshe Justman, Alan Kirman and Sophie Lecostey are gratefully acknowledged for helpful comments on earlier versions.
2. We shall not deal in this paper with the dynamic considerations of learning that governs such evolution, but it is important to recognize that such processes permanently feed the SFT menu from which economic agents are choosing.
3. Contrary to ours, von Ungern-Sternberg's model refers to a circular space of characteristics where each firm competes under uniform mill pricing with two neighbours, one on its right and the other on its left.
4. In any case, we feel justified in ordering the technology-location sequence the way we did. Although the degree and focus of specialization are obviously linked, it is the choice of the former that determines the commitment value involved in choosing the latter. The influence of the degree of flexibility on the strength of such a commitment effect has been examined for instance by Vives (1986). The degree of flexibility there is an exogenous parameter, not a strategic variable, and concerns the ability to switch between different product characteristics. But it appears as pre-determined at the stage in which capacities (analogous to our locations) are chosen. Also, Brander and Eaton (1984) adopt a similar sequential structure in their discussion of product line rivalry where scope decisions are made before line decisions.
5. The implications of assuming instead a two-stage game, with a simultaneous choice of technologies and locations, are briefly considered before the concluding section.
6. If $C(t_j) + t_j/2 \le C(t_i)$, firm j takes the whole market by simply locating at the centre of the interval $[0,1]$.
7. We denote $\partial_1 \Pi(t_i, t_j)$ the partial derivative of Π with respect to its first argument.
8. For an equilibrium (t^*, t^*) to exclude either extreme flexibility ($t^* = \theta$) or extreme specialization ($t^* = 1$) the slope $C'(t^*)$ of the technological frontier at t^* must be equal to $-1/6$. This is precisely the value which must take the limit, as θ tends to 1, of $(C(\theta) - C(1))/(\theta - 1)$ in order to exclude either extreme flexibility or extreme specialization when the technological frontier is concave (as seen from Figure 7.4 and using conditions (6.14) and (6.15)).
9. Since the game is symmetric, if (t_i, t_j), with $t_i \ne t_j$, is an equilibrium, so is (t_j, t_i).
10. The bias in favour of flexibility introduced by competition between firms is even larger under uniform mill pricing. Transposing von Ungern-Sternberg's symmetric oligopoly equilibrium (based upon the simultaneous choice of mill prices and technologies, with exogenous locations at 1/4 and 3/4) to our setup, we also obtain his condition $C'(t^*) = -1/4$, leading to a value of t^* still lower than in our equilibrium.
11. Optimal solutions can be asymmetric for a lower degree of convexity of the technological frontier. This is true in particular for a constant degree of convexity ρ (the example examined above), with $\rho < 1/2$ and γ small enough.

REFERENCES

Arrow, Kenneth J. (1974), *The Limits of Organization*, New York: Norton & Co.

Arthur, B.W. (1989), 'Competing technologies, increasing returns, and lock-in by historical small events', *Economic Journal*, **99** (394), 116–131.

Baumol, William J., John C. Panzar and Robert D. Willig, (1982), *Contestable Markets and the Theory of Industry Structure*, New York: Harcourt Brace Jovanovich.

Boyer, M. and M. Moreaux (1997), 'Capacity commitment versus flexibility', *Journal of Economics & Management Strategy*, **6** (1), 347–376.

Brander, J.A. and J. Eaton (1984), 'Product line rivalry', *American Economic Review*, **74** (3), 323–334.

Chandler, A. (1990), *Scale and Scope: The Dynamics of Industrial Capitalism*, Cambridge, MA: Harvard University Press.

Dixit, A. and J. Stiglitz (1977), 'Monopolistic competition and optimum product diversity', *American Economic Review*, **67** (3), 297–308.

Dos Santos Ferreira, R. and J.-F. Thisse (1996), 'Horizontal and vertical differentiation: the Launhardt model', *International Journal of Industrial Organization*, **14** (4), 485–506.

Eaton, B. and R. Lipsey (1979), 'A comment on location and industrial efficiency with free entry', *Quarterly Journal of Economics*, **93** (3), 447–450.

Eaton, B. and N. Schmitt (1994), 'Flexible manufacturing and market structure', *American Economic Review*, **84** (4), 875–888.

Hoover, E. (1937), 'Spatial price discrimination', *Review of Economic Studies*, **4** (3), 182–91.

Hotelling, H. (1929), 'Stability in competition', *Economic Journal*, **39** (153), 41–57.

Lancaster, K. (1975), 'Socially optimal product differentiation', *American Economic Review*, **65** (4), 567–585.

Launhardt, Wilhelm (1885/1992), *Mathematische Begründung der Volkswirtschaftslehre*, Leipzig; English translation: *Principles of Mathematical Economics*, Aldershot, UK and Brook field, VT, USA: Edward Elgar.

Lederer, P. and A. Hurter (1986), 'Competition of firms: discriminatory pricing and location', *Econometrica*, **54** (3), 623–40.

MacLeod, W., G.Norman and J.-F. Thisse (1988), 'Price discrimination and equilibrium in monopolistic competition', *International Journal of Industrial Organization*, **6** (4), 429–446.

Milgrom, P. and J. Roberts (1990), 'The economics of modern manufacturing: technology, strategy, and organization', *American Economic Review*, **80** (3), 511–528.

Stigler, G. (1939), 'Production and distribution in the short run', *Journal of Political Economy*, **47** (3), 305–327.

Teece, D. (1982), 'Towards an economic theory of the multiproduct firm', *Journal of Economic Behaviour and Organization*, **3** (1), 39–63.

von Ungern-Sternberg, T. (1988), 'Monopolistic competition and general purpose products', *Review of Economic Studies*, **55** (2), 231–246.

Vives, X. (1986), 'Commitment, flexibility and market outcomes', *International Journal of Industrial Organization*, **4** (2), 217–229.

Willinger, Marc and Ehud Zuscovitch (1988), 'Towards the economics of information intensive production systems: The case of advanced materials', in G. Dosi et al. (eds), *Technical Change and Economic Theory*, London and New York: Pinter Publishers, pp. 239–255.

APPENDIX

The Equilibrium Regime in the Location Game

We first show that the regimes represented in Figures 7.2 and 7.3, with a cost advantage of firm 1 in some interval $(z,1]$, where $z > a_2$, cannot correspond to equilibria of the location game. Recall that, by convention, $a_1 \leq a_2$ and $t_1 < t_2$ (hence $c_1 > c_2$). To begin with, we take the case of Figure 7.2, where $c_1 \geq c_2 + t_2(a_2 - a_1)$, so that firm 2 has a cost advantage in the interval (x,z), such that $0 \leq x \leq a_1 \leq a_2 < z < 1$ and with

$$x = \max\left\{\frac{t_2 a_2 - t_1 a_1 - (c_1 - c_2)}{t_2 - t_1}, 0\right\} \text{ and } z = \frac{t_2 a_2 - t_1 a_1 + (c_1 - c_2)}{t_2 - t_1} \quad (7.32)$$

The mathematical expectation of firm 2 profit in this regime is

$$\int_x^z \left[c_1 + t_1 |a_1 - \alpha| - c_2 - t_2 |a_2 - \alpha|\right] d\alpha \quad (7.33)$$

with a derivative with respect to a_2:

$$t_2(x + z - 2a_2) + \left[t_2 a_2 - t_1 a_1 + (c_1 - c_2) - (t_2 - t_1)z\right]\frac{\partial z}{\partial a_2} +$$

$$\left[t_2 a_2 - t_1 a_1 - (c_1 - c_2) - (t_2 - t_1)x\right]\frac{\partial x}{\partial a_2} \geq \frac{2t_1 t_2}{t_2 - t_1}(a_2 - a_1) \quad (7.34)$$

The expression after the inequality sign is positive for $a_2 > a_1$, so that firm 2 has always an incentive to move to the right in this regime. Similarly, in the case of Figure 7.3, where $c_1 < c_2 + t_2(a_2 - a_1)$, so that firm 2 has a cost advantage in the interval (y,z), such that $a_1 < y < a_2 < z < 1$, with z as above and

$$y = \frac{t_1 a_1 + t_2 a_2 - (c_1 - c_2)}{t_1 + t_2} \quad (7.35)$$

The mathematical expectation of firm 2 profit is then

$$\int_y^z \left[c_1 + t_1(\alpha - a_1) - c_2 - t_2 |a_2 - \alpha|\right] d\alpha \quad (7.36)$$

with a derivative with respect to a_2:

$$t_2(y + z - 2a_2) + \left[t_2 a_2 - t_1 a_1 + (c_1 - c_2) - (t_2 - t_1)z\right]\frac{\partial z}{\partial a_2} +$$

$$\left[t_1 a_1 + t_2 a_2 - (c_1 - c_2) - (t_1 + t_2)y\right]\frac{\partial y}{\partial a_2} = \frac{2t_1 t_2}{t_2^2 - t_1^2}\left[c_1 - c_2 + t_1(a_2 - a_1)\right] (7.37)$$

which is again positive, expressing an incentive for firm 2 to move to the right.

We finally show that a regime with market areas $[0,x)$ and $(x,1]$ for firms 1 and 2, respectively, is also excluded as an equilibrium regime. Indeed, the firm 1 profit is then

$$\int_0^x \left[c_2 + t_2 (a_2 - \alpha) - c_1 - t_1 (a_1 - \alpha) \right] d\alpha \qquad (7.38)$$

with a derivative with respect to a_1:

$$-t_1 x + \left[t_2 a_2 - t_1 a_1 - (c_1 - c_2) - (t_2 - t_1) x \right] \frac{\partial x}{\partial a_1} = -t_1 x \qquad (7.39)$$

which is negative for $x > 0$, expressing an incentive for firm 1 to move to the left. We conclude that the equilibrium regime is necessarily characterized by market areas $[0,y)$ and $(y,1]$, for firms 1 and 2 respectively, with $y \in [a_1, a_2]$. Notice that this is also the sole possible equilibrium regime in the case of equal costs ($t_1 = t_2$). Of course, we ignore the case where one of the two firms is excluded from the market by a self-defeating technological choice at the first stage.

Asymmetric equilibria when the technology is convex

We assume $C(t) = \gamma \left(1 - t^{1-\rho} \right)$, with $\gamma > 0$, $1/2 < \rho < 1$, and $0 \le t \le 1$. Thanks to the strict quasi-concavity of the payoff function, we may concentrate on the first order conditions, which are then sufficient for a global maximum:

$$(i)\ \partial_1 \Pi \left(t_i, t_j \right) = 0 = \partial_1 \Pi \left(t_j, t_i \right) \text{ with } 0 < t_i < t_j < 1, \text{or} \qquad (7.40)$$

$$(ii)\ \partial_1 \Pi \left(t_i, 1 \right) = 0 \le \partial_1 \Pi \left(1, t_i \right) \text{ with } 0 < t_i < 1 \qquad (7.41)$$

We are restricting our analysis to asymmetric equilibria, with both firms choosing interior technological solutions in case (*i*), or one firm choosing extreme specialization in case (*ii*) (we recall that extreme flexibility is never an optimal solution under this specification of the cost function). Using (7.11) and denoting $\tau = t_i / t_j \in (0,1)$, we find that the above conditions are equivalent to

$$\frac{t_j^\rho}{2\gamma} = h(\tau, \rho) \le h(1/\tau, \rho) \tau^{-\rho} \qquad (7.42)$$

with the latter relation restricted to an equality if $t_j < 1$, and with $h(\tau, \rho)$ defined as follows:

$$h(\tau,\rho) \equiv \frac{2(1+\tau)(2+\tau)}{3+\tau}(1-\rho)\tau^{-\rho} + 1 - \tau^{1-\rho} \qquad (7.43)$$

In order to establish existence of an interior asymmetric equilibrium, we may then proceed in two stages. First, we look for the solutions in τ (over $(0,1)$) to the equation

$$H(t,\rho) \equiv h(1/\tau,\rho)\tau^{-\rho} - h(\tau,\rho) = 0 \qquad (7.44)$$

Second, we compute $t_j = (2\gamma h(\tau,\rho))^{1/\rho}$, checking that it is smaller than 1. Equation (7.44) has two solutions $\underline{\tau}(\rho)$ and $\overline{\tau}(\rho)$ in $(0,1)$ if $\rho < \hat{\rho} \approx 0.5223$, and no solution in the same interval if $\rho > \hat{\rho}$. This is shown in Figure 7.10, representing the graphs of functions $H(\cdot,0.52)$ and $H(\cdot,\hat{\rho})$ (the thin and thick curves, respectively), with the two roots $\underline{\tau}(0.52)$, $\overline{\tau}(0.52)$ of the former and the root $\hat{\tau} \approx 0.07$ of the latter. As ρ decreases from $\hat{\rho}$ to $1/2$, the graph of $H(\cdot,\rho)$ moves up, so that the smallest root $\underline{\tau}(\rho)$ decreases from $\hat{\tau}$ to 0 while the largest root $\overline{\tau}(\rho)$ increases from $\hat{\tau}$ to 1.

Also, we see that $H(\tau,\rho) \geq 0$ if and only if $\underline{\tau}(\rho) \leq \tau \leq \overline{\tau}(\rho)$, so that no asymmetric equilibrium exists, whether interior or not, if $\rho > \hat{\rho}$. We get equilibrium uniqueness with symmetry in this case. If $\rho = \hat{\rho}$, we obtain the pair of equilibria $(\hat{\tau},1)$ and $(1,\hat{\tau})$, provided $\gamma \leq 1/2h(\hat{\tau},\hat{\rho})$. Otherwise, the only equilibrium is again the symmetric one. If $\rho < \hat{\rho}$, we must check that $2\gamma h(\tau,\rho) < 1$ for $\tau = \underline{\tau}(\rho)$ or $\tau = \overline{\tau}(\rho)$. As $h(\cdot,\rho)$ is a decreasing function, $\gamma = 1/2h(\tau,\rho)$ is uniquely determined, so that we obtain in particular:

$$\gamma = \frac{1}{2h(\overline{\tau}(\rho),\rho)} = \overline{\gamma}(\rho) < \frac{1}{6(1-\rho)} = \frac{1}{2h(1,\rho)}$$

$$\gamma = \frac{1}{2h(\underline{\tau}(\rho),\rho)} = \underline{\gamma}(\rho) < \overline{\gamma}(\rho) \qquad (7.45)$$

In Figure 7.5, the graph of the function $\overline{\gamma}$ is represented by the thick decreasing curve and the graph of the function $\underline{\gamma}$ by the lower thin increasing curve. For $\gamma < \underline{\gamma}(\rho)$, there are two pairs of interior asymmetric equilibria (t_i,t_j) (for $i \in \{1,2\}$ and $j \in \{1,2\} \setminus \{i\}$), with $t_i = \tau t_j$, $t_j = (2\gamma h(\tau,\rho))^{1/\rho} < 1$, and $\tau = \underline{\tau}(\rho)$ or $\tau = \overline{\tau}(\rho)$. For $\underline{\gamma}(\rho) \leq \gamma < \overline{\gamma}(\rho)$, there is a single pair of interior asymmetric equilibria, with $\tau = \underline{\tau}(\rho)$, and none for $\gamma \geq \overline{\gamma}(\rho)$.

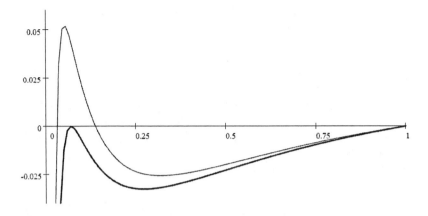

Figure 7.10   Graph of $H(\tau,0.52)$ (thin) and $H(\tau,\hat{\rho})$ (thick)

In order to establish existence of an equilibrium $(t_i,1)$ such that only t_i is interior, we may again proceed in two stages, but reversing their order: first, we look for the solution $\tilde{\tau}(\rho,\gamma)$ in τ (over $(0,1)$) to the equation $2\gamma h(\tau,\rho)=1$, and then we check that such solution satisfies $H(\tau,\rho)\geq0$, that is, that $\underline{\tau}(\rho)\leq\tilde{\tau}(\rho,\gamma)\leq\overline{\tau}(\rho)$ (if $\rho<\hat{\rho}$ and for $\gamma\in\left[\underline{\gamma}(\rho),\overline{\gamma}(\rho)\right]$). Putting together all our findings, we may state:

- If $\rho>\hat{\rho}$, or $\rho\leq\hat{\rho}$ and $\gamma>\overline{\gamma}(\rho)$, the equilibrium is unique and symmetric.
- If $\rho<\hat{\rho}$ and $\underline{\gamma}(\rho)\leq\gamma\leq\overline{\gamma}(\rho)$, besides the symmetric equilibrium there are two pairs of asymmetric equilibria, one interior and the other with extreme specialization (the only that subsists in the limit case of $\rho=\hat{\rho}$).
- If $\rho<\hat{\rho}$ and $\gamma<\underline{\gamma}(\rho)$, besides the symmetric equilibrium there are two pairs of interior asymmetric equilibria.

Quasi-Convexity of the Total Cost Function

The total cost function G is strictly quasi-convex if the Hessian matrix $\partial^2G(t_1,t_2)$ is positive definite when evaluated at *any* interior critical point $(t_1,t_2)\in(\theta,1)^2$ or, equivalently, if its principal minors are all positive at any such point. We have seen in the first part of our sixth subsection on optimality that $\partial_{ii}^2G(t_1,t_2)>0$ for $i=1,2$ at a critical point provided $-C''(t)t/C'(t)>1/2$ for any $t\in(\theta,1)$. Hence, in order to prove the strict quasi-convexity of G under this assumption on C, we must show that the Hessian $\det\left(\partial^2 G(t_1,t_2)\right)$ is itself positive, or equivalently that

$$\left(\frac{\partial_{12}^2 G(t_1,t_2)}{\partial_{11}^2 G(t_1,t_2)}\bigg|_{\partial_1 G(t_1,t_2)=0}\right)\left(\frac{\partial_{21}^2 G(t_1,t_2)}{\partial_{22}^2 G(t_1,t_2)}\bigg|_{\partial_2 G(t_1,t_2)=0}\right)<1 \qquad (7.46)$$

Notice that, by the implicit function theorem, this condition is nothing else than the condition that $(\phi\circ\phi)'(t)=\phi'(\phi(t))\phi'(t)<1$ at any fixed point of $\phi\circ\phi$ (with ϕ as defined by (7.31)), a condition stated in the last part of the sixth subsection.

From (7.24) and (7.25) we can compute:

$$\partial_{12}^2 G(t_1,t_2)\big|_{\partial_1 G(t_1,t_2)=0} = -\left(1+2C'(t_2)+4C'(t_1)\right)\frac{C'(t_1)}{t_1+t_2} \qquad (7.47)$$

Using this equation, together with (7.26) and again (7.25), we may then give an explicit formulation of the above condition:

$$\frac{(1-y^*)/y^*}{-2\frac{t_1+t_2}{t_1}\frac{C''(t_1)t_1}{C'(t_1)}-1} \frac{y^*/(1-y^*)}{-2\frac{t_1+t_2}{t_2}\frac{C''(t_2)t_2}{C'(t_2)}-1}<1 \qquad (7.48)$$

This inequality is clearly satisfied if $-C''(t)t/C'(t)>1/2$ for any t, since its left-hand side is then smaller than $\left(t_1(1-y^*)/t_2y^*\right)\left(t_2y^*/t_1(1-y^*)\right)=1$.

8. Division of Labour and Division of Knowledge in Firms' Innovative Networks: an Essay on Ehud Zuscovitch's Theoretical Perspectives

Patrick Cohendet, Jean-Alain Héraud and Patrick Llerena

INTRODUCTION

In a series of contributions, from his PhD dissertation to his latest articles, Ehud Zuscovitch progressively elaborated an illuminating vision of the process of development of new technologies. This vision, which borrows from the pioneering evolutionary works (Dosi 1982; Nelson and Winter 1982), is based on stimulating ideas and concepts that the author insistently shaped and improved. Among these, Ehud Zuscovitch emphasized the role and the limits of 'networks of firms' with the emergence in the late 1980s of a new regime of growth that he used to call the 'Information Intensive Production System' (hereafter, IIPS), which corresponds to a large extent to what is called today 'the knowledge-based economy'. Economic development, he says, 'relies on increasing specialization that passes a new threshold of complexity due to the tremendous potential of product variety made possible by the rapid dissemination of information technologies' (Zuscovitch 1998, p. 243). This new regime is intensive in knowledge and information:

> Technical knowledge is not sufficient. The very definition of specific applications calls for cooperation with users, and it follows that firms must develop learning abilities in general and discriminating capabilities in particular, both on the supply and demand sides (see Teubal and Zuscovitch 1993). As a matter of fact, every micro-market defined as a complete environment of its own and as such, calls for numerous specialities. This gives rise to the information-intensive production systems (Zuscovitch 1998, p. 253).

This IIPS regime differs from the preceding regime based on increasing returns from the production of standardized commodities. In particular, according to Ehud Zuscovitch, the conditions of surplus creation associated with innovation (as a creation of new knowledge) have fundamentally changed with the emergence of IIPS, the challenge being now to deal with increasing variety while maintaining economic efficiency: this is the role of networks of firms. The role of networks of firms, he argues, is explained by the fact that the differentiation of goods calls for the differentiation of skills, something that it is very difficult for firms to address. In the previous regime of growth, the mass production regime, specialization remained in the private (and, if possible, secret) domain of firms. This was possible because variety was limited. But in IIPS even specialization must be shared. A highly specialized skill can only be maintained if competence is shared among many users. Partnership becomes the condition for viability. Co-operation enables partners to develop skills in a mutual beneficial way: Each party specializes and agrees to share learning according to some modality. This is why the network as a social process may be thought of as a new industrial organization. Surplus creation is no more (mainly) the result of division of labour within the firm, but shared among several actors. In parallel, as we will argue in the following parts of this paper, the necessary sunk costs have probably to be shared by some community of actors as well. This mechanism was something Ehud Zuscovitch seemed to be looking for without achieving the theoretical goal.

Ehud Zuscovitch's questioning of the viability of the industrial system in the IIPS regime is a very modern one. This questioning is not only on the viability of networks, it also concerns the viability of the firm itself and its ability to cope with ever increasing levels of specialization. In such a perspective, the aim of this contribution is first to briefly synthesize Ehud's conception of the role of networks of firms in the new IIPS regime, in order to highlight its richness and modernity. Then we suggest an extension of his ideas in the light of the recent progress of the academic literature on the domain:[1] we discuss the issue of the limits of networks and advocate the need to bring into the economic analysis the notion of knowing communities as one of the main sources of creation of surplus in an IIPS regime. Finally we specify the role of knowing communities in the formation of networks.

THE RELATIONSHIP BETWEEN SPECIALIZATION AND SURPLUS

According to Ehud Zuscovitch the dynamics of growth relies on the relationship between specialization and surplus creation. He considers that the nature of this relationship has drastically changed with the emergence of IIPS. He noted first that whatever the approach (Smith, or Schumpeter, or spillovers/externalities) the surplus is the consequence of encounters between two different structures and the subsequent reorganization that follows. It appears as a function of a reorganization:

> When moving to a more efficient technology or production method, the surplus is generated not by the application of the method by itself, but rather as a consequence of one structure being superimposed on the other, causing the agents to adjust to and integrate the novelty, thus expending much productive energy (Zuscovitch 1998, p. 249).

In the Smithian model for instance (illustrating the mass production system), the overall process of increasing returns is a sequential process characterised by an initial exogenous increase of demand, followed by adjustments in production units leading to increasing capacity. Ehud Zuscovitch points out that for Adam Smith theory, 'the invisible hand is a metaphor for the discussion of resource allocation (or the exchange co-ordination problem) which arises because of specialization (division of labour) and the surplus it generates' (Zuscovitch 1998, p. 248). This gives birth to a reorganization of process together with some process innovation which tends to increase efficiency. In this regime of standardization, with a reasonable division of labour, the firm could be practically independent: the real competences and skills that are required could be developed 'in-house'.

For Schumpeter, surplus creation is strongly related to innovation, which is an internal mechanism of the firm, but also to the perturbation and successive adjustments it introduces into market structures. On the other hand, for the classical industrial organization (hereafter, IO) model, the spillovers of knowledge and technology dissemination are the fundamental sources of surplus. These visions apply generally well to mass production regime of standardization where scale effects generate increasing returns.

In the new regime of IIPS, that explores the potential of infinite product variety made possible by the dissemination of Information and Communication Technologies, Ehud Zuscovitch underlines that the generation of surplus arises principally from alternative mechanisms in which the co-operative dimension is essential. To better explain this property, the author proposes to analyse in depth the relationships between specialization and surplus creation in this new regime.

In IIPS, Ehud Zuscovitch advocates that the new regime calls for a 'network organization' that superimposes itself on the production system with a multiplicity of micro-markets with particular specifications for smaller production runs. There are thus a growing number of bodies of knowledge that one has to master, and the only possible access to such diversity is through cooperation with other producers and users of the products. This hypothesis requires to better capture Ehud Zuscovitch's understanding of networks which are at the centre of the relationship between specialization and surplus creation under IIPS. Under its various forms, differentiation generates an extremely high potential for cross-fertilization: skills combination may stimulate creativity and productivity. In a Schumpeterian perspective, it continuously stimulates new combinations. In short, network is an arena where both creation and allocation of resources are at play simultaneously. New solutions elaborated in networks are permanently 'superimposed' on former structures.

The 'networks structures' are thus the key units of IIPS. Ehud Zuscovitch views 'networks as constellations of firms which are linked to each other by partnership arrangements to confer mutual advantages to the participants' (Zuscovitch 1998, p. 244). It is a new form of industrial structure that tackles the fundamental challenge of simultaneously increasing variety and efficiency. Partner-contingent specialization increases mutual benefits and ultimately joint profits, but at the same time it increases individual risk: it must therefore include a risk-reducing device which is precisely what networks offer through the progressive building of 'trust'. Ehud Zuscovitch considers trust as a tacit agreement in which rather than seeking out the best opportunity at every instant, each agent takes a longer perspective of the transaction, so long as his traditional partner does not go beyond some mutually accepted norms. Thus, because of their ability to internalise externalities, networks offer a flexible organizational solution for joint specialization, provide some protection for property rights of intangible assets, and more importantly alleviate the capital accumulation constraint on the division of labour and growth. In IIPS even specialization must be shared. A highly specialized skill can only be maintained if competence is shared among many users. The network turns specialization essentially into a social process and creates the same separation between specialization and ownership as the limited liability feature did in the case of capital mobilisation. In technological partnerships, spillovers are mastered to a large degree by reciprocity arrangements and partners do find that the benefits of sharing and sometimes even diffusing knowledge overcome the welfare or profits losses.[2]

Network can also be considered as an extension of the domain(s) of competence of firms. The firm's belonging to networks appears in the form of *goodwill* (see also Kogut 2000) and is an essential asset that is part of its portfolio of competences. This reinforces the idea suggested by Ehud Zuscovitch that networks are mechanisms built to avoid transaction costs in the construction) of knowledge and also reinforces the importance of trust (to mitigate opportunistic behaviours) in networks. For a given firm network delineates those firms with which the interactions are regulated by the rules of building and reinforcing knowledge, and those firms (which do not participate in the network) with which the interactions are essentially regulated by transaction costs. Finally, Ehud Zuscovitch claims that network offers the possibility internalizing externalities. In technological partnerships, spillovers are mastered to a large extent by reciprocity arrangements and partners do find that the benefits of sharing and sometimes even diffusing knowledge overcome the welfare or profits losses. Network is a mechanism to which the weak appropriation hypothesis of the traditional model (Arrow 1962) does not apply. When product variety is limited, any leakage of information may entail serious losses simply because the total output is affected. Under increasing variety, increased differentiation drives the system towards multiple micro-markets where imitation is much more difficult.

However, while emphasizing the advantages of networks as the key mechanism of the IIPS regime, Ehud Zuscovitch repeatedly questions the viability of such a regime based on networks. Sustainable differentiation or the ability of the industrial structure to manage large product variety is a major concern in all his works. He suggests that in order to advance understanding of the relationship between networks, differentiation, and surplus creation, the principles of interactivity must be thoroughly understood. To a large extent, recent progress in the literature confirms, and beyond, the illuminating insights of Ehud Zuscovitch's perspective. What he addresses is the fundamental issue of viability of the industrial system as a whole under what we are now used to calling the 'Knowledge Based Economy'.

In fact, he was rather sceptical about the possibility of networks of firms maintaining on a sustainable basis an efficient answer to the problem of articulating increasing specialization (of firms) to face increasing multiple markets. For him, an ever increased specialization bears too much on the firm side, while co-ordinating an increasing diversity of firms bears too much on the network side, in particular in terms of related conditions of trust which are more and more demanding. Our view is that if the debate on the viability of the industrial system under IIPS is restricted to the sole categories of firms and network, Ehud Zuscovitch's rather pessimistic vision is probably verified. This would signify a gradual erosion of the possibility of creation of surplus in the economy and a drastic slowdown of the rate of growth in the economy.

Our proposal in the following part of the contribution is to go beyond these two categories and explore the micro dimension of IIPS, by looking at the intra-firm level. At this intra-firm level we propose to highlight the functioning of 'knowing communities' as the active units of specialization, and as the active sources of creation of surplus in the IIPS regime that can under certain conditions compensate for firms and networks failures in the creation of surplus in the IIPS regime. Situated at the interstices of the hierarchical structures of firms, knowing communities play the unique role of innovative slack that permanently contributes to the creation of surplus of the economic system.

THE VIABILITY OF THE NEW PRODUCTION REGIME: THE LIMITS OF IIPS SPECIALIZATION AND THE ROLE OF KNOWING COMMUNITIES

As a new form of industrial structure that tackles the fundamental challenge of simultaneously increasing variety and efficiency, networks of firms have limits. As pressures for an ever larger variety is expressed by the economic environment, there is a need for an increasing proliferation of specialized and distinct firms to be integrated by network structures. For example as Boland and Tenkasi (1995) underlined, 'the first generation of cellular phones used five sub technologies, but their third generation incorporated fourteen distinct sub technologies.... The increasing proliferation of specialized and distinct knowledge communities and the need for their integration has also resulted in the emergence of new organizational forms.' The building of a sufficient level of trust within the network may succeed in diminishing the transaction costs between partners or at least may keep them at a reasonable level, but it cannot prevent the growing constraint of a different source of costs: the fixed (sunk costs) associated with the building of knowledge.

If we consider a given firm, the ability to integrate an ever diverse number of specialized bodies of knowledge is not infinite. First, because ever growing absorptive capabilities (which are far from being a free good) are required for understanding external knowledge; second, because the ability to design cognitive platforms[3] of integration is required for shaping the external knowledge in a form suitable for further exploitation by the firm; and third because in this system the firm is compelled to specialize ever further in its domain of specialized knowledge. This requires the building of an infrastructure of knowledge (models, grammar, codes, etc.) that generates ever increasing sunk costs[4] with the growing risk that these costs could not be compensated anymore by the advantages of networks.

Moreover, a natural tendency of these networks of firms is to put pressure on firms for them to become super-specialized units in a given domain of knowledge. We consider that this is not the vocation of firms (at the very limit the natural consequence of this phenomenon is the dissolution of firms into markets). Firms are not machines to produce an ever more advanced type of specialized knowledge: they are places of co-ordination of different bodies of knowledge that assure an efficient organization of an existing division of work, and matrices where the delicate integration of disperse forms of knowledge is permanently elaborated and refined.

The risk is thus high that the development of networks will face a limit, as firms might be when dealing with too complex knowledge. To some extent, such a situation is comparable to the risk of an overflow of information that leads the firms as, A. Chandler (1962, 1977) for instance clearly explained to abandon the functional forms of organization for the multidivisional form in order to cope more efficiently with information. This problem was solved by a kind of division of work between the hierarchy in charge of the strategic decision making and the divisions in charge of operational decisions. However, here in the IIPS system, firms have to cope with a much stronger problem of complexity. They have to deal with an overflow of knowledge – which cannot be solved by a simple reorganization of internal structures of firms: it implies to revisit both the intra- and inter- dimensions of interactions of specialized units of knowledge.

After the managerial evolution described by Chandler (ibid.), large firms have developed a functional division of labour to such an extent that the corresponding divisions behaved like internal service providers, with professional competences very specific to the function but relatively common to all firms. Following Gaffard's analysis (2003), the further step of the historical process appears when large firms start externalizing the functional divisions, leading to the creation of new sectors. Then the quasi-integration of the former firms with these new business services can lead to a specific type of network co-ordination. This is a relevant view of today's business organization, mixing various types of co-ordination mechanisms and labour division, optimising knowledge management as well. But with the concept of knowing communities we go even further in the complexity of organizational arrangements.

Our view is that this risk of a knowledge overflow calls for another form of collaborative organization to cope with variety and efficiency: we argue in the following that this form could not rely on simple 'networks of firms', but on more 'complex networks' associating firms and these elementary sources of specialized knowledge: the 'knowing communities'. The reasons for considering knowing communities are at least twofold: first they are the natural loci of formation of a specialized knowledge (the 'elementary active units of specialization'), second they take charge in their functioning of the fixed costs associated with the building of a specialized piece of knowledge.

A 'knowing community' can be defined as a gathering of 'individuals who accept to exchange voluntarily and on a regular basis about a common interest or objective in a given field of knowledge'. Through this regular exchange, common cognitive platforms and common social norms are built that assure the cohesion of the community and guide the newcomers' behaviours. The critical role of 'knowing communities' in the building of useful knowledge for society has been recently popularized by successful examples such as the Linux open source community, or the role of the community of repairmen ('reps') at Xerox.

Let us consider the latter example, described by Orr (1990). According to the author, the job of a rep is best described as a continuous improvisation taking place in a network of relationships between clients, machines and other reps. Reps work autonomously. They intervene at Xerox clients' places where they have to repair a machine, by themselves most of the time. Together, they form a community of practice, which allows mutual help and the collective problem solving of unusual breakdowns. When they talk about machines, technicians actually build up a common identity while exchanging what each of them gained from various experiences. They create a stock of operational competences in sharp contrast with handbooks and user guides that are promoted by the hierarchy. This constantly actualized repertoire is transmitted through oral culture. It allows reps to cope with managerial evolutions that downplay their role by increasingly relying on work methods disconnected from the reality of workers and machines. The highly technical work of reps appears as a resource socially distributed, stored and diffused above all by informal conversations. Moreover, through their ability to maintain constant interactions with other communities (engineers, designers, etc.) in the organization, reps are at the origin of many creative ideas at Xerox.

These examples underline the role of communities as modes of economic co-ordination that 'economize' on hierarchy to produce useful knowledge. As the knowledge-based economy expands, knowing communities play an increasing role, because they can take on some significant parts of the 'sunk costs' of the process of generation or accumulation of specialized subsets of knowledge.[5] These costs correspond for instance to the progressive construction of languages and models of action and interpretation that are required for the implementation of new knowledge, that cannot be covered through the classical signals of hierarchies (or markets). This setting is likely to compensate for some organizational limitations (learning failures) that firms face when confronted with the need to continuously innovate and produce new knowledge.

Knowing communities might be found in traditional work divisions and departments, but they also cut across functional divisions, spill over into after-work or project-based teams, and straddle networks of cross-corporate and professional ties:

For example, within firms, classical communities include functional groups of employees who share a particular specialization corresponding to the classical division of labour (e.g. marketing or accounting). They also include teams of employees with heterogeneous skills and qualifications, often coordinated by team leaders and put together to achieve a particular goal in a given period of time (Amin and Cohendet 2004).

We could also refer to the communities of engineers working in different (and therefore competing) firms but sharing the same problems and objectives, who often help one another independently from – and out of view of – their own hierarchies. Such behaviours do not really confront or substitute for hierarchies: they just complement them, as a kind of parallel co-ordination mechanism. Knowing communities can be of a different nature in the way they deal with knowledge: some of them may focus on the accumulation and exploitation on a given field of knowledge ('communities of practice'), some of them (others) on the exploration of a new field of knowledge ('epistemic communities'). As Wenger (1998) noted, a community drawing on interaction and participation to act, interpret and innovate, acts 'as a locally negotiated regime of competence'. Therefore communities are suppliers of sense and collective beliefs for agents, and play a central role of co-ordination in the firm.

Following Boland and Tenkasi (1995), we can view knowledge intensive firms as organizations composed of multiple communities with highly specialized technologies, expertise and knowledge domains:

Organizations are characterised by a process of distributed cognition in which multiple communities of specialized knowledge workers, each dealing with a part of overall organizational problem, interact to create the patterns of sense making and behaviour displayed by the organization as a whole. Organizations are necessarily characterised by distributed cognition because their critically important processes and the diversity of environments and technologies to be dealt with are too complex for one person to understand in its entirety. Communities develop unique social and cognitive repertoires which guide their interpretation of the world (Boland and Tenkasi 1995).

If knowing communities in firms could thus be seen as elementary units of specialized knowledge, they also provide another potential advantage to firms: they strongly contribute to equipping firms with absorptive capabilities. Knowing communities are never bound within the limits of organizations. They permanently interact in their specialized domains of knowledge with the outside world collecting new ideas and benchmarking the best conditions of practice. They nurture the organization by continuously bringing new pieces of specialized knowledge which have just been tested and validated in the outside world. The different communities in the organization could thus been seen as a set of diverse sources of absorptive capabilities that potentially allow firms to benefit form a diversity of knowledge. As Cohen and Levinthal (1990) remarked,

> ... diversity of knowledge plays an important role: in a setting in which there is uncertainty about the knowledge domains from which potentially useful innovation may emerge, a diverse background provides a more robust basis for learning because it increases the prospect that incoming information will relate to what is already known. In addition to strengthening assimilative power, knowledge diversity also facilitates the innovative process by enabling the individual to make novel associations and linkages.

However, as Cohen and Levinthal also emphasized,

> ... absorptive capabilities refer not only to the acquisition or assimilation of information by the organization, but also to the organization's ability to exploit it. Therefore, an organization's absorptive capacity does not simply depend on the organization's direct interface with the external environment. It also depends on transfers of knowledge across and within subunits that may be quite removed from the original point of entry. To understand the sources of a firm's absorptive capacity, we focus on the structure of communication between the external environment and the organization as well as among the subunits of the organization, and also the character and distribution of expertise within the organization.

These remarks lead to the crucial issue of both the interactions between a community and the hierarchical structures of the firm, and the interactions between knowing communities as a source of creation of surplus in the IIPS regime.

DIVISION OF LABOUR AND DIVISION OF KNOWLEDGE WITHIN THE FIRM: THE DYNAMICS OF KNOWLEDGE THROUGH THE FUNCTIONING OF KNOWING COMMUNITIES

Under the Smithian vision, the process of specialization that leads to a further division of labour was supposed to be conceived, supported and controlled by the firm and to be achieved within the firm. Our main hypothesis, in line with Ehud Zuscovitch's vision, is that under the IIPS regime, firms do not have anymore the possibility of fully controling the process of increased specialization within their hierarchical structures. As explained above, they are confronted with increasing fixed costs of building the cognitive platforms required for handling ever more complex levels of specialization. That is the reason why the process leading to the new division of knowledge will be increasingly delegated to these informal groups, or knowing communities that can take in charge (each community in its own domain of competence) at negligible costs the efforts of accumulating and developing knowledge. The new division of knowledge that results from the interactions between these communities (in this dynamics, new communities continuously emerge, others disintegrate) depends on the preceding division of labour, but to some extent only. As we have seen, it is possible that communities emerge from functional divisions. However, this is far from being the rule. In general communities do not coincide with the existing hierarchical structures of the organization. They are transversal to these structures. In short, in the IIPS regime, the division of knowledge does not in general correspond to the division of labour, and it is precisely by comparing the dynamics of these two structures (division of knowledge and division of labour) that we locate the new sources of surplus in the IIPS regime.

In the following paragraphs we develop these arguments, by distinguishing between two main cases. First, we consider the specific case of knowing communities confined within an existing functional department. In such a case we are in a context which could be seen as an extension of the perspection drawn by Adam Smith, with some important nuances that are introduced, in particular the possibility of outsourcing the new source of knowledge and developing 'vertical networks of activities'. Second, we consider the general case of knowing communities that develop interactions and contacts far beyond the limits of any functional department. They generally spread 'horizontally' rather than 'vertically', and through their activities of knowledge they tend to activate the formation of 'horizontal' networks.

Knowing Communities Confined Within an Existing Functional Department

When knowing communities are 'confined' within an existing functional department, their dynamics are compatible with the formation of 'vertical' networks of quasi-integrated firms that result from the process of externalization of the functional divisions of firms (as analysed in particular by Gaffard 2003). In this movement of externalization it is often the communities which were formally in a given functional department of the firm that constitute the active units of reproduction and extension of knowledge in the new outsourced companies. It is also often thanks to these communities that have maintained contacts and practices of co-ordination with their former structures that the vertical networks of activities hold and remain coherent. One can even advocate that in some cases it is the knowing community itself that has provoked the movement of separation with the former structure. In the case for instance of American Airlines, Evans and

Wuster (2000) mentioned a significant externalization of activities that was achieved in the late 1970s, with the outsourcing as a subsidiary of Sabre, a company that concentrated all the activities of seat reservations. The authors underlined that the active unit of the outsourcing process was a community of engineers within American Airlines that strongly believed in this new venture, and succeeded in convincing the hierarchy of American Express of the interest of outsourcing this new business.

When knowing communities undertake their knowledge activities within a given functional department as in the above case of American Airlines, they circulate and accumulate knowledge within the existing division of labour. The division of labour entails a process of learning by doing that contributes to increasing skills and expertise within each specialized hierarchical unit (functional departments, business units, etc.), and thus to enhancing the accumulation of specialized knowledge. This is in line with the classical Smithian vision, with the nuance that the dynamics of accumulation of knowledge is undertaken by the knowing community and not placed under the direct control of the hierarchy of the firm. From this accumulation, new productivity gains can then be obtained. In this context, to the extent that competences and routines are developed by learning-by-doing (and/or have tacit components that transfer only in face-to-face interaction), the division of labour not only defines the problems to be solved, but also the direction, potential, participants, etc., of the learning that can take place. In other words, the division of labour does not only lead to (static) efficiency outcomes. It also determines (by defining the setting for learning) the learning outcomes, and thus the competences and routines that will develop inside the firm. The division of labour drives and shapes the division of knowledge.

Knowing Communities are not Confined within a Given Department

In general knowing communities are not confined within a given department: they cross the boundaries of functional departments and Strategic Business Units (hereafter, SBU). Within and across organizations, there are many different kinds of communities, which vary in terms of structures and memberships. Some of these communities emerge spontaneously from the hierarchical structures of the firm (some workshop staff may constitute a community of practice overlapping with the functional division of operations in the firm), while some communities may result from adherence to a common passion of very dispersed individuals within the firm (for instance, a community of practice of people interested in computing in a given organization will not in general overlap with the staff of the computer department, but may comprise agents of the firm working in different positions, departments and even locations of the firm). Such communities, bound by relations of common interest, purpose, or passion, and held together by routines and varying degrees of mutuality, are now being considered as key sites of knowledge formation and exchange, and learning. Communities thus defined seem to embody the pragmatic, situated, interactive, and enacted knowledge routines that have been outlined above. These are characteristics that, as we have seen, cannot be captured by individual-centred or classical organization-centred approaches. Instead, they do seem to fit with the workings of project- or task-focused groupings caught up in daily processes of interaction and practices of knowing through the combination of conscious and unconscious rhythms of work.

According to Brown and Duguid's interpretation (1991) the firm can be viewed

> ... as a collective of communities, not simply of individuals, in which enacting experiments are legitimate, separate community perspectives can be amplified by inter-changes among communities. Out of this friction of competing ideas can come the sort of improvisational sparks necessary for igniting organizational innovation. Thus large organizations, reflectively structured, are perhaps well positioned to be highly innovative and to deal with discontinuities. If their internal communities have a reasonable degree of autonomy and independence from the dominant worldview, large organizations might actually accelerate innovation.[6]

It is through the dynamic interactions between communities that new configurations of the knowledge net emerge by creating new meanings, new linguistic routines, and new knowledge. The creation of new knowledge in an organization is often the result of an open system transformation of that organization's communities of knowing as they question and revise routines and create new processes and relationships between themselves. Producing knowledge to create innovative products and processes in such firms requires the ability to draw up strong perspectives within a community, as well as the ability to take the perspective of another into account. Thus, a critical role of the hierarchy of the firm is to contribute to organizing efficient platforms of knowledge within firms in order to facilitate the interaction between knowing communities.

This conception of the role of knowing communities suggests that through the interactions between knowing communities there is an accumulation of innovative potential of new knowledge or a 'creative slack' that is activated by 'horizontal' relationships between the active units of knowledge. To sum up the discussion at this point, we have underlined that knowing communities when confined to functional departments can be considered as the active units of knowledge that favour the movement of increasing specialization and the formation of vertical networks that follows an increasing division of labour. While, in general through their dynamic interactions that cross the frontiers of any hierarchical structure, knowing communities are reservoirs of creative ideas that emerge from permanent horizontal interactions.

We have thus suggested that in the IIPS regime, a growing part of the creation of surplus will result form the daily functioning and interactions between knowing communities. From their activities a creative potential of innovative ideas and principles emerge. However, the main question is now to explain how this creative potential is then turned into actual industrial activities. How the new potential division of knowledge can drive the division of work. The answer to this key question depends on the delicate matching between the formal structures of the firm and the informal structures of its knowing communities. Firms should design on a permanent basis the mechanisms that assure a satisfactory circulation of the knowledge held by knowing communities to the formal structures of the firm. From the above analysis, the firm in the IIPS regime can be progressively viewed as a specific organizational design in charge of continuously matching a division of labour (that is expressed by the 'hard architecture' of formal divisions such as functional departments, business units, formal team structures, etc.) with a division of knowledge (that is expressed by the different informal knowing communities, each being specialized in a given domain of knowledge). In order to better assess the implications of such a statement, we pinpoint in the following the differences between the firm viewed in a classical mass production regime and the firm embedded in the IIPS regime.

More precisely, along this perspective, we can interpret the role of firms in the IIPS regime as institutional designs that continuously assure the matching between two structures: a formal structure that embodies the division of labour and an informal structure that expresses the division of knowledge based on the evolution of specialized knowing communities. The two structures co-evolve in the following way: the division of labour partly drives a further division of knowledge; but in turn, due to the active functioning of knowing communities, a new division of knowledge is formed that tends to superimpose itself on the former division of labour. This is the source of surplus at the level of the firm. And the role of the manager-entrepreneur is to arrange and reorganize the former division of labour by taking into account the new productive combinations suggested by the informal structure of knowledge.

As the firm faces more and more unpredictable environments, the division of work might no more be the driver of the division of knowledge, but on the contrary, the boundaries between activities and hence the division of work, less and less stabilised, could be interpreted as the outcome of the evolution of knowledge and competences that products or technologies mobilize or might mobilize. As Langlois (2002) noted, 'the problem of defining boundaries of encapsulation (between tasks) becomes even more challenging in a dynamic setting. For example the tasks in an innovative development project cannot be partitioned in advance, since knowledge is continually changing'. In this knowledge-based perspective, the firm can be seen as a platform of coherent distinctive competences (a 'nexus of competences') which result from the matching between the formal and informal.

To reinterpret Ehud Zuscovitch's hypothesis, 'the nature of the relationship between specialization and surplus creation has drastically changed with the emergence of IIPS'. The surplus is the consequence of encounter between two different structures and the subsequent reorganization it follows. It appears as a function of 'reorganization'. When moving to a more efficient technology or production method, the surplus is generated not by the application of the method by itself, but rather as a consequence of one structure being added on top of the other, causing the agents to adjust to and integrate the novelty, thus expending much productive energy.

To sum up, under the mass production system, the overall process of increasing returns is a sequential process characterised by an initial exogenous increase of demand, followed by adjustments in production units leading to increased capacity. This gives birth to a reorganization possibly accompanied by outsourcing operations together with some process innovation which tends to increase efficiency. In this regime of standardization, with a reasonable division of labour, the firm could be practically independent: the real competences and skills that are required could be developed 'in-house'. In IIPS, Ehud Zuscovitch advocates that the firm has to cope with the necessity mastering a growing number of bodies of knowledge: the only possible access to such diversity is through co-operation with other producers and users of the products. The new regime calls for a 'network organization' that superimposes itself on the production system with a multiplicity of micro-markets with particular specifications for smaller production runs. This hypothesis suggests extending Ehud Zuscovitch's understanding of networks along the perspective described below, in the last part of this article.

REINTERPRETING THE ROLE OF NETWORKS: FROM NETWORKS OF 'FIRMS' TO COMPLEX NETWORKS OF INSTITUTIONS AND COMMUNITIES

The above interpretation suggests a revised understanding of innovative networks. Increasing specialization passes a new threshold of complexity due to the growing potential of product variety. In what could be called an 'advanced' IPPS regime, networks should not be seen anymore as a mere constellation of firms viewed as specialized units of knowledge. Innovative networks are complex co-operative mechanisms that articulate firms as distinctive platforms of competences (or nexus of competences) relying on knowing communities as specialized active units of knowledge. In other words, to tackle the fundamental challenge of simultaneously increasing variety and efficiency, an innovative network is the matrix where a two-stage 'interactive process' takes place.

First, a network is the scene for a fundamental process of 'differentiation of competences' between firms. Each firm seeking to build a distinctive competence focuses on a given domain of knowledge by articulating together different specialized units of active knowledge which reside under the boundary of the firm (knowing communities). However, whatever the richness and diversity of these internal sources of specialized knowledge, the firm always needs to set up co-operative agreements with other firms. The necessity to access more differentiated skills to cater for micro-market requirements always calls for the need to negotiate access to complementary competences held by other firms.

In this process of mutual building of distinctive competences, there is another strong reason for the existence of networks: the firm developing a distinctive competence faces the risk of 'competence trap' which implies being locked in an isolated domain of knowledge. As a result firms need to invest simultaneously in building a distinctive competence and in building with other firms the 'generic' body of knowledge (Nelson 1987) which expresses the common features of technology, understanding of problems, problem-solving heuristics, beliefs widely shared among a specific group of firms or in the industry.[7] Thus, networks are places where the diversity and heterogeneity of competences between firms at the micro-level and the emergence of common patterns of behaviour or common characteristics at the meso- and macro-levels (Nelson 1991; McKelvey 1998) are simultaneously built. Networks can thus be seen as devices through which firms can develop principles of co-ordination and co-operation in order to sustain the co-construction process between distinctive competences (firm level) and collective competences (industry level).[8] Common knowledge building[9] is necessary in order to share and integrate more effectively aspects of knowledge which are dispersed and distributed among complementary firms.

This interpretation of network is somewhat similar to the distinction made by Kogut (2000) between two approaches to network analysis. The first approach emphasizes the individual advantages gained by firms in accessing to external knowledge. This vision of networks focuses on the distinctive benefits individual firms derive by extending their relationships and their opportunities through access to network resources. The focus is on the distinctive capability of firms to combine internal and external knowledge on their own. The second approach, as Kogut (2000) underlines imputes part of the value of a firm to the capability of its embedded network. 'The network is itself knowledge, not in the sense of providing access to distributed information and capabilities, but in representing a form of coordination guided by enduring principles of organization.' As one takes into account the systemic dimension of learning one shifts from learning at the firm level to network level learning where the 'the structure of a network implies principles of coordination that not only enhance the individual capabilities of member firms, but themselves lead to capabilities that are not isolated to any one firm.'

With respect to the distinctive and common competence co-construction process, firms can only exploit effectively their distinctive competences once part of their private and proprietary knowledge becomes common knowledge. In this case participation in networks through disclosure eases the diffusion of knowledge and speeds up the emergence of common competences to improve the co-ordination process within the network. As Van de Ven (1993) notes:

> ... there is an ongoing tension for each industry participant to organize its own proprietary functions and distribution channels as opposed to contributing to the creation of the industry's resources and institutional arrangements. Although the former may advance the firm's position as a first mover in the short run, the latter provides the infrastructure that ultimately influences the collective survival of the emerging industry.

Second, a network is the scene of a process of *increasing specialization of knowing communities*. Increased specialization is inherent to the functioning of knowing communities. Each community is generally attached to a given firm (or lab) and its evolution is based on and strengthens or exacerbates distinctive competences. However, as we have seen in the preceding part, these communities do not act in isolation, and their cognitive efforts are not confined within the boundaries of firms. Each community involved in the emerging phase of an innovation deploys considerable efforts to 'command the attention' of other communities (generally attached to other firms) to convince them of the relevant interest of the knowledge it has elaborated. If they succeed, the building of a common base of knowledge by communities attached to different firms or labs can be undertaken and the process can accelerate through different tests and elaboration of diverse codes. Through generalization, the use of knowledge in new contexts favours different degrees of exploration and variety generation leading to further steps of differentiation.

As we have underlined, the process of generation of variety cannot be analysed by looking at the sole role of institutions (firms and labs). Institutions are not the active units of elaboration of this common base indispensable for the development of a specific innovation. The active units which undertake the codification process are in our view the diverse communities that participate in the development of innovation. These communities are essential in the phase of emergence of novelty, then their role diminishes (and the role of institutions increases) as the knowledge base is increasing and reinforced.

These two fundamental processes that take place within a network – the process of differentiation of competences of firms and the process of *increasing specialization of knowing communities* – continuously co-evolve with mutual adjustments. The distribution of competences that drives the allocation of knowledge between firms is based on the prior production and accumulation of knowledge achieved by the knowing communities attached to each respective firm. In turn, the distribution of competences shapes the cognitive efforts of knowing communities in a new round of production of new knowledge. Network is thus at the centre of the relationship between specialization and surplus creation under the advanced regime of IPPS. In its various forms, differentiation generates an extremely high potential for cross-fertilization: skills combination may stimulate creativity and productivity. In a Schumpeterian perspective, it continuously stimulates new combinations. In short, network is an arena where both creation and allocation of knowledge resources are at play simultaneously. New solutions elaborated in networks come permanently on top of former structures.

CONCLUSION

Our aim in this contribution was to investigate Ehud Zuscovitch's concern about the viability of networks in what he called the IIPS system (which he would probably accept to call today the 'knowledge-based economy'). Our view is that if we restrict the concept of network to the sole network of firms considered as the ultimate units of specialization of knowledge, then the system will face severe limitations. The questioning of the viability of the industrial system in the IIPS regime concerns the viability of the firm itself and its ability to cope with ever increasing levels of specialization. There are unavoidable limits to the ability of hierarchical structures to afford the sunk costs associated with the building of new knowledge.

We have suggested that the necessary 'slack' of innovative resources which constitutes the source of surplus in the new regime of growth comes from knowing communities. These economic elements are active units of knowledge specialization that offer the unique advantage of bearing a significant amount of the sunk costs associated with the building of specialized pieces of new knowledge: they are an indispensable complement to the hierarchical structures for the survival of firms in a regime of permanent innovation.

Seen through these lenses, the firm tends to become a 'community of communities' to refer to Brown and Duguid's vision. More precisely, we suggest that firms in the IIPS regime are viewed as nexus of competences that articulate hierarchical structures and knowing communities. As a consequence, networks should not be seen anymore as networks of firms (in terms of hierarchical structures) but rather as networks of nexus of competences (firms articulating hierarchical structures and knowing communities) in which the viability and the sources of surplus come from the active role of knowing communities in the generation of new knowledge.

The perspective suggested by Ehud Zuscovitch raises a series of important issues for economic analysis. According to us two main issues at least should be emphasized.

First, Ehud Zuscovitch's vision clearly invites revisiting the traditional Smithian conception of the relation between division of labour and division of knowledge. The Smithian perspective, considers the division of knowledge as a 'consequence' of the division of labour. One can argue that in innovative environments, the causality tends to be reversed: the division of knowledge tends to precede the division of labour. However, much more importantly, we think that in the new regime of growth, what matters is the constant interactions and feedback between the division of knowledge and the division of labour. In particular through the working of knowledge communities, a new division of knowledge tends to emerge and to separate from the preceding division of labour. This is precisely where the source of surplus comes from, and this is precisely where the role of networks is indispensable: networks can be considered as the mechanisms which rearticulate the new division of knowledge with the division of work, where the new solutions elaborated in the system are superimposed on former structures. Networks can thus be seen as tools providing an essential coherence for the economic system.

Second, Ehud Zuscovitch's vision calls for an in-depth reconsideration of the evolutionary theory of the firm. There is much to be done in the perspective drawn by Brown and Duguid and some others, to place knowing communities at the heart of the conception of the evolutionary firm. For instance, among the difficulties is the need for reinterpreting the role of routines as the key building blocks of the evolutionary firm. To a large extent, routines have been conceived as resulting from an existing division of labour in the firm. Analysing knowing communities seems to suggest a renewed way to look at routines, in particular at their formation and emergence in the processes of creation of new knowledge.

NOTES

1. This extension is in particular based on the continuation of the research done in Strasbourg along Ehud Zuscovitch's perspective. Ehud worked during the most of his career, including his PhD, in the community of researchers of BETA, a joint unit in economics and management science between CNRS and University Louis Pasteur, Strasbourg. He benefited from and gave a lot to this community, specifically in the areas of innovation economics and Science & Technology programmes evaluation.
2. By including priority-to-members mechanisms, networks necessarily introduce inefficiencies and welfare losses. However, this can be justified if these costs are offset by efficiency gains in the form of enhanced capacity to differentiate skills and products, and hence to contribute to economic growth.
3. Ciborra (1996) defines a platform as a 'meta-organization shaping structures and routines into typical forms like hierarchies or networks.'
4. As the use of markets or hierarchies generates specific costs, 'networking costs' arise when firms develop network coordination. They typically have the nature of sunk costs because they are very specific (rather cognitive than physical) assets.
5. See for instance Cowan, David and Foray (1997).
6. Brown and Duguid's suggestion opens an interesting agenda of research: large firms may find in the functioning and activation of their communities considerable potential of innovation that could contribute to counter balance the traditional bureaucratic handicap of large firms towards innovation.
7. Dosi (1982) used the technological paradigm and technological trajectory concepts in order to underline the fact that such generic knowledge bases are highly structured, and tend to evolve along structured trajectories. This collective aspect of knowledge refers mainly to general knowledge, in the sense that it is applicable to many situations, codified knowledge and common knowledge which can easily be shared among a large set of firms in a sector (i.e. engineering or technical communities within or across industries).
8. This dialectic process between distinctive and common competences is also underlined through the 'discovery cycle' proposed by Nooteboom (2000) which combines exploitation and exploration dynamics. Nooteboom considers the discovery cycle as an interactive process between consolidation, generalization, differentiation and reciprocation stages. Consolidation of knowledge is based on two rationales at the industry and organizational levels. The first is to improve efficiency through standardisation, codification and better co-ordination between systemic linkages. The second is to favour generalization that is the expansion and transfer of knowledge to new contexts: 'consolidation serves as a platform for expansion and new applications.' Both consolidation and generalization have to do with convergence of competences, variety reduction, and dissemination and diffusion of the same knowledge base in varied settings (different products, organizations and industries).
9. Common knowledge building within networks can take different forms: developing a common language; developing common cognitive frameworks, interpretative capabilities and patterns; developing shared understanding; favouring some commonality of specialized knowledge in order to improve the absorptive capacity of platform members; etc.

REFERENCES

Amin, A. and P. Cohendet (2004), *Architectures of Knowledge: Firms, Capabilities and Communities*, Oxford, UK: Oxford University Press.

Arrous, J. and E. Zuscovitch (1984), 'La diffusion intersectorielle des matériaux synthétiques' in Cohendet P. et al. (eds), *La Chimie en Europe: Innovations, Mutations et Perspectives*, Economica, pp. 141–238.

Arrow, K. (1962), 'Economic welfare and the allocation of resources for invention', in NBER (ed.), *The Rate and Direction of Inventive Activity: Economic and Social Factors*, Princeton University Press, pp. 609–625.

Boland, R. and R. Tenkasi (1995), 'Perspective making and perspective taking in communities of knowing', *Organization Science*, 6 (4), 350–372.

Brendle, P. and E. Zuscovitch (1985), 'Organisation des entreprises: l'impact des technologies de l'information', *Revue Française de Gestion*, 51 (1), 115–121.

Brown, J. and P. Duguid (1991), 'Organizational learning and communities of practice: toward a unified view of working, learning and innovation', *Organization Science*, 2 (1), 40–57.

Chandler, A. (1962), 'Strategy' and 'Structure': Chapters in the *History of the Industrial Firm*, Cambridge MA: MIT Press.

Chandler, A. (1977), *The Visible Hand: The Managerial Revolution*, Cambridge, MA.: Harvard University Press.

Ciborra, U. (1996), 'The platform organization: recombining strategies, structures, and surprises', *Organization Science*, 7 (2), 103–118.

Cohen, W. and D. Levinthal (1990), 'Absorptive-capacity – a new perspective on learning and innovation', *Administrative Science Quarterly*, 35 (1), 128–152.

Cowan, R., P. David and D. Foray (2000), 'The Explicit Economics of Knowledge Codification and Tacitness', *Industrial and Corporate Change*, 9 (2), 212–253.

Dosi, G. (1982), 'Technological paradigms and technological trajectories', *Research Policy*, 11 (3). 147–162.

Evans, P. and T. Wuster (2000), *Blown to Bits*, Boston, MA: Harvard Business School Press.

Gaffard, J.-L. (2003), 'Coordination, marché et organization: essai sur l'efficacité et la stabilité des économies de marché', *Revue de l'OFCE*, 85 (April), 235–270.

Kogut, B. (2000), 'The network as knowledge: generative rules and the emergence of structure', *Strategic Management Journal*, 21 (3), 405–425.

Langlois, R. (2002), 'Modularity in technology and organization', *Journal of Economic Behavior & Organization*, 49 (1) 19–37.

McKelvey, M. (1998), 'Evolutionary Innovations: learning, entrepreneurship and the dynamics of the firm', *Journal of Evolutionary Economics*, 8 (2), 157–175.

Nelson, R. (1987), *Understanding Technical Change as an Evolutionary Process*, Amsterdam: North-Holland.

Nelson, R. (1991), 'How do firms differ, and how does it matter?', *Strategic Management Journal*, 12 (special issue), 61–74.

Nelson, R. and S. Winter (1982), *An Evolutionary Theory of Economic Change*, Cambridge, MA: Harvard University Press.

Nooteboom, B. (2000), 'Transformation: puzzles, perspectives and proposals', Inaugural lecture, Erasmus University, Rotterdam.

Orr, J. (1990), *Talking About Machines: an Ethnography of a Modern Job*, Ithaca, NY: Cornell University Press.

Teubal, M. and E. Zuscovitch (1993), 'Knowledge differentiation and demand revealing through network evolution', in B. Johansson et al. (eds), *Patterns in a Network Economy*, Berlin: Springer Verlag, pp. 15–32.

Van De Ven, A. (1993), 'The emergence of an industrial infrastructure for technological innovation', *Journal of Comparative Economics*, 17 (2), 338–365.

Wenger, E. (1998), *Communities of Practice: Learning, Meaning and Identity*, Cambridge: Cambridge University Press.

Willinger, M. and E. Zuscovitch (1988), 'Towards the economics of information-intensive production systems', in G. Dosi, C. Freeman, R. Nelson and L. Soete (eds), *Technical Change and Economic Theory*, London: Frances Pinter, pp. 239–255.

Zuscovitch, E. (1983), 'Informatisation, flexibilité et division du travail', *Revue d'Économie Industrielle*, **25** (3), décembre, 50–61.

Zuscovitch, E. (1985), La dynamique du développement des technologies – éléments d'un cadre conceptuel, *Revue Économique*, **36** (5), 897–916 (on PERSEE website).

Zuscovitch, E. (1998), 'Networks, specialization and trust', in Cohendet P. et al. (eds), *The Economics of Networks*, Berlin: Springer Verlag.

9. The Implementation of National Competition Policy Law and the Dynamics of Price–Cost Margins: Evidence from Belgium and the Netherlands 1993–1999

Jozef Konings, Patrick Van Cayseele and Frédéric Warzynski

INTRODUCTION

One of the main economic aims of the European integration process was to foster growth through the benefits of increased competition (see e.g. the famous Cecchini Report 1988). Another complementary aspect of integration was to modify and harmonize the existing domestic regulations to make the economic environment more 'competition friendly'. National legislations related to the defence of a competitive environment were adapted from the European law, i.e. Articles 85 and 86 of the Treaty of Rome and the merger legislation. The speed at which this convergence took place varied to a large extent among the different countries.

Behind the reassessment of the importance of competition policy, we find a strong belief that the promotion of competition has a positive effect not only on innovation and productive efficiency, but also on allocative efficiency. Consumer and total welfare are higher in a more competitive environment and governments have an interest in establishing and maintaining a competitive product market.

A natural question to ask is whether competition policy is effective. The empirical literature has been surprisingly silent about it, while theoreticians and practitioners have been debating about the pro and contra of various aspects of antitrust policy enforcement. Warzynski (2001 2003) analysed the dynamics of price–cost margins in U.S. manufacturing using sector level data, and linked it to the history of antitrust enforcement: pricing was found to be less competitive during the lax enforcement period. However, we also raised the issue that firm level data was needed to study the dynamics of markups. Using firm level data, we provided in a previous paper (Konings, Van Cayseele and Warzynski 2001) a simple test to assess the effectiveness of competition policy by comparing two countries with a different approach towards the protection of competition: Belgium which had adopted a law protecting competition that came into effect in 1993; and the Netherlands where competition authority only became active in 1998 and where cartels were tacitly tolerated (de Jong 1990). During the period 1993–1997, price–cost margins were found to be higher in the Netherlands than in Belgium.

In this paper, we apply the methodology of Roeger (1995) to analyse the dynamics of price–cost margins (PCMs) using a large microeconomic dataset of Belgian and Dutch firms and relate it to the introduction of a new competition law and to the importance of import competition. We update the previous paper by using a different methodology, extending the period of analysis (1993–1999) and by examining more in details the importance of cyclicality and trade.

The effect of competition policy should be approached from a dynamic perspective (rather than a static one) because the competitive process is itself dynamic. We will analyse the evolution of PCMs as suggested by the recent work of Sutton (1991, 1997): equilibrium prices P (or PCMs) are a declining function of the number of firms (N) on the market; however the slope may differ depending on the degree of competition (defined as a conduct) in the market. The theoretical framework is sufficiently robust to allow for all types of interactions between firms and therefore captures all possible oligopoly models. While strategic interactions between firms affect the position and slope of the $P(N)$ function, a number of exogenous parameters, such as the toughness of competition policy, also influence the position of the function.

We make various contributions: first, we test whether the toughness of competition policy has an effect on the $P(N)$ function, that is, the toughness of price competition. We approximate the toughness of price competition in two ways: through a cross-country comparison and through a within-country dynamic comparison. In our first approach, we compare PCMs in two countries, one of them having a well documented weak protection of competition over most of the period. In the second approach, we analyse the dynamics of PCMs in a given country that experienced a dramatic switch of regime: in 1998, competition policy was toughened in the Netherlands with the creation of the Dutch competition policy authority (known under its Dutch acronym, NMa, for Nederlandse Mededingingsautoriteit), as part of a general strategy to increase competitiveness of the Dutch economy. By studying the dynamics of PCMs we try to get some insights into the effectiveness and role of competition policy. Most other papers in the literature (starting with Hall 1986; see also e.g. Domowitz, Hubbard and Petersen 1988; Roeger 1995) have focused on a static approach to the pricing behaviour of firms, using aggregate time series data to estimate the average PCM in an industry over a very long time period. The second contribution of the chapter lies in the data and in the methodology that we follow. We use an extensive firm level dataset covering a large proportion of firms in the Belgian and Dutch manufacturing over the period 1993–1999. Using firm level data allows us to increase the number of observations, to capture the heterogeneity of behaviour in an industry and to analyse the short-run dynamics of PCMs in a given industry. We find that: first, PCMs are still estimated higher in the Netherlands than in Belgium; second, however, they have declined in the Dutch manufacturing industry following the introduction of the new competition law and have converged to the level observed in Belgium; third, moreover trade appears to discipline the industry as the PCMs are positively linked to import price index. We introduce our methodological framework based on Hall (1986, 1988) and Roeger (1995) after we present the change in policy in Belgium and in the Netherlands. We then describe our dataset and discuss our results before we conclude.

COMPETITION POLICY IN BELGIUM AND THE NETHERLANDS: THEORY AND PRACTICE

Belgium

The system of price regulation was aimed at fighting inflation and maintaining consumer purchasing power, as well as correcting for undesirable market outcomes by guaranteeing fair prices. It forced firms to notify the Ministry of Economic Affairs of price increase to obtain its approval. The system was increasingly criticized, as economists questioned its relevance on macroeconomic ground in a small open economy where the price level is mainly fixed by exogenous factors. The policy was moreover seriously criticized on a microeconomic ground as facilitating co-operation between firms and as distorting the signalling role of prices. In the late 1980s the price regulation system was abolished. The regulatory system was mainly replaced by a new competition law that came into effect in April 1993. The new law was designed very similarly to the European Union legislation, i.e. Articles 85 and 86 of the Treaty of Rome and the Merger regulation. Three institutions were established to put law into practice:

- An investigation body under the authority of the Ministry of Economic Affairs (the Service for Competition) Committee;

- A mixed advisory body, composed half of economic experts and half of representatives of the Ministry (the Central Economic Council) firm does not innovate to grow rapidly (at the time of innovation);
- An independent decision body (the Council for Competition);

The organizational structure reveals that the Ministry of Economic Affairs plays an important role both directly and indirectly: it grants exemptions, can ask the Service to investigate a case and more importantly, the Service is part of the Ministry. This casts '*doubt about the independence and effectiveness of the court*' since it must rely on information received from the Ministry.

Moreover the Service suffers from *lack of financial resources and understaffing*. As a result only merger cases are investigated at the expense of the fight against anticompetitive practices and the treatment of demand for exemptions. Between 1993 and 1996, 170 notifications of concentration were presented to the Council which, for 22 of them, there was no time to analyse the case, so that the mergers were implicitly allowed to proceed. Out of 70 complaints only 19 were investigated. Out of 40 demands of exemption, only nine were treated and three decisions were taken (*Le Soir*, 19 February 1997, 'L'autorité anti-cartel belge dénonce les promesses oubliées'). A drift toward dangerous amateurism was denounced. All these factors led to an increasing feeling of frustration of the members of the Council: some resigned, others spoke to the press about the structural problems encountered by the authority (*Le Soir*, 24 December 1996, 'Le Conseil de Concurrence risque l'implosion'). The chairman of the Council has been changed repeatedly (for various reasons). Politicians promised to act so as to improve the situation (*Le Soir*, January 1997, 'Elio Di Rupo s'est engagé à doter l'institution anti-cartel de moyens suffisants à l'exercice de sa tâche'), but it is only recently (the new law was voted in 1999) that the law has been modified to provide more resources to the competition authority. The turnover threshold above which firms have to report their proposed mergers was raised, and the resources were increased sixfold: as a consequence, 40 additional investigators were hired by the Service of Competition and it was decided that four members of the Council would have a permanent position, while all members used to be part-timers before that.

These problems suggest that the competition authorities have not been operating as they should have and that a period of adjustment is necessary before establishing credibility.[1]

Netherlands

Compared to Belgium, the Dutch political authorities have been slower to adapt the legislation to the European standard. They were traditionally more inclined to tolerate or even favour cartels (de Jong 1990). These were numerous and were fought only if they injured general interest (abuse principle), a notion that was not defined in the law.

This attitude gradually changed under pressure from the EU. In 1991, the existing law from 1956 was amended. Later a new competition law inspired by the European principles was introduced. The NMa, the Dutch Competition Authority, was created and started operating in January 1998. Contrary to Belgium, a single institution is responsible for investigating, judging and punishing. It is divided in three sections:

- Investigation, Supervision and Dispensations (OTO);
- Control of Concentrations (CoCo);
- Decisions, Objections and Appeals (BBB);

Although the new body is also part of the Ministry of Economic Affairs, the new law ensured that the Ministry's intervention would be presented to the parliament in an annual report and that the current structure would be revised after three years, making the NMa a transient body before a more independent institution is established.[2]

In a report presented to the Organisation for Economic Co-operation and Development (OECD), the Dutch delegation stated that 'the NMa must build up a reputation and image of irreproachable conduct, reliability and independence, and must meet the usual Dutch standards for supervisory authorities in the financial sectors or the standards of the Bundeskartelamt in Germany' (OECD 1997). In their first year of operations, the NMa has been flooded with demands for exemption in the context of the transitional regime (1040 while they had expected only 350), has received 266 complaints (139 were settled) and 154 mergers have been reported. The importance of the complaints has impeded the NMa pursuing their own investigations, but devoted attention to investigations which should be started in 1999. In 1999, the reduction in the number of exemptions freed resources for other activities, which will be used 'first and foremost to investigate hidden cartels and abuses of dominant position ... A focus on the sectors and/or practices where the highest prosperity gains can be realized will benefit the effectiveness of enforcement policy' (NMa 1999, p.6). In that year, the NMa received 158 notifications of proposed concentration, 92 new complaints, while the demand for exemptions was significantly reduced: 16 new applications were received. Of the complaints 29% were processed, 65% withdrawn, sometimes after informal contacts, and 6% discontinued as the necessary information had not been provided. Most complaints concerned services, construction, telecommunications, utilities and agricultural sector, and almost not the manufacturing industry, except the printing, publishing and media industry.

The general assessment of the work of the NMa after two years of operation is relatively positive, compared to Belgium. The competition authority was well prepared to accomplish the tasks delegated by the legislator and has been successful in handling in a limited amount of time the large number of cases which it was faced with. We would expect that the improvement in the protection of competition would be effective and lead to a more competitive environment, and we test this in this paper.

THEORY

The Model

A firm i in time t operates according to a production function

$$Q_{it} = \Theta_{it} F(N_{it}, M_{it}, K_{it})$$

where Θ is an index of technical progress, N is the level of employment, M is the amount of intermediary input needed for production and K is capital. In a competitive environment, assuming constant returns to scale and competitive pricing in the input market, it can be shown that:

$$\Delta q_{it} = \alpha_{N_{it}} \Delta n_{it} + \alpha_{M_{it}} \Delta m_{it} + \upsilon_{it} \tag{9.1}$$

where

$$\alpha_{N_{it}} = \frac{W_{it} N_{it}}{P_{it} Q_{it}}$$

$$\alpha_{M_{it}} = \frac{P_M M_{it}}{P_{it} Q_{it}}$$

$$\Delta x_{it} = \Delta \log\left(\frac{X_{it}}{K_{it}}\right), \ X = Q, N, M$$

$$\upsilon_{it} = \Delta \log\left(\Theta_{it}\right)$$

However, when firms have market power, they will set a higher price that exceeds the marginal cost. In this case: $p/c \equiv \mu \geq 1$. Equation (9.1) then can be generalized as:

$$\Delta q_{it} = \mu_{it}(\alpha_{N_{it}}\Delta n_{it} + \alpha_{M_{it}}\Delta m_{it}) + \upsilon_{it} \qquad (9.2)$$

This also can be written as:

$$\Delta q_{it} - \alpha_{N_{it}}\Delta n_{it} - \alpha_{M_{it}}\Delta m_{it} = \Delta y_{it} = \beta_{it}\Delta q_{it} + (1-\beta_{it})\upsilon_{it} \qquad (9.3)$$

where β_{it} is the Lerner index ($\beta_{it} \equiv (p_{it}-c_{it})/p_{it} = 1-1/\mu_{it}$). The above equations are directly derived from production theory, *without any explicit link to behaviour in the product market. The model does not even constrain profit maximization* (see Basu and Fernald 2001, footnote 15). A more structural approach, following Levinsohn (1993), which yields the same equations as above, is presented in the next subsection.

The Structural Model

Profit maximization with respect to output levels implies (time index is omitted for convenience):

$$\left(1+\frac{s_i \lambda_i}{\eta_j}\right)^{-1} = \frac{P_i}{MC_i} = \mu_i$$

or

$$\beta_i = \frac{P_i - MC_i}{P_i} = 1 - \frac{1}{\mu_i} = \frac{s_i \lambda_i}{|\eta_j|} \qquad (\text{PCM})$$

where s stands for market share, η_j stands for the price elasticity of demand for a given good in industry j and $\lambda_i \equiv \partial Q/\partial Q_i$ stands for the conjectural variations term with $Q = Q_0 + \lambda_i Q_i$ and Q_0 is taken as given by the firm. If $\lambda = 1$ then firms engage in Cournot competition. If $\lambda = 0$ the firm is price taker and sets price equal to marginal cost. The parameter λ is the most important focus of the so called New Empirical Industrial Organization (hereafter, NEIO) literature (see Bresnahan 1989). It is interpreted as the average conduct and can vary depending on various factors, such as the emergence of new competitive forces. In this paper we prefer to link β to the notion of toughness of price competition such as described in Sutton (1991, 1997). This function relates the equilibrium price, or price–cost margin, to the market structure of a given industry in a static view, but also in a dynamic view, describes how price–cost margins evolve following entry and/or switches in the competitive environment. To derive the firm demand for inputs, rewrite the profit function as:

$$\Pi_i = P_i Q_i - W_i N_i - P_{M_i} M_i - R_i K_i$$

where W is the wage paid to labour, P_M is the price of intermediate goods and R is the cost of capital.

Maximizing profit with respect to inputs implies:

$$\Theta_i \frac{\partial F_i}{\partial N_i} = \left(1 + \frac{s_i \lambda_i}{\eta_j}\right)^{-1} \frac{W_i}{P_i}$$

$$\Theta_i \frac{\partial F_i}{\partial M_i} = \left(1 + \frac{s_i \lambda_i}{\eta_j}\right)^{-1} \frac{P_{M_i}}{P_i}$$

$$\Theta_i \frac{\partial F_i}{\partial K_i} = \left(1 + \frac{s_i \lambda_i}{\eta_j}\right)^{-1} \frac{R_i}{P_i}$$

Totally differentiating the production function yields:

$$dQ_i = \Theta_{it} \left(\frac{\partial F_i}{\partial N_i} dN_i + \frac{\partial F_i}{\partial M_i} dM_i + \frac{\partial F_i}{\partial K_i} dK_i\right) + F_i \, d\Theta_i$$

Substituting the partial derivatives of F_i in the latter gives:

$$dQ_i = \mu_i \left(\frac{W_i}{P_i} dN_i + \frac{P_{M_i}}{P_i} dM_i + \frac{R_i}{P_i} dK_i\right) + F_i \, d\Theta_i$$

This is basically the same equation as in Levinsohn (1993) working with discrete changes and is similar to the approach of Hall. To see this divide both sides of the latter equation by Q_i so that:

$$\frac{dQ_i}{Q_i} = \mu_i \left(\frac{W_i N_i}{P_i Q_i} \frac{dN_i}{N_i} + \frac{P_{M_i} M_i}{P_i Q_i} \frac{dM_i}{M_i} + \frac{R_i K_i}{P_i Q_i} \frac{dK_i}{K_i}\right) + \frac{d\Theta_i}{\Theta_i}$$

Using different notations and assuming constant returns to scale one obtains (9.2) which, as before, also can be written to be equivalent to (9.3). Therefore by regressing the Solow residual Δy over Δq we obtain a simple testable equation yielding an estimate of the Lerner index. We also look at the evolution of this parameter.

Econometric Concerns

Applying this method to estimate PCMs suffers from a number of shortcomings that could lead to unreliable and high estimates.

Endogeneity

In our specification both Δy and Δq should be viewed as endogenous. Then estimating Equation (9.2) by OLS yields biased and inconsistent estimates since $E(\Delta q' v) \neq 0$.

When using aggregated U.S. data, the usual instruments are the growth of real GDP, the price of oil, the political party of the president or the growth of military purchases (Hall 1986 and 1988, Hakura 1998, Jun 1998, Domowitz et al. 1988). Blanchard (1986) and Roeger (1995) criticized these instruments on the basis that productivity shocks are likely to be correlated with the instruments as well. We might deal with this issue in two different ways: first, in Konings et al. (2001) we estimated the model using instrumental variables (IV) for the endogenous variable Δq. We used General Method of Moments estimates *à la* Arellano and Bond (1991) using as instruments lagged values of the level of output in firm i for $t-2$ onwards. Second, to avoid the search for instruments, Roeger (1995) has modified Hall's model so that he could estimate markups by OLS in a consistent and unbiased way. In this paper, we follow the latter approach. This method has another important advantage: we do not have to search for the right deflator as the estimation proceeds with nominal values. The usual practice is to deflate sales with the producer price index and cost of materials with a material price index at the industry level. A methodology using nominal values does not constrain identical prices and allows some heterogeneity in the pricing behaviour.

Identifying restrictions on β_{it}

As is clear from equation (PCM) the price–cost margin is indexed at the level of the firm i and varies with time t. Such an estimation is obviously impossible and we have to define a subset where we assume common behaviour in terms of PCMs. We estimate the average PCMs for the entire sample and in a given industry j for a given year. The elasticity of demand can be assumed to be similar for all firms in a given industry if the good is homogeneous. However, the firm specific term of market share remains. Ideally one could try to define market share by dividing firm output by the industry sales (including imports and excluding exports), if the relevant market at the product level could be identified, but this is not possible with our dataset, because the degree of industry aggregation is too important. We try to control for this issue by letting PCMs vary by size class. However, as already noted by Levinsohn (1993), estimates were not very different. This might be because our dataset only contains (by definition) relatively large firms with an established product market.

Treatment of outliers
One problem in analysing inter-industry differences using extensive firm level data is the existence of outliers. Misreporting and improper analysis of the changes in a firm life cycle (i.e. change in the unit of analysis due to vertical integration or disintegration) can influence the estimates and lead to the wrong conclusions. To remedy this problem, we use different techniques of robust regression. The results provided in the paper follow the method of Beaton and Tukey (1974).

The Roeger Method

Knowing the problem of finding good instruments in a sector level analysis, Roeger (1995) proposed an extension of the Hall methodology that incorporates information about the dual, or price based, Solow residual under imperfect competition. Under constant returns to scale, the cost function of firm i in time t is written as (omitting firm and time index to simplify notations):

$$C(W, R, P_M, Q, \Theta) = \frac{G(W, R, P_M)Q}{\Theta}$$

Marginal costs is then:

$$\frac{\partial C}{\partial Q} \equiv MC = \frac{G(W, R, P_M)}{\Theta}$$

Logarithmic differentiating marginal cost, we get:

$$\Delta mc = \frac{\partial G}{\partial W}\frac{W}{G}\Delta w + \frac{\partial G}{\partial P_M}\frac{P_M}{G}\Delta p_M + \frac{\partial G}{\partial R}\frac{R}{G}\Delta r - \upsilon$$

Using Shephard's lemma (Varian 1992, p. 74), we also have that:

$$\frac{\partial G}{\partial W} = \frac{\Theta N}{Q}, \ \frac{\partial G}{\partial P_M} = \frac{\Theta M}{Q}, \ \frac{\partial G}{\partial K} = \frac{\Theta K}{Q}$$

Therefore

$$\Delta mc = \frac{\Theta N}{Q}\frac{W}{G}\Delta w + \frac{\Theta M}{Q}\frac{P_M}{G}\Delta p_M + \frac{\Theta K}{\partial Q}\frac{R}{G}\Delta r - \upsilon$$

or

$$\Delta mc = \frac{WN}{C}\Delta w + \frac{P_M M}{C}\Delta p_M + \frac{RK}{C}\Delta r - \upsilon$$

Finally:

$$(1-\beta)P = MC = \frac{G(W,R,P_M)}{\Theta}$$

so that we get an expression for the dual Solow residual:

$$\alpha_N \Delta w + \alpha_M \Delta p_M + (1-\alpha_N - \alpha_M)\Delta r - \Delta p = -\beta(\Delta p - \Delta r) + (1-\beta)\upsilon \quad (9.4)$$

Subtracting Equation (9.4) from Equation (9.3) we get:

$$(\Delta q + \Delta p) - \alpha_N(\Delta n + \Delta p_N) - \alpha_M(\Delta m + \Delta p_M) - (1-\alpha_N - \alpha_M)(\Delta k + \Delta p_K) \quad (9.5)$$

where $\Delta x = \dfrac{\Delta X}{X}$, $X = Q, P, N, M, K, P_N, P_M, P_K$. Equation (9.5) simplifies to:

$$\beta[(\Delta q + \Delta p) - (\Delta k + \Delta p_K)]$$

Renaming the left-hand side as *SR* and the term under bracket in the right hand side as x, one obtains a simple testable equation that can be estimated by OLS.

What Does the PCM Say about Conduct?

The (PCM) equation is derived under assumption of Cournot competition. The expression becomes slightly more complicated in the case of Bertrand competition with differentiated products, and β would then depend on the own price elasticity and the cross price elasticity (see e.g. Röller and Sickles 2000). Such an analysis therefore assumes to a large extent that an homogeneous good is produced in the industries investigated, which is clearly an overstatement for some. We must keep in mind this limitation in interpreting the results.

The conjectural variations term reflects the belief that one firm has of the other firms output decisions in reaction to its own choice and therefore reflects the intensity of competition in a given market. The use of conjectural variations has been widespread in the NEIO literature (Bresnahan 1989).

Shapiro (1989) defends to some extent its empirical use as 'a convenient way of parameterizing oligopolistic behavior', which moreover 'can be quite useful for comparative statics purposes'. However, he also claims that 'the idea behind conjectural variations is logically flawed': they 'are an attempt to capture a dynamic concept, response in a static model'.[3]

We adapt our methodology to the limitations of the dataset and to the theoretical weaknesses of the conjectural variations approach. In any case, Equation (9.5) remains valid under general conditions of industry pricing, but its interpretation depends on the type of competition within the industry and on other characteristics. This approach is very much in line with the philosophy of the bounds approach to inter-industries studies in empirical industrial organization. In contrast with the NEIO tradition which relies on institutional, technological and product specific features of the industry to write down a detailed structural model and test it, the bounds approach will look for mechanisms that hold good across industries. In our case, we will analyse a potential effect of a switch of regime due the introduction of a new competition law.

Consider the function $p(I|\theta)$ where p is price, I is the number of firms present in the market, and θ is a shift parameter indexing the toughness of competition. This function summarizes the properties of the final subgame in a multi-stage game-theoretic model. By assumption, $p_I(I|\theta) < 0$. Assume also that $p_\theta(I|\theta) < 0$.

> The parameter [θ] captures the effect of exogenous influences such as legal restraints in competition, or changes in transport costs that intensify competition between remote firms. Changes in such factors lead to a shift in the functional relationship between equilibrium price and profit, for any given market structure (Sutton 1997, pp.70–71).

To make it simple, we test whether the introduction of a new competition law led to a switch in the toughness of price competition.

Our Specification

Our methodology will be to look at the evolution of β (as an aggregate function of elasticity, market structure and conduct in link with our structural model or simply as a useful indicator of pricing behaviour) in a set of industries. We will therefore estimate the average PCM in a given industry j in a given year t. We also test the effect of various factors:

- Cyclicality of PCM: game theoretical models have provided two contradicting theories of cyclical pricing behaviour. According to Green and Porter (1984), PCMs are procyclical because collusion is less sustainable in recessions than in booms; Rotemberg and Saloner (1986) argue the opposite. Both models are equally plausible and therefore, ultimately, the answer to this question is an empirical one (Rotemberg and Woodford 1990 document the existing evidence). We test the effect of the cyclicality by interacting our x variable with the growth of real Gross Domestic Product (ΔGDP), as a *conjectural indicator*:

$$SR_{it} = \beta x_{it} + \beta_2 x_{it} \times \Delta GDP_{ct} \qquad (9.6)$$

where c is a country index.

- Did the implementation of a competition policy law have any effect on markups?: Unfortunately the toughness of competition policy enforcement is difficult to establish quantitatively. We approximate it by capturing the dynamics of markups, controlling for all other potential candidates, and by comparing PCMs in two different environments:

  - We look at the evolution of the PCMs in a country before and after a 'switch of regime' occurred. In Belgium the new competition authorities started to operate from April 1993 on. This means that if competition policy was effective in disciplining the industry, we should observe a decline in the markup ratio after this date. Our dataset only starts in 1993 and we are not able to say much about the dynamics.[4] Our emphasis in this paper, at least in terms of dynamic evolution, is on the Dutch case. In the Netherlands, the switch of regime should have taken place from 1998 onwards. Therefore, if firms changed their behaviour after the appearance of a competition policy authority, this should be reflected by a lower PCM.

$$SR_{it} = \beta_3 x_{it} + \beta_4 x_{it} \times D9899 \qquad (9.7)$$

where $D9899$ is a dummy equal to 1 if the year is 1998 or 1999, and 0 otherwise. We also control for the previous aspects analysed. In line with what has been written previously in Sutton's terminology, we check whether the policy change led to an increase in the toughness of price competition.

  - We compare PCMs between the two countries, therefore capturing institutional details which might lead to differences in pricing behaviour.

$$SR_{it} = \beta_4 x_{it} + \beta_6 x_{it} \times NED \qquad (9.8)$$

The analysis is done at two levels. First, we analyse the effect of these factors for manufacturing industry as a whole. Then, we disaggregate the manufacturing industry to 22 subsets and test the relevance of these factors within a given industry.

- Finally we check whether a change in the import price index (*IPI*) induces a decrease in the markup. The price of imports should better reflect the competition effect of imports than their volume:

$$SR_{it} = \beta_7 x_{it} + \beta_8 x_{it} \times IPI_{jt} \qquad (9.9)$$

DATA

Our dataset combines various editions of the Amadeus CD Rom Top 200000, which provides information of the top 200,000 European companies. The dataset is compiled by a private company, Bureau van Dijk, on the basis of initial information supplied by national partners. By definition, the dataset does not cover the entire population of firms but only the largest ones. As a consequence, and in line with the theoretical model proposed in the previous section, we would expect price–cost margins to be higher since these firms are firms with an established market and probably a high market share for their specific product(s). Therefore, an important point to stress is that our conclusions are only valid for the subsample that we analyse. However, these firms constitute the bulk of the activity of the manufacturing sector in both countries and the identification of potential differences in pricing behaviour would be indicative of differences in the economic environment. Another important point to stress is that these data are comparable across countries, as the Bureau Van Dijk harmonizes the various accounting practices in the European Union.

Using firm level panel data for the estimation of price–cost margins has a number of advantages over aggregate sector level data: first it increases the number of observations and allows us to capture the heterogeneity of pricing behaviour among firms; second, it allows us to estimate the PCM for every year and to follow its evolution on a relatively long time period (1993-1999); third, the estimating equation derives from the theory of the firm and therefore requires firm level data.[5]

Table 9.1 displays the summary statistics of our samples in 1998: the average Dutch is much larger than the average Belgian firm (around 7 times larger in terms of revenue but the variance is much larger too, and the median is only around twice bigger, indicating the presence of outliers). The share of labour costs in turnover α_N was around 18–19 % on average, and the share of material costs α_M in turnover was much larger (between 52 and 55%).

Table 9.1 Summary statistics in 1998

	Nr. Obs.	mean	std. dev.	median
Belgium				
Operating revenue (*Q*)	1769	2850.70	8177.40	940.40
Tangible fixed assets (*K*)	1795	478.10	1765.20	123.60
α_N	1751	0.19	0.13	0.16
α_M	1730	0.55	0.20	0.56
δ (depreciation rate)	1720	0.46	1.00	0.31
Netherlands				
Operating revenue (*Q*)	1213	729.70	4015.90	117.50
Tangible fixed assets (*K*)	1776	130.30	795.10	14.20
α_N	1019	0.18	0.11	0.17
α_M	529	0.52	0.18	0.51
δ (depreciation rate)	1233	0.24	0.42	0.18

Note: Q and K are expressed in millions Belgium Francs; α_N, α_M , and δ are percentages.

RESULTS

The Dynamics of PCMs

We start with estimating Equation (9.4) for each year and for the entire sample. This illustrates the evolution of the average PCM. Table 9.2 shows that the estimates of the Lerner index are statistically different from 0, indicating a sign of market power in every period. Average estimates are higher in the Netherlands than in Belgium. However, they are moving closer to each other, as the Dutch average PCM has fallen from 0.31 in 1993 to 0.25 in 1999. The difference between the Belgian and the Dutch average is significant for all years except 1996 and 1999.

We also analyse the cyclicality of the PCM by linking the dynamics of our estimates to the evolution of real GDP growth as in Equation (9.6). Results are shown in the first column of Table 9.3. The main result remains valid: average PCMs remain higher in the Netherlands than in Belgium. The difference is estimated at 0.05 (i.e. an 18% difference) and is statistically significant. We moreover find evidence of countercyclical price–cost margin in the Netherlands. Finally, we find a significant decrease in PCM after 1998 in the Netherlands of 0.04. However, we should not put too much emphasis on these estimates, as it is an average across industries which are likely to be very different in terms of structure, conduct and elasticities. We prefer to analyse the dynamics within sectors.

Table 9.2   Estimates of average PCM in Belgian and Dutch manufacturing

	Belgium		Netherlands	
	β	Nr. obs.	β	Nr. obs.
average	0.232*** (0.001)	9060	0.282*** (0.002)	2345
1993	0.225*** (0.003)	952	0.311*** (0.007)	343
1994	0.218*** (0.004)	1030	0.264*** (0.006)	336
1995	0.212*** (0.003)	1383	0.292*** (0.007)	323
1996	0.256*** (0.003)	1404	0.247*** (0.006)	287
1997	0.231*** (0.002)	1463	0.288*** (0.006)	399
1998	0.232*** (0.002)	1562	0.251*** (0.007)	412
1999	0.244*** (0.003)	1542	0.254*** (0.008)	251

Note: Standard errors in parentheses; ***/**/* indicates significance at 1%/5%/10%.

Table 9.3   Estimates of average PCM in Belgian and Dutch manufacturing (controlling for cyclicality)[*]

	β	β
Belgium		
β	0.241*** (0.003)	0.231*** (0.002)
β_2	–	3×10^{-4} (7×10^{-4})
Netherlands		
β	0.307*** (0.005)	0.312*** (0.005)
β_2	–	-0.011*** (0.002)

Note: See Table 9.2, footnotes.

PCMs by Industry

The presence of significant market power in our sample is further confirmed by the results in Table 9.4. We disaggregate the manufacturing industry in 22 2-digit subindustries, then estimate β in each subset. The Lerner index is significantly different from zero in all subindustries. Moreover, the PCM is higher in the Netherlands than in Belgium in 15 out of 18 subindustries where we can compare them. There are substantial differences across sectors. These differences might be due to different factors that we investigate below and might hide different dynamic evolutions. We then analyse the dynamics of PCM within sectors and try to explain this heterogeneity. We analyse the link between GDP growth and PCMs by sector in Table 9.5.

Table 9.4 Estimates of average PCM (β) in Belgian and Dutch subindustries

	Belgium	Netherlands
NACE 15: Food and beverages	0.165 (0.002)	0.180 (0.004)
NACE 16: Tobacco	0.209 (0.016)	
NACE 17: Textiles	0.233 (0.003)	0.267 (0.011)
NACE 18: Clothing	0.224 (0.006)	0.397 (0.055)
NACE 19: Leather, luggage and footwear		
NACE 20: Wood, straw and plaiting materials	0.219 (0.005)	0.204 (0.017)
NACE 21: Pulp, paper and paper products	0.271 (0.005)	0.272 (0.007)
NACE 22: Publishing, printing and media	0.296 (0.005)	0.405 (0.006)
NACE 23: Coke, refined petroleum and nuclear fuel	0.251 (0.012)	
NACE 24: Chemicals and chemical products	0.277 (0.003)	0.325 (0.007)
NACE 25: Rubber and plastic products	0.273 (0.004)	0.294 (0.008)
NACE 26: Other non-metallic mineral products	0.323 (0.004)	0.407 (0.008)
NACE 27: Basic metals	0.230 (0.005)	0.309 (0.010)
NACE 28: Fabricated metal products	0.201 (0.004)	0.284 (0.006)
NACE 29: Machinery and equipment nec	0.233 (0.004)	0.237 (0.007)
NACE 30: Office machinery and computers	0.206 (0.015)	0.145 (0.013)
NACE 31: Electrical machinery and apparatus nec	0.212 (0.005)	0.166 (0.007)
NACE 32: Radio, TV and communication equipment	0.248 (0.012)	
NACE 33: Medical, precision and optical instruments	0.254 (0.011)	0.396 (0.040)
NACE 34: Motor vehicles, trailers and semi-trailers	0.143 (0.005)	0.268 (0.012)
NACE 35: Other transport equipment	0.194 (0.017)	0.239 (0.026)
NACE 36: Furniture, manufacturing nec	0.195 (0.005)	0.327 (0.009)

Note: Standard errors in parentheses. All reported coefficients are significant at the 1% level. NACE stands for the French definition: The Statistical Classification of Economic Activities in the European Community.

Innovation, economic growth and the firm

Table 9.5   Cyclicality of PCMs in Belgian and Dutch subindustries

NACE	Belgium β	β_2	Netherlands β	β_2
15	0.184	−0.009	0.286	−0.033
16	0.195		−	−
17	0.230		0.092	0.055
18	0.215		−	−
19	0.449	−0.162	−	−
20	0.236	−0.007**	0.152**	
21	0.251	0.010	0.260	
22	0.285	0.006*	0.358	0.019
23	0.328	−0.037	−	−
24	0.274		0.390	−0.023
25	0.293	−0.013	0.257	
26	0.330		0.456	−0.021
27	0.223		0.340	
28	0.201		0.296	
29	0.234		0.251	
30	0.271		0.462	−0.097
31	0.205		0.142	
32	0.247		−	−
33	0.208		0.940	−0.167
34	0.136		−0.140	0.105
35	0.149	0.020*	0.307	
36	0.173	0.011	0.693	−0.110

Note: See Table 9.4. Standard errors are not reported and are available upon request. We do not report coefficients with a non-significance level larger than 10%. Coefficients are significant at the 1% level except for coefficients with superscript **/* which indicates significance at 5%/10%.

Once we have controlled for cyclicality we can re-examine the PCM differential between Belgium and the Netherlands. We find a positive and significant estimate in 8 of the 18 sectors for which a comparison is feasible (see Table 9.6 where only estimates for β_3 are shown; note that the estimated regression equation is: $SR_{it} = \beta x_{it} + \beta_2 x_{it} \times \Delta GDP + \beta_3 x_{it} \times NED$). In the other 10 sectors the difference is not significant. This provides further support for our hypothesis that different institutional regimes and more specifically different approaches to the protection of competition leads to different firm pricing behaviour. Of course, *other explanations are possible.* Even at the industry level, it might well be the case that firms are operating along different product lines and that Dutch firms have specialized in different activities. The Dutch economy is also characterized by the presence of many multinationals relatively to Belgium. These firms have the possibility to use transfer pricing and compete at a different level (market share are usually computed at the national level, as concentration indices).

However, multinational enterprises are also present in industries characterized by scale economies and imperfect competition (Markusen 1995, p. 169), i.e. what we try to capture. In our summary statistics, we have noticed that Dutch firms were larger on average than the typical Belgian firm. However, we also noticed that price–cost margins did not vary by size class.

Table 9.6   The PCM differential between Belgium and the Netherlands

NACE	β_3
18	0.207 (0.059)
24	0.079 (0.016)
26	0.193 (0.019)
27	0.049** (0.024)
28	0.135 (0.019)
33	0.244 (0.060)
34	0.137 (0.036)
36	0.256 (0.053)

Note: See Table 9.5.

We should stress again though that we are limited in our analysis by the difficulty to identify the relevant product market in our dataset. It might be also that Dutch firms are more efficient, but this is not what is at stake here. What we analyse is the level and evolution of the Lerner index, and not the welfare implications in terms of trade off between productive efficiency and allocative efficiency. However, it is important to stress once more than the consensual view of competition is that it also leads to better incentives to innovate and to produce efficiently.[6] Another interesting characteristics of the Netherlands is the so called Polder model, an institutionally organized discussion between the government, firms and trade unions, which has introduced more labour market flexibility and moderate wage increase. But Belgium has also experienced a period of wage moderation which would have benefited the firms by limiting the bargaining power of workers. The Netherlands has also been assumed to have lower profit tax. However, the average corporate tax rate was relatively similar between the two countries (around 24% according to the European Commission). Moreover, any difference should be reflected in the price of capital. Lower tax rate would make capital cheaper, what provides incentives for more investment.

We now concentrate on the Dutch manufacturing and analyse the switch of regime variable (see Table 9.7 where only estimates for β_3 from the following regression equation: $SR_{it} = \beta x_{it} + \beta_2 x_{it} \times \Delta GDP + \beta_3 x_{it} \times D9899$). The results suggest that some sectors were more affected than others, in particular we observe a significant reduction in PCM for three sectors: food and beverages (NACE 15), publishing, printing and media (NACE 22) and basic metals (NACE 27). In those sectors there was certainly scope for improvement, and the fact that PCMs have declined in the manufacturing industry on average, and in these sectors more specifically, would act as evidence of an effective enforcement of competition policy, mostly as a deterrent. For one sector in particular (NACE 22: publishing, printing and media), the authorities have been extremely active and have clearly targeted their operations. In 1999, several exemptions and mergers have been rejected, 5 complaints have been submitted and the authority has imposed sanctions in 2 of them (NMa 1999). There appear to have been no interventions in the other sectors, so that it is difficult to link the evolution to direct intervention, but the establishment of a more credible threat might have deterred firms in these sectors to act in a anti-competitive way.

Table 9.7   The post-1998 effect in Dutch subindustries

NACE	$\Delta\beta = \beta_3$
15	−0.047 (0.015)
22	−0.055 (0.019)
24	0.087^{**} (0.042)
27	-0.069^{**} (0.033)

Note: See Table 9.5.

The effect of Import Prices

We also tested whether import prices could affect the pricing behavior of domestic firms. We use the Import Price Index provided by Eurostat at the 2-digit NACE Rev.1 level. In Konings et al. (2001), it was found that imports, measured by the import penetration ratio, did not discipline the industry in the Netherlands. We use here a different measure of import competition. Results are provided in Table 9.8 below (the regression equation is $SR_{it} = \beta x_{it} + \beta_2 x_{it} \times \Delta GDP + \beta_3 x_{it} \times IPI$ and estimates are reported only for β and β_3).

Table 9.8   Estimates of interactive effects of import penetration ratio

NACE	Belgium	Netherlands
x	0.174 (0.014)	0.238 (0.031)
$x \times IPI$	0.107 (0.013)	0.108 (0.033)

Note: See Table 9.5.

First, we see that the average PCM varies in the same direction as the import price index, which reflects a competitive effect of imports as a decline in import prices is associated with a decline in PCM. Second, the difference between the average PCM in the Netherlands and Belgium remains robust to the introduction of trade; third, the effect of import price index is almost exactly the same in Belgium than in the Netherlands.

We also experimented with other measures of import discipline like the ratio of import price over producer price and the evolution of this ratio. Results were relatively similar. Controlling for the cyclical behaviour of PCMs also yielded the same results. Replicating this analysis at the 2-digit level, we found a positive and significant effect in seven industries and a negative and significant effect in three industries for Belgium (among them the chemical industry); for the Netherlands, we found a positive and significant effect for five industries and a negative and significant effect for three industries (among them the printing and publishing industry and the chemical industry). This would suggest again (like in the previous chapter) that between-industries differences explain most of the results in Table 9.8, although there is a dynamic effect as well in some industries.

CONCLUSION

In this paper we analysed PCMs in the Belgian and Dutch manufacturing industry using firm level data, while most other studies used aggregate industry level data. We followed the approach developed by Roeger (1995) and added to this methodology by looking at 'switch of regime' aspects to represent different regimes of competition policy.

In the Netherlands, PCMs decreased after the competition authority became active, as the law was implemented coherently by a well prepared organization. This contrasts with Belgium where lack of preparation, amateurism and lack of resources impeded competition policy to be enforced effectively. Import prices were also found to discipline the industry, in contrast with our previous finding that import quantities did not. We believe that the methodology that we have taken is informative to assess the extent of market power as well as the effectiveness of policy measures in a dynamic setting. Competition is a dynamic process, hence competition policy should not be judged on the basis of static considerations alone.

Our 'switch of regime' analysis simply approximates the toughness of competition policy. In the future one would like to use an index of the toughness of competition policy built on objective or subjective information about the effectiveness of the competition authorities' actions, so that this type of analysis could be replicated in more general environments.

NOTES

1. For a more detailed description of the evolution of competition policy in Belgium, see Sleuwaegen and Van Cayseele (1998) and OECD (1998).
2. For an overview of the evolution of competition policy in the Netherlands see Brusse and Griffiths (1998) and OECD (1997).
3. A harsher critical view has recently been developed in Corts (1999).
4. In Konings et al. (2001), we had a dataset covering the years 1994–1996 and concluded that PCM remained constant after 1993. However, Warzynski (2002) provides results based on a previous time period (1988–1995) and shows that PCM did not fall after 1993. See the discussion in section 3.2 of that paper for an explanation.
5. A fourth reason is not important here in contrast with Konings et al. (2001): it allows the finding of 'good' instruments by using lagged variables as instruments for the firm-level variable (Arrelano and Bond 1991).
6. What we could have done is to compute the true productivity shock, corrected for imperfect competition and compare the average productivity growth in both countries. Unfortunately it was impossible to find a good deflator for materials.

REFERENCES

Arellano, M. And S. Bond (1991), 'Some tests of specification for panel data: Monte Carlo evidence and an application to employment equations', *Review of Economic Studies*, **58** (2), 277–297

Basu, S. and J.G. Fernald, (2001), 'Aggregate productivity and aggregate technology', *European Economic Review*, **46** (6), 963–991.

Beaton, A.E. and J.W. Tukey, (1974), 'The fitting of power series, meaning polynomials, illustrated on band-spectroscopic data', *Technometrics*, **16** (2), 145–185.

Blanchard, O. (1986), 'Market structure and macroeconomic fluctuations: comments', *Brookings Papers on Economic Activity*, **17** (2), 323–328.

Bresnahan, T. (1989), 'Empirical studies of industries with market power', in: R. Schmalensee and R. Willig (eds), *Handbook of Industrial Organization*, **2**, North Holland, Amsterdam, pp. 1012–1057.

Brusse, W.A. and R. Griffiths, (1998), 'Paradise Lost or Paradise Regained? Cartel Policy and Cartel Legislation in the Netherlands', in S. Martin (ed.), *Competition Policies in Europe*, Elsevier, pp. 15–39.

Cecchini Report (1988), The European Challenge 1992, European Commission.

Conseil de Concurrence, (2000), Rapport annuel.

Corts, K.S. (1999), 'Conduct parameters and the measurement of market power', *Journal of Econometrics*, **88** (2), 227–250.

de Jong, H.W. (1990), 'Nederland: het kartelparadijs van Europa?', *Economisch Statistische Berichten*, **75** (3749), 244–248.

Domowitz, I., R.G. Hubbard and B.C. Petersen, (1988), 'Market structure and cyclical fluctuations in U.S. manufacturing', *Review of Economics and Statistics*, **70** (1), 55–66.

Green, E.J. and R.H. Porter (1984), 'Noncooperative collusion under imperfect price information', *Econometrica*, **52** (1), 87–100.

Hakura, D.S. (1998), 'The Effects of European Integration on the Profitability of Industries', *IMF Working Paper*, 98/85.

Hall, R.E. (1986), 'Market structure and macroeconomic fluctuations', *Brookings Papers on Economic Activity*, **17** (2), 285–322.

Hall, R.E. (1988), 'The relation between price and marginal cost in U.S. industry', *Journal of Political Economy*, **96** (5), 921–947.

Jun, S. (1998), 'Procyclical multifactor productivity: tests of the current theories', *Journal of Money, Credit and Banking*, **30** (1), 51–63.

Konings, J., P. Van Cayseele and F. Warzynski (2001), 'The dynamics of industrial markups in two small open economies: does national competition policy matter?', *International Journal of Industrial Organization*, **19** (5), 841–859.

Levinsohn, J. (1993), 'Testing the imports-as-market-discipline hypothesis', *Journal of International Economics*, **35** (1–2), 1–22.

Markusen, J.R. (1995), 'The boundaries of multinational enterprises and the theory of international trade', *Journal of Economic Perspectives*, **9** (2), 169–189.

NMa (1999), Annual reports.

NMa (1998), Annual reports.

OECD (1997), 'Annual report on competition law and policy in the Netherlands', Mimeo.

OECD (1998), 'In-depth examination of competition policy in Belgium', Mimeo.

Roeger, W. (1995), 'Can imperfect competition explain the difference between primal and dual productivity measures? Estimates for U.S. manufacturing', *Journal of Political Economy*, **103** (2), 316–330.

Röller, L.-H. and R.C. Sickles, (2000), 'Capacity and product market competition: measuring market power in a 'puppy-dog' industry', *International Journal of Industrial Organization*, **18** (6), 845–865.

Rotemberg, J. and J. Saloner, (1986), 'A super-game theoretic model of business cycles and price wars during booms', *American Economic Review*, **76** (3), 390–407.

Rotemberg, J. and M. Woodford, (1990), 'Cyclical markups: theory and evidence'. *NBER Working Paper*, 3534.

Shapiro, C. (1989), 'Theories of Oligopoly Behavior', in R. Schmalensee and R.D. Willig (eds), *Handbook of Industrial Organization*, **1**, Elsevier Science Publishers, 329–414.

Sleuwaegen, L. and P. Van Cayseele (1998), 'Competition policy in Belgium', in Martin, S. (ed.), *Competition Policies in Europe*, Elsevier, 185–204.

Sutton, J. (1991), *Sunk Costs and Market Structure*, MIT Press.

Sutton, J. (1997), 'Game Theoretic Models of market Structure', in D. Kreps and K. Wallis (eds), *Advances in Economics and Econometrics*, Cambridge: Cambridge University Press.

Varian, H. R. (1992), *Microeconomic Analysis*, London: Norton.

Warzynski, F. (2001), 'Did tough antitrust policy lead to lower markups in the US manufacturing industry?' *Economics Letters*, **70** (1), 139–144.

Warzynski, F. (2002), 'The dynamics of price cost margins in Belgian manufacturing: 1989–1995', Mimeo, K.U. Leuven.

Warzynski, F. 2003. The Dynamic Effect of Competition on Price Cost Margins and Innovation. Ph.D. Dissertation, K.U. Leuven.

10. Export Prices and Increasing World Competition: Evidence from French, German, and Italian Pricing Behaviour

Sarah Guillou and Stefano Schiavo

INTRODUCTION

The paper investigates the pricing behaviour of firms operating in foreign markets by looking at export prices set by French, German and Italian exporters for a large number of products and destinations. A large literature has established that firms often absorb part of exchange rate fluctuations in their own margins so as to limit the impact of such shocks on the price faced by foreign consumers. Moreover, this behaviour is often found to be heterogeneous across destination markets, a phenomenon labelled as pricing-to-market (hereafter, PTM). There are several reasons to rationalize such pricing strategies by profit maximizing firms, among which the existence of different demand price elasticities, and of different market conditions (competition level) stand out. We argue that firms decide to internalize part of exchange rate changes, i.e. to price-to-market, only when they have not enough market power to pass them through to final consumers, a choice that can be easily rationalized in terms of the need to conquer or preserve market shares. Hence, a better understanding of the PTM strategies adopted by exporting firms can shed light on the external competitiveness of an economy. Our detailed comparison of French, German and Italian export prices represents the first contribution of the paper as it allows us to draw some inference on the competitive position of these countries in the last three decades.

Existing works on the topic focus almost exclusively on estimating the elasticity of export prices to the exchange rate; here, on the contrary, we make one further step and investigate also the dynamic of profit margins, i.e. the part of the price that depends neither on production costs nor on the exchange rate. This focus is new to the literature and is a second way of contributing to research on the topic. More precisely, our empirical specification postulates that the export price is determined by a mark-up over the marginal cost. A fixed time effect over all destination markets proxies for the marginal cost or, better, for the average marginal cost faced by all firms located in a given country and exporting a given product. The difference between the marginal cost and the export price is then further decomposed into two parts. The first depends on exchange rate variations and it is often referred to as signalling PTM. The second is a fixed effect depending only on the destination: this gives information about the profit margins of firms on that particular export market. Our empirical analysis is based on export unit values for a sample of 178 manufactured goods commonly exported by France, Italy and Germany to 35 destination markets (which are again common to the three source countries) over the last three decades (1973–2003).

Contrary to what is usually reported in the literature, PTM is not widespread among French and German exporters, and concerns around one third of products exported by Italian firms. Also, the standard claim that PTM behaviour displays strong product specific features needs to be better specified: while we do find that PTM coefficients vary with products, our results suggest that export pricing is mainly determined by the characteristics of source and destination markets. This appears to be true both for the part of export price variation that responds to exchange rate changes and for profit margins.

The paper is organized as follows: next section contains a brief overview of the literature, and then we present our empirical methodology and the data. The remaining sections offer a detailed discussion of results, after which we perform some robustness tests. Finally, we draw some conclusions and outlines possible future research paths.

A GLANCE AT THE LITERATURE

The empirical literature has uncovered a widespread PTM behaviour by exporting firms: this is a pricing strategy aimed at selling the same product at different prices in different markets. Since the seminal work by Krugman (1987) exchange rate variations have been identified as one of the major causes of this behaviour. Subsequent theoretical analysis has established that in presence of segmented markets and of a non-constant elasticity of demand a monopolist shipping its products to several markets will adopt a PTM strategy (Goldberg 1995; Bergin and Glick 2005). More generally, when the exporting firm chooses voluntarily not to pass-through all exchange rate variations and so to stabilize prices in local (consumers') currency – either because of the need to defend its market share (as in Froot and Klemperer 1989), or for reputation motives (as in Krugman 1987) – then export to non-integrated markets will translate into price **Erreur ! Signet non defini.** differentials. Moreover, the variation in export prices expressed in the exporter's currency will have as a counterpart a variation of the profit margin of the opposite sign, which will depend on the exchange rate change.

This kind of behaviour has been documented by means of a number of empirical studies.[1] Complete pass-through of exchange rate changes into import prices is strongly rejected at short horizons, whereas in the long run it becomes larger and approaches unity. An incomplete pass-through implies a PTM strategy, whereas when the import price moves one-to-one with the exchange rate there is no PTM. The empirical literature claims that PTM behaviour has a product specific dimension (Knetter 1993; Gil-Pareja 2000; Parsley 2004), meaning that the degree of reaction of export prices to exchange rate variations is not uniform and varies sensibly with products exported by the same country. In more detail, PTM appears to be less diffused for differentiated products (Stahn 2006). Some sort of consensus exists as well on importance of export country characteristics, and in particular most studies find that U.S. exporters do not adopt PTM (Mann 1986; Knetter 1993; Goldberg and Knetter 1997; Gordon et al. 2002). Moreover, it seems that the degree of PTM depends negatively on the market share enjoyed in the destination market (Froot and Klemperer 1989; Feenstra et al. 1996; Asplund et al. 2001) as well as on the size of the latter (Gaulier et al. 2006). In truth, the claim that product specific characteristics are (among) the main determinants of PTM appears not to be very well founded. In particular, it is difficult to find product specific PTM coefficients that are independent of the source country; in other words, while one does see that the PTM coefficient differs for different products; one does not detect any true regularity common to different products exported from different countries.[2] For what concerns price–cost margins, works focusing on export margins are very few. Theoretical models based on imperfect competition predict that increased competition due to economic integration leads to a downward pressure on profits and hence on margins. Moreover, margins on foreign sales are supposed to be lower than domestic ones due to higher competition. Bernstein and Mohnen (1991) and Moreno and Rodríguez (2004) find results consistent with this view using data on Canadian and Spanish firms.

SPECIFICATION AND EMPIRICAL STRATEGY

The empirical specification we will be following in the analysis builds on Knetter (1989) and embodies the basic idea that with imperfect competition the price set by the exporter in its own currency is a mark-up over marginal cost, with the former being determined by the elasticity of demand in each destination market. Hence, Knetter (1989) proposes a decomposition of the export price into the marginal cost and a mark-up made up of two parts: one depending on exchange rate variations and one being destination-specific. In order to actually use this framework, one should be able to measure either the marginal cost or the mark-up. Knetter (1989) solves this problem by adopting a fixed effect regression model of the form:

$$\ln p_{jt} = \theta_t + \sum_{i=1}^{J} d_{ij}\lambda_i + \beta \ln s_{jt} \qquad (10.1)$$

where the time effect θ_t measures the marginal cost as it captures the part of the export price that is common across all destinations but varies over time; $d_{ij} = 1$ if $i = j$ and zero otherwise. The residual variation in the data represents then the mark-up, which can be divided into a part driven by exchange rate variations, and one that is destination-specific. The fact that the mark-up depends on exchange rate fluctuations results from the decision by the exporter to stabilize prices in the buyer's currency by absorbing part of the price change due to exchange rate movements. This in turn implies an incomplete pass-through. Now, although the phenomenon under scrutiny is the same, a sort of habit has emerged in the empirical literature whereby studies analysing the impact of exchange rate variation on 'import' prices label the phenomenon 'exchange rate pass-through' (hereafter, ERPT), whereas those focusing on 'export' prices name it 'pricing-to-market' (see Goldberg and Knetter 1997).[3]

Throughout the paper we will use a specification in first differences (as in Knetter 1993) to account for the fact that series are not stationary. Thus the model becomes an analysis of covariance model whereby export price variations are explained by a time specific effect common to all destinations (θ_t), a destination specific effect (λ_j), and a part resulting from exchange rate changes.[4] The main difference with respect to the specification adopted in Knetter (1993) is that we do not assume the mark-up to be constant over time, so that the destination specific terms appear also when the model is specified in first differences. It is worth stressing that neither equation (10.1), nor the following ones that we will actually estimate, aims at explaining 'why' export prices move the way they do, or to look into the 'determinants' of PTM. What the model allows one to do is rather a 'decomposition' of export price changes into marginal costs shocks and mark-up changes.

Our empirical strategy is threefold: we start from a pooled regression where for each of the export countries we analyse the behaviour of export prices over all products and all destination markets:

$$\Delta \ln p_{kjt} = \theta_{kt} + \sum_{i=1}^{J} d_{ij}\lambda_i + \beta\Delta \ln s_{jt} + \varepsilon_{kjt} \qquad (10.2)$$

Here p_{kjt} is the export price of product k sold in destination j at time t, while s_{jt} represents the bilateral exchange rate between the source country (France, Germany or Italy) and the destination j at time t. The λs are assumed to be destination specific, which implies that different products shipped to the same destination are characterized by the same (change in the) profit margin.[5] As it is clear, equation (10.2) provides us with an average behaviour over all products and destinations; while this allows us to draw a first interesting comparison between the three export countries, it nonetheless hides important details on the difference across products and destinations.

As the literature often claims that PTM behaviour by exporting firms is product specific, our second step entails applying the export price decomposition to each product separately. The estimating equation becomes:

$$\Delta \ln p_{jt} = \theta_t + \sum_{i=1}^{J} d_{ij}\lambda_i + \beta\Delta \ln s_{jt} + \varepsilon_{jt} \qquad (10.3)$$

where the notation has the same meaning as before and is therefore self-explanatory. Equation (10.3) delivers an estimated coefficient and a set of estimated λs for each product.[6]

Finally, we complete our investigation by pooling data by product and running separate regressions for each destination market. This latter specification provides us with a description of the average PTM behaviour over all products for partner country. Hence, it represents a logical complement of the analysis by product and it grants us the possibility to analyse the presence of destination-specific effects. When we run a regression for each destination, the exchange rate becomes a time specific effect, so that it is no longer possible to use time dummies to capture marginal costs. To obviate this, we adopt the same strategy as Gaulier et al. (2006) and proxy marginal costs by means of a time trend:

$$\Delta \ln p_{kt} = t + \sum_{i=1}^{K} d_{ik}\lambda_i + \beta\Delta \ln s_t + \varepsilon_{kt} \qquad (10.4)$$

Also, in equation (10.4) the λs assume the function of product-specific effects and therefore represent the part of export price variation that does not respond to exchange rate changes but is rather specific to each product.

Throughout the empirical analysis we drop observations characterized by an (yearly) exchange rate variation larger (in absolute value) than 50%: the rationale for this is the desire to focus on the pricing strategies of exporting firms under normal conditions, abstracting from extreme episodes possibly due to sharp devaluations or exchange rate collapses that are likely to have disruptive effects.

DATA

The analysis is based on manufacturing 178 products exported from France, Germany and Italy to 35 destination markets between 1973 and 2003, as collected in the Organisation for Economic Co-operation and Development (OECD) International Trade by Commodity Statistics (ITCS). Export prices not being available, we employ export unit values obtained dividing the value of exports by their volume for each specific product. Unit values are good approximation of export prices only at highly disaggregated level: we therefore focus on 5-digit data, the finest level available using the SITC Rev. 2 classification (which is the only classification system allowing us to get consistent data from 1973 onward).[7]

As one of the goals of our paper is to provide a detailed and systematic comparison of PTM behaviour between France, Germany and Italy, we have assembled a sample of products and destination markets that is 'common' to the three exporting countries under consideration. The 178 products have been selected on the basis of their importance within the export structure of each source country, and basically represent the common pool of the exported most 200 manufacturing products. Destination markets have been selected to represent a significant portion of the main clients of the three exporting countries. Working on such a long time span poses some problems with respect to this, as favourite destination markets have changed significantly in the last 30 years. In order not to limit ourselves to the first obvious and almost unchanged 10 partners, we have put together a list of 35 destination markets covering between 80 and 90% of total export. We have tried to grant a broad geographic coverage including, beside the obvious European partners, the U.S. and Japan, also a few South American and African countries, as well as some Asian markets whose importance has rapidly expanded in the last decade.

In addition to export unit values we build an exchange rate variable against the French franc, the Deutsche mark, and the Italian lira starting from the domestic currency/U.S. dollar rate taken from various versions of the Penn World Tables. For euro area member countries, the post-1999 exchange rate series is a notional figure obtained converting the euro/dollar rate back into the (dismissed) national currency using the permanently fixed conversion rate against the euro. A real exchange rate (used in the robustness analysis) is also built for most countries using producer price indexes published by the IFM International Financial Statistics.[8]

RESULTS

We move now to the core of the paper, where we present our results and try attaching an economic interpretation to them. Unlike the other studies on the subject, we do not limit ourselves to study the estimated PTM coefficients (β s) of the different regressions, but exploit also the information on the λ s, which we label profit margin even if in truth it represents the part of the variation in mark-up that is destination (or product) specific and does not respond to exchange rate variations. In what follows we will then present at first results concerning the PTM behaviour (i.e. results on the estimated β s) for the three aforementioned specifications, and then move to describing results for the λ s.

Pricing-to-Market Behaviour

Pooled regression

Estimation results on the pooled dataset reveal a significant PTM behaviour for the three export countries, although a clear heterogeneity emerges among them, with the value of the β being much larger for Italy than for France and Germany (see Table 10.1). The small difference registered between the latter two countries is nonetheless statistically significant as a T-test rejects the null hypothesis of the two coefficients being equal.

Table 10.1 PTM behaviour: pooled regression

		Chow stability test	
Country	estimated β	p-value	Result
France	−0.10	0.29	cannot reject
Germany	−0.17	0.00	reject
Italy	−0.44	0.84	cannot reject

Note: All estimated β are significantly different from zero at the 1% level. For the Chow stability test the breakpoint is assumed in 1990.

Results reported in Table 10.1 are consistent with the rejection of the hypothesis of complete pass-through that finds widespread validation in the literature (see for instance, Menon 1995). Also, results appear in line with previous empirical evidence for the three countries under consideration: Falk and Falk (1998) estimate a coefficient of −0.18 over the period 1990–1994, while Stahn (2006) reports a PTM coefficient for Germany ranging between −0.03 and −0.19 over the period 1976–2004; results for Italy (Basile et al. 2006) give a β coefficient estimate of −0.34. The higher value found for

Italian exports is consistent with two possible phenomena, which are not necessarily mutually exclusive: PTM is less often adopted by French and German exporters vis-à-vis their Italian counterparts, on the other hand a higher PTM coefficient may also result from the decision to pass-through a lower share of exchange rate variations to final consumers.[9]

To study whether the reaction of export prices to exchange rate variations has changed over time we perform a Chow test for stability postulating the existence of a structural break in 1990.[10] The null hypothesis of stability is strongly rejected in the case of Germany, whereas *p*-values for France and Italy are far from being significant.

Regression by product
When we pool over all destination markets (and therefore estimate one equation for each product) we observe that the majority of estimated β s are not significantly different from zero. More specifically, Table 10.2 shows that only 23 products over 151 display significant PTM behaviour for France, a number that grows to 41 over 164 for Germany and 41 over 156 for Italy. Hence, only a small share (ranging from 15 to 26 per cent) of products exported by the three countries is characterized by PTM behaviour. The postulated (in the existing literature) product effect seems not particularly relevant in our sample, as for only three products we find significant PTM in all the three source countries (while for 53 products the estimated coefficient are simultaneously not significant).

Table 10.2 PTM behaviour: regressions by product

Country	regressions	significant β s [a]	stability test [b]	poolability test
France	151	23 (18)	9	cannot reject
Germany	164	41 (34)	18	cannot reject
Italy	156	41 (40)	21	reject

Notes:
[a] The number of rejections. The number of significantly negative β s is between parentheses.
[b] The breakpoint is assumed in 1990.

The usual stability test is performed on each single regression and results suggest no structural break in most of the cases, not even for Germany. Last, we also run a Chow test for poolability to test the null hypothesis of equality of the β s across products: in other words we test whether the pooled specification (10.2) can be considered a good representation of the average behaviour in each export country or, on the contrary, the constraint imposed by assuming homogeneous PTM coefficients across all products delivers a distorted picture. The last column of Table 10.2 suggests that poolability can only be rejected in the case of Italy, whereas the degree of heterogeneity across products is not enough to reject it for France and Germany. This finding as well questions the standard result of PTM being a product specific phenomenon. One possible explanation to this is the fact that most previous studies did not work on a common sample of products and destinations, and also that the number of products included in the studies was rather limited.

Figure 10.1 provides one with a good representation of the results obtained in the specification by product: it represents the distribution (in terms of a kernel density plot) of estimated β s for each exporting country.

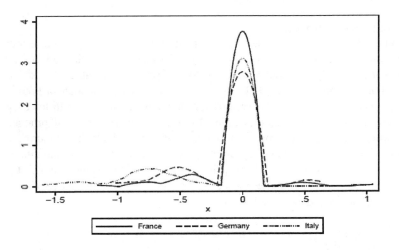

Figure 10.1 Distribution of estimated β: regression by product

It is easy to see that the majority of coefficients are not significantly different from zero, and those which are significant have the expected negative sign. Moreover, the three distributions display a second much lower modal value for negative values the PTM coefficients, with the peak being leftmost for Italy, which is consistent with our previous findings. The comparison between the three distributions can be formalized by means of a Kolmogorov–Smirnov test, where the null hypothesis of equality of distributions is tested for each country pairs. Results (not reported but available upon request) tell that it is not possible to reject the null of equality when we compare the French and the German distribution, whereas this is the case when the comparison involves Italy and France (a p-value of 0.005) and Italy and Germany (although in this latter case one rejects at 10% but not at 5%). This suggests that the behaviour of Italy does display an idiosyncratic behaviour with respect to Germany and France, which are closer among themselves.

Regression by destination

Table 10.3 reports results obtained from the estimation of equation (10.4). We see that this time between 60 and 90% of regressions are characterized by a significant PTM coefficient, and that the latter has always the expected negative sign. Italy displays the largest number of significant coefficients, consistently with the idea of its exporters adopting more often a PTM strategy. The presence of a structural break is detected in very few of the regression equations, supporting what we have found in the regression by product and suggesting that this is not a very relevant issue. On the contrary, poolability is strongly rejected by the data so that the PTM strategies adopted by French, German and Italian exporters appear to be strongly influenced by the characteristics of the destination market.

Interestingly enough, there are 13 (out of the possible 34 common destinations) cases where a significant PTM coefficient is found for the three exporting countries simultaneously, plus two destinations for which PTM is not applied by any of them. Hence, in almost 50% of the cases our analysis uncovers an homogeneous behaviour by French, German and Italian exporters. Among the 13 aforementioned destinations characterized by a significant β, the coefficient is largest (in absolute value) for Italy.[11]

Figure 10.2 shows the kernel density estimate of the distribution of the β coefficients for the three export countries. Once again one can appreciate the different behaviour of Italy vis-à-vis France and Germany: the modal values is shifted to the left, thus corresponding to higher (in absolute value) PTM coefficients, and the corresponding peak of the distribution is higher than for the other two countries, thus suggesting that it occurs with higher frequency.

Table 10.3 PTM behaviour: regressions by destination

Country	regressions	significant βs [a]	stability test [b]	poolability test
France	35	20 (20)	3	reject
Germany	35	21 (21)	1	reject
Italy	35	31 (31)	4	reject

Notes:

[a] The number of rejections. The number of significantly negative βs is between parentheses.
[b] The breakpoint is assumed in 1990.

As before, we also compute a Kolmogorov–Smirnov test for equality of distributions on the three country pairs and still find that the distribution of the estimated β s for Italy is different from those of the other two countries; on the contrary, we cannot reject the null of equality among the French and the German distribution.

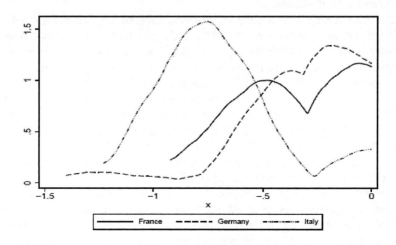

Figure 10.2 Distribution of estimated β: regression by destination

The Evolution of Margins: Lambdas

We move now to explore the dynamic of the profit margin, i.e. the part of the change in the export price that does not depend on exchange rate changes and that is destination (or product) specific.

Pooled regression

Estimation results for equation (10.2) are reported in Table 10.4: we find that only for France the growth rate of profit margins has been significantly different from zero for the vast majority of destination markets. Moreover, estimated λ s are all positive testifying for an increase in the mark-up during the last three decades. An F-test on the equality of the λ s cannot be rejected in the case of France, suggesting that the dynamic of profit margins has been homogeneous over all destinations. The picture is rather different for Germany and Italy, which are characterized by few significant λ s coefficients: seven out of 35 in the former case, only 2 for Italy. Also, the sign of significant coefficients is negative in the regression for Germany, whereas the two λ s display different signs in the case of Italy. The small number of significant coefficients is probably the driving force behind the rejection of the null hypothesis of equality of the λ s for Germany and Italy, although those few coefficients do have the same order of magnitude.

Table 10.4 Evolution of profit margins: pooled regression

Country	significant λ s	sign	*F*-test *
France	30/35	positive	cannot reject
Germany	4/35	negative	reject
Italy	2/35	mixed	reject

Note: H_0: equality of the λ s within regressions.

Regressions by product

When we estimate equation (10.3) we end up with a set of 35 λ s for each product, which results in almost 5,500 estimated coefficients for each exporting country. This forces us to discuss results in aggregate terms and omit most of the details. To present our findings in the clearest possible form we consider each set of λ s (each regression) as a single item and investigate what happens inside it by means of an *F*-test on the equality of the λ s.

Table 10.5 presents, for each exporting country, the number of regressions actually estimated (which falls short of 178 because we dropped products with less than 100 degrees of freedom) together with the number of them characterized by none of the estimated λ s being significant, the number of regressions with less than 10% of the λ s being significant and, finally, those with at least 75% of them being significant. In this latter case the table reports (in parenthesis) the number of regressions characterized by positive λ s.[12]

Table 10.5 Evolution of profit margins: regressions by product

Country	regressions	significant λ s [a]			*F*-test [c]
		none	<10%	>75% [b]	
France	151	105	28	15 (6)	5
Germany	164	90	44	20 (13)	5
Italy	156	56	47	41 (20)	25

Notes:

[a] Number of regressions characterized by none, less than 10% or more than 75% of the λ s significantly different from 0.

[b] In parenthesis the number of regressions where at least 75% of the λ s are significantly positive.

[c] Number of rejections.

As one can see by summing the three items, we observe a bimodal distribution in the significance of the estimated λs, whereby either the vast majority of them is significant or almost none of them is different from zero. Table 10.5 also shows that most of the estimated λs are not significant, suggesting that the profit margins have not moved a lot beside over and beyond the change due to variations in production costs. In fact, if we sum the number of regressions for which less than 10% of the coefficients are significant and those characterized by none of them being different from zero, we can see that the share is as high as 88% for France, reaching 80% for Germany and still 66% for Italy. The latter country displays the largest number of regressions with most of the λs different from zero (41), half of which are positive. France and Germany as well display a dynamic of profit margins that changes sign depending of the specific products, with the share of negative and positive sign being almost equal. A first look at results from the *F*-test for the equality of λs within each regression suggests that the null hypothesis is not often rejected; nonetheless a closer look indicates that when most of the estimated λs are significant, rejection occurs between 25 and 50% of the times. Hence, some sort of price discrimination seems to actually occur: when profit margins display a non-zero rate of change, they move differently in the various export markets considered in the study.

To compare the behaviour of profit margins across different products we reason in terms of statistical distributions and consider the set of estimated λs associated with each product as a random draw from a population, and test the null hypothesis of the different samples coming from a unique population. This is done by means of a nonparametric Friedman test: the *p*-values of the tests (not reported) do not allow us to reject the null and therefore suggest that even for profit margins there is no clear product specific effect.

Regression by destination

Turning to the specification by destination we find, as we did with respect to PTM coefficients, that many more regression equations display significant λs. Recall that as specified in equation (10.4), the λs are product specific, so for each of the 35 destination markets there is a set of 178 λs.

As Table 10.6 reports, the specification by destination generates a clear-cut distinction between regressions characterized by significant coefficients and those where the latter are not significant. In other words, the feature by which either (almost) all of none of the estimated λs are significant gets amplified in the present context. We find that for France 80% of the regressions displays coefficients significantly different from zero, a share that goes down to 60% and 40% for Italy and Germany, but remains nonetheless higher than the corresponding figure in the regression by product. When significant, the change in the profit margin is always positive; in addition to that the null hypothesis of the various coefficients being equal among them within each regression cannot be rejected save once in the case of Italy.

Table 10.6 Evolution of profit margins: regressions by destination

| Country | regressions | significant λ s [a] | | | F-test [c] |
		none	<10%	>75% [b]	
France	35	7	0	28 (28)	0
Germany	35	18	1	16 (16)	0
Italy	35	11	3	21 (21)	1

Notes:

[a] Number of regressions characterized by none, less than 10% or more than 75% of the λ s significantly different from 0.
[b] In parenthesis the number of regressions where at least 75% of the λ s are significantly positive.
[c] Number of rejections.

The Friedman test is applied also to the estimated λ s from the regression by destination and leads us to strongly reject the null hypothesis of the different sets of coefficients coming from the same population. In other words we find that the behaviour of profit margins is not homogeneous across destination markets, something that is consistent with our previous results.

ROBUSTNESS ANALYSIS

Weighted OLS

We test the robustness of our results by applying weighted ordinary least squares (OLS) regression to our data (as in Gaulier et al. 2006). This allows one to control for the relative importance of each product and destination when estimating the β s and the λ s. For each source country and each year, weights are based on the value of each bilateral flow normalized to the relevant total amount of trade in the dataset. Hence, denoting with X_{jkt} the value of export of product k shipped to country j in year t, weights for the pooled regression are just $X_{jkt} / \sum_j \sum_k X_{jkt}$, i.e., the value of export divided by total exports of all products to all destinations in time t. For the specification by product observations are weighted by total trade in each year and product (so that the denominator becomes $\sum_j X_{jkt}$), whereas in the regressions by destination total trade means the sum of all exports shipped to that destination in that year ($\sum_k X_{jkt}$).

Results for the PTM coefficients are reported in Table 10.7. For what concerns the pooled regressions, the only relevant change is the inversion in the ranking between France and Germany, the latter now displaying the smallest coefficient (0.16 compared to 0.22 for France and 0.44 for Italy). The difference lies mostly in the change experienced by the French coefficient as the other two estimated β s are almost identical to those reported in Table 10.1: we continue to find that PTM is much more widespread among Italian exporters.

Table 10.7 PTM behaviour: results using weighted OLS

Panel I, Pooled Regression	
Country	estimated β [a]
France	−0.22
Germany	−0.16
Italy	−0.44

Panel II, Regression by Product			
Country	regressions	significant β s [b]	stability test [c]
France	151	70 (66)	31
Germany	164	77 (70)	16
Italy	156	98 (96)	13

Panel III, Regression by Destination			
Country	regressions	significant β s [b]	stability test [c]
France	35	26 (24)	13
Germany	35	29 (28)	5
Italy	35	35 (34)	15

Notes:

[a] All coefficients are significantly different from zero at the 1% level of significance.
[b] In parenthesis is the number of significantly negative β s.
[c] The breakpoint is assumed in 1990.

The specification by product (panel II of the table) yields many more significant coefficients than before. We still find a rather similar behaviour for Germany and France for which around 45% of regressions display a significant coefficient; this share goes up to above 60% in the case of Italy.

Almost all β s have the expected negative sign, and stability is not often rejected (only around 10 to 20% of the times). Figure 10.3 reports the kernel density estimate for the distribution of the estimated β s: the difference between Italy and the other two countries is more marked than before (see Figure 10.1), especially for what concerns the right peak around zero, which is much lower and thick, and the 'fatness' of the left tail. As before, a Kolmogorov-Smirnov test on the equality of the distributions rejects the null of equality when Italy is compared with the other two countries, whereas it cannot reject equality between the French and German distributions.

Finally, panel III contains results form the specification by destination. Here again weighted OLS result in more significant PTM coefficients: in particular we find that all estimated β s are significant for Italy, 26 out of 35 for France and 29 for Germany. The distribution of the coefficients is depicted in Figure 10.4: contrary to our previous findings weighted analysis yields quite different distributions for France and Germany. Formal testing carried out by means of a Kolmogorov–Smirnov test confirms the visual impression and this time it leads to reject the null of equality between the two distributions, so that none of them is equal to another. Italy is still characterized by a distribution shifted to the left and displaying a thicker left tail. Nonetheless we still find a lot of symmetry in the PTM strategy adopted by exporters operating in the three exporting countries. In fact the number of destinations characterized by a significant PTM coefficient irrespective of the source of exports reaches 21 out of 34 potential markets. Among these, in 13 cases the Italian coefficient is the largest (in absolute value).

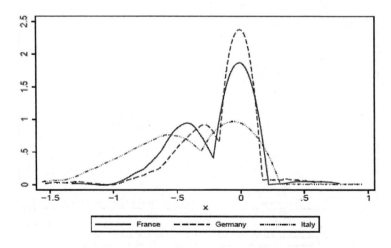

Figure 10.3 Distribution of estimated β: weighted regression by product

Overall the picture that emerges with respect to PTM behaviour is similar to that which we had obtained using plain OLS estimation. Coefficients are more often significant, but still there is a big gap between the specification by product, where less than one half of the regressions displays a non-zero β, and the specification by destination, which appears to be more informative.

Table 10.8 summarises results on the dynamics of the profit margins obtained using weighted OLS regression analysis. For what concerns the pooled regression, panel I of the table suggests that on average profit margins have not moved in any significant way beyond the change dictated by exchange rate changes and cost shocks. The specification by product confirms this impression as between 97 and 98% of the regressions is characterized by either none or less than 10% of the λ s being significant. Moreover, in panel III we see that running one regression for each destination market (and pooling over all products) yields many significant results. For France we have 25 regressions with at least 75% of the λ s being positively significant; this number is similar to the German figure (22), though the sign of the coefficients varies depending on the destination and is positive in 13 cases. Italy displays the highest share of regressions with significant coefficients (30) and, as for France, most of the destination markets are characterized by growing profit margins. Finally, while for what concerns the specification by product a Friedman test does not allow us to reject the hypothesis that different λ s come from the same population, this homogeneity is strongly rejected in the case of the regressions by destination. Our results again confirm that export pricing strategies are determined primarily in a destination specific fashion.

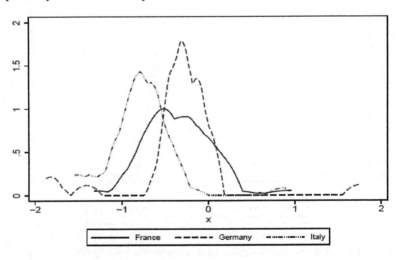

Figure 10.4 Distribution of estimated β: weighted regression by destination.

Real Exchange Rates

So far we have been investigating the role of nominal exchange rate changes on export prices. We claim that this is the most rational choice as we wish to separate cost shocks from destination specific (demand) effects. Some authors have nonetheless used real exchange rate changes (for instance Penkova 2005; Gaulier et al. 2006) so that we have decided to follow this path as well in order to test the robustness of our results (Parsley 2004).

Table 10.8 Evolution of profit margins: results using weighted OLS

Country	Panel I, Pooled Regression	
	significant λ s	Sign
France	0	–
Germany	0	–
Italy	3	positive

Country	Panel II, Regression by Product				
		significant λ s [a]			
	regressions	none	<10%	>75% [b]	F-test [c]
France	151	127	22	1 (0)	25
Germany	164	154	7	3 (2)	37
Italy	156	150	2	3 (1)	16

Country	Panel III, Regression by Destination				
		significant λ s [a]			
	regressions	none	<10%	>75% [b]	F-test [c]
France	35	7	2	25 (25)	25
Germany	35	12	1	22 (13)	28
Italy	35	3	1	30 (29)	24

Notes:

[a] Number of regressions characterised by none, less than 10% or more than 75% of the λ s significantly different from 0.

[b] In parenthesis is the number of regressions where at least 75% of the λ s are significant and positive.

[c] Number of rejections.

Table 10.9 reports results concerning the PTM coefficients for the three different specifications. The pooled regression gives roughly the same results, although this time the German coefficient is no longer significantly different from zero. On the contrary the estimated βs for France and Italy are very close to those reported in Table 10.1 above. Another difference lies in the fact that a Chow stability test leads us to reject the hypothesis of structural stability for all the three countries. Panel II of the table summarises results obtained from the regression by product. Once again there is compelling evidence about the fact that pooling across all different destinations washes away most information and generates a rather blurred picture. Few coefficients are in fact significant (between 14 and 23 per cent), with Italy still displaying the highest percentage. The general picture is very close to the one obtained using nominal exchange rates and therefore confirm our previous discussion.

Table 10.9 PTM behaviour: results using real exchange rates

	Panel I, Pooled Regression	
Country	estimated β s [a]	stability test
France	−0.09***	reject
Germany	−0.01	reject
Italy	−0.34***	reject
	Panel II, Regression by Product			
Country	regressions	significant β s [b]	stability test [c]	poolability-test
France	151	31 (23)	11	reject
Germany	164	23 (10)	15	reject
Italy	156	36 (32)	24	reject
	Panel III, Regression by Destination			
Country	regressions	significant β s [b]	stability test [c]	poolability-test
France	29	11 (10)	3	reject
Germany	29	18 (17)	2	reject
Italy	29	25 (24)	4	reject

Notes:

[a] '***' means significantly different from zero at the 1% level of significance.

[b] In parenthesis is the number of significantly negative β s.

[c] The breakpoint is assumed in 1990.

In panel III of Table 10.9 we find results from specification (10.4), i.e. from the regression by destination country. The number of export markets falls short of 35 due to the fact that for a handful of countries we could not find a reliable producer price index and therefore no real exchange rate series was calculated. Generally speaking results are again very similar to the original ones, although the share of significant PTM coefficients is now lower for each source country. Italy still displays the highest share followed by

Germany and France, with almost all of the estimated β s having the expected negative sign. Moreover, we continue to find symmetry in the PTM behaviour of the three countries: height destinations (out of 28) are in fact characterized by a significant independently of the source country, and in other three cases the estimated β is always not different from zero. As before, the Italian PTM coefficient is the highest of the three.

Moving now to the dynamic of profit margins, the foremost change in the results contained in panel I of table 10 vis-à-vis those reported in Table 10.4 above is that most estimated λ s are no longer significant for France (and those significant are negative), whereas the opposite occurs for Germany who now displays many negative and significant coefficients.

Table 10.10 Evolution of profit margins: results using real exchange rates

Panel I, Pooled Regression			
		Chow stability test [a]	
Country	significant λ s	Sign	F-test
France	4	negative	accept
Germany	26	negative	reject
Italy	0	–	accept

Panel II, Regression by Product				
		significant λ s [b]		
Country	regressions	none	<10%	>75% [c]	F-test [d]
France	151	129	11	8 (2)	6
Germany	164	80	46	30 (11)	8
Italy	156	74	42	30 (19)	20

Panel III, Regression by Destination				
		significant λ s [b]		
Country	regressions	none	<10%	>75% [c]	F-test [d]
France	29	7	0	22 (20)	0
Germany	29	17	2	10 (8)	1
Italy	29	14	1	14 (13)	0

Notes:

[a] H0: equality of the λ s within regressions.

[b] Number of regressions characterized by none, less than 10% or more than 75% of the λ s significantly different from 0.

[c] In parenthesis is the number of regressions where at least 75% of the λ s are positively significant.

[d] Number of rejections.

The regression by product (panel II) yields almost the same results as with nominal exchange rates and therefore still conveys the usual picture. Similarly, results from the specification by destination (panel III) are similar to those reported in Tables 10.4–10.6: profit margins display a positive and significant rate of growth for 75% of French export destinations, 30% of German, and 50% of Italian ones. Moreover, we still cannot reject the null hypothesis of the estimated λ s being equal for the various products exported to each destination market.

CONCLUSION

The paper compares the export price strategies of three large European countries (France, Germany and Italy) using a large and common pool of manufacturing products and destination markets. Contrary to what is often reported in the literature, our results suggest that PTM is not widespread: this is especially true for French and German exporters. We find that on average Italian exporters adopt more often a PTM strategy and we interpret this as a sign of the weaker competitive position of that country in international markets, due to its specialization in traditional, lower-end products (see Faini and Sapir 2005).

The specification by product does not add much, vis-à-vis the pooled regression, to our understanding of the phenomena under scrutiny: coefficients are seldom significant, so that pooling over all destinations for each single product seems to wash away most of the information contained in the data. Consistently with the previous literature we find that regression analysis for different products yields different PTM coefficients; nonetheless we find no regularity in terms of products when we compare the behaviour of French, German and Italian exporters. Hence, we claim that product specific characteristics do not play a major role in determining the PTM behaviour of exporting firms. On the other hand, the specification by destination is much more informative and it appears that export price changes are mainly determined in a destination specific fashion. Pooling across products exported to each destination market yields significant PTM coefficients more than 60% of the times.

Something similar applies to profit margins as well, with the specification by destination yielding many more significant estimates. Margins appear to move rather homogeneously across products, pointing to the fact that the price of exports shipped to the same destination tend to move in a homogeneous way. On the contrary, the hypothesis of a homogeneous behaviour across countries (even for the same product) is strongly rejected. Within this latter heterogeneity, we find that on average profit margins have either remained stable or augmented in the last three decades, so that increased international integration seems not to have reduced firm market power. In conclusion we claim that export price changes are mainly determined on the basis of the characteristics of the source and of the destination markets. Further research is needed to investigate and better determine the actual determinants of different pricing strategies of exporting firms. Our results, hinting at the interplay of source and destination country characteristics need to be further extended and systematized, with a particular focus on explaining the different behaviours we have documented in the present work.

NOTES

1. See for instance Knetter (1989), Gagnon and Knetter (1995), Adolfson (1999), Gordon et al. (2002), Mahdavi (2002), Campa and Goldberg (2002), Gaulier et al. (2006). Goldberg and Knetter (1997) represents an excellent review of early work on the subject.
2. In the first comparative study on the subject Knetter (1993) test the null hypothesis of equality across of PTM coefficients for Germany, Japan, the UK and US on a product-by-products basis. He cannot reject it, yet his study is limited to only seven products that although 'comparable' are not strictly the same.
3. The main difference in the two streams of the literature concerns the focus of the analysis, which concerns the behaviour of exporting firms in multiple markets in the case of PTM, whereas ERPT is more focused on the effect of exchange rate shocks on domestic prices.
4. As Knetter (1993) points out, the time effect captures primarily shocks to the marginal cost of the producer, but also changes in the mark-up that are common to all destinations.
5. This assumption is mainly driven by technical reasons: letting the λ s be destination and product specific would generate a set of dummy variables too large to be handled and therefore prevents the estimation.
6. The actual number of regressions (and hence results) for each source country can be smaller than 178 as we do not consider those with less than 100 degrees of freedom.
7. Two problems remain. First, unit value changes reflect not only prices changes but also composition changes due to shifts in import demand. Second, unit values reflect also quality changes which are impossible to track.
8. Time coverage varies by country. French data refer to the producer price of intermediate goods, data for Thailand are from the Bank of Thailand, whereas for Taiwan they come from the Groningen Growth and Development Centre '60 industry database'.
9. Gaulier et al. (2006) claim that German exporters are relatively not very inclined to adopt a PTM strategy.
10. Beside cutting the sample into two pieces of approximately equal length, 1990 is also the year of German unification, which represented a major shock not only for Germany itself but also for its main trading partners.
11. A few instances occur where the estimated PTM coefficient is larger than 1, thus hinting to an over-reaction of export prices to exchange rate variations. This uncommon behaviour is nonetheless quite rare and, also, is not new to the empirical literature and therefore does not spoil our results.
12. We have observed that when most of the estimated λ s are significant, they display the same sign.

REFERENCES

Adolfson, M. (1999), 'Swedish export price determination: pricing to market shares?', *Working Paper Series in Economics and Finance* 306, Stockholm School of Economics.

Asplund, M., R. Eriksson and N. Strand (2001), 'Price discrimination in oligopoly: evidence from Swedish newspapers', *Working Paper Series in Economics and Finance* 468, Stockholm School of Economics.

Basile, R., de Nardis, S. and A. Girardi (2006), 'Pricing to market of Italian exporting firms', *ISAE Working Papers* 70, Institute for Studies and Economic Analyses (Roma, Italy), ideas.repec.org/p/isa/wpaper/70.html.

Bergin, P. and R. Glick. (2005), 'Tradability, productivity and understanding international economic integration, *NBER Working Paper*, 11637.

Bernstein, J. and P. Mohnen (1991), 'Price-cost margins, exports and productivity growth: with an application to Canadian industries', *Canadian Journal of Economics*, **24** (3), 638–659.

Campa, J. and L. Goldberg (2002), 'Exchange rate pass-through into import prices: a macro or micro phenomenon?,' *IESE Research Papers* D/475, IESE Business School.

Faini, R. and A. Sapir (2005), 'Un modello obsoleto? crescita e specializzazione dell'economia italiana', in T. Boeri et al. (eds), *Oltre il Declino*, Bologna: Il Mulino: pp. 19–81.

Falk, M. and R. Falk (1998), 'Pricing to market of German exporters: evidence from panel data', *ZEW Discussion Papers* 98-28, ZEW - Zentrum für Europäische Wirtschaftsforschung.

Feenstra, R., J. Gagnon and M. Knetter (1996), 'Market share and exchange rate pass-through in world automobile trade', *Journal of International Economics*, **40** (1-2), 187–209.

Froot, K. and P. Klemperer (1989), 'Exchange rate pass through when market share matters', *American Economic Review*, **79** (4), 637–654.

Gagnon, J. and M. Knetter (1995), 'Markup adjustment and exchange rate fluctuations: evidence from panel data on automobile exports', *Journal of International Money and Finance*, **195** (4123), 289–310.

Gaulier, G., A. Lahreche-Revil and I. Mejean (2006), 'Exchange-rate pass-trough at the product level', *CEPII Working Papers* 2006-02, CEPII.

Gil-Pareja, S. (2000), 'Exchange rates and European countries export prices: an empirical test for asymmetries in pricing to market behavior', Weltwirtschaftliches Archiv.

Goldberg, P. (1995), 'Product differentiation and oligopoly in international markets: the case of US automobile industry', *Econometrica*, **63** (4), 891–951.

Goldberg, P. and M. Knetter (1997), 'Goods prices and exchange rates: what have we learned?', *Journal of Economic Literature*, **35** (3), 1243–1272.

Gordon, M., B. Dumas and R. Marston (2002), 'Pass-through and exposure', *The Journal of Finance*, **57** (1), 199–231.

Knetter, M. (1989), 'Price discrimination by US. and German exporters', *American Economic Review*, **79** (1), 198–210.

Knetter, M. (1993), 'International comparisons of price-to-market behavior', *American Economic Review*, **83** (3), 473–486.

Krugman, P. (1987), 'Pricing to market when the exchange rate changes', in S. Arndt and D. Richardson (eds), *Real-Financial Linkages among Open Economies*, Cambridge MA: MIT Press, pp. 49–70.

Mahdavi, S. (2002), 'The response of the US export prices to changes in the dollar's effective exchange rate: further evidence from industry level data', *Applied Economics*, **34** (17), 2115–2125.

Mann, C. (1986), 'Prices, profit margins, and exchange rates', *Federal Reserve Bulletin*, June, 366–379.

Menon, J. (1995), 'Exchange rate pass through', *Journal of Economic Surveys*, **9** (2), 197–231.

Moreno, L. and D. Rodríguez (2004), 'Domestic and foreign price/marginal-cost margins: an application to Spanish manufacturing firms', *Review of International Economics*, **12** (1), 60–80.

Parsley, D. (2004), 'Pricing in international markets: a 'small country' benchmark', *Review of International Economics*, **12** (3), 509–24.

Penkova, E. (2005), 'Pricing-to-market or hysteresis? An empirical investigation of German exports', *Discussion Papers in Economics* 05/03, University of Dortmund, Department of Economics.

Stahn, K. (2006), 'Has the export pricing behaviour of German enterprises changed? Empirical evidence from German sectoral prices', *Discussion Paper Series* 1: *Economic Studies* 2006/37, Deutsche Bundesbank.

Index